PLANNING YOUR
GARDEN

PLANNING YOUR
GARDEN

ANNE de VERTEUIL
&
VAL BURTON

Collins
8 Grafton Street, London W1X 3LA

First published in 1987 by
William Collins Sons & Co Ltd
London · Glasgow · Sydney
Auckland · Toronto · Johannesburg

British Library Cataloguing in Publication Data
De Verteuil, Anne
  Planning your garden.
  1. Gardens——Design 2. Gardening
  I. Title II. Burton, Val
  712'.6   SB473
  ISBN 0-00-412261-5

Photo typeset by AKM Associates (UK) Ltd,
Ajmal House, Hayes Road, Southall, London

Printed and bound in Singapore through Print Buyers' Database

This book was designed and produced by
The Paul Press Ltd
41-42 Berners Street, London W1P 3AA

Art Director   Stephen McCurdy
Project Editor   Elizabeth Longley
Contributors   Denys De Saulles (*Garden Design Projects*)
Suzy Powling (*Best Plants for Your Garden*)
Art Editor   Stephen Bull
Artists   David Ashby, Craig Austin, Lynn Chadwick,
Pamela Dowson, Shirley Felts, Elizabeth Pepperell
Picture Research   Vickie Walters
Index   Kathy Gill
Editorial Director   Jeremy Harwood

CONTENTS

INTRODUCTION

In the course of our garden design work, we are faced with a variety of different dilemmas to solve. Our clients present us with hosts of original ideas that they would dearly love to see put into operation in their own gardens, and part of our job is to rationalize these ideas in the light of practicality and, of course, our own capabilities. We like to feel that although it is impossible to construct an entire water garden, for instance, in the confined space of a city garden, we can realistically satisfy our clients' tastes by installing an ornamental fountain or pool.

Sustained creativity in the light of practical necessity, therefore, is what our business is all about and **Planning Your Garden** demonstrates, we hope, exactly how you can make the most of your garden and of your personal garden design ideas. Every garden, like every individual, has its own character, which is determined by factors such as its outlook, its size and its architectural surroundings. It should never be your aim to erase every trace of your garden's natural personality; you should rather attempt to highlight its better qualities and perhaps introduce new ways of presenting its existing features. The aim throughout the book is to guide you through an analysis of your garden's various elements, so that you can begin to assess its potential – and its limitations – as a whole.

The section of the book that deals with different specific design features provides you with all the necessary, practical knowledge to enable you to face the prospect of improving your garden with professional confidence. The route to success is a simple one, provided you remember that design is a progressive business – there is no clear-cut middle and end – and therefore all its disparate facets should be approached in a clear logical order. When you begin work on any of the selected designs, you should discipline yourself not to cut any corners which might jeopardize a successful end result. None of the steps described in the section are superfluous to requirement!

The book concludes with a directory of some of the more unusual plants that you might like to use in your garden. The plants are arranged according to type and function, together with details of their flowering season, size, cultivation and any potential problems so that you can see at a glance whether they will be suitable in the particular environment you have in mind.

We hope that **Planning Your Garden** will inspire you to bring a touch of creativity to your garden, no matter how wild or how tiny it is, and convince you that an exciting garden is not beyond the bounds of possibility.

BASIC PRINCIPLES OF GARDEN DESIGN

The keys to good garden design are patience and careful planning, and planning begins with a detailed analysis of your garden in its context. This includes obvious facts such as the climate, type of soil and the kind of effect you wish to achieve, and takes into account the features which cannot be changed, and whether you wish to incorporate or effectively disguise them.

The design itself is largely a matter of personal choice, tempered by a realistic assessment of your garden's potential. You must start with the "framework" it dictates – its shape, fixed features, and so on – and build around it a structure that pleases you. This may be simply a pleasant place in which to relax, or one that fits a definite image or style. The finishing touch will be the degree of colour and you have hundreds of plants from which to choose to create your design.

THE GARDEN IN CONTEXT

Regional characteristics of climate and topography are influential factors in the broadest sense, establishing the general context in which the garden lies. In country areas, for example, their visual impact on the garden will be evident in the form of the landscape, colour of the local stone, and characteristic buildings, and in the distribution and type of natural vegetation.

Differences in the local climate may vary greatly over a single area, depending on whether the region itself is to the north or south of the country, is coastal or inland, predominantly hilly or flat. Those situations which are the extreme of the climatic range getting least sun will generally be less favourable to certain types of planting, as will those in any extreme position, such as on high and upland areas, and on open and exposed ground. In general, the greater the number of moderating factors – whether man-made or natural – which intervene between the garden and the weather, the more benign the conditions for a wider number of plants.

Gardens naturally vary in shape, size and the results you can expect to achieve. Soil, aspect and the immediate surroundings are all factors that must be taken into account before starting any design scheme. Whatever the individual situation, however, there are basic principles to bear in mind before you embark on planting. The advantages of a pleasant setting can be reflected in the way the design takes shape, while still, as here, maintaining a character of its own through well-composed plant groups.

Immediate surroundings

The biggest single influence on the design of a garden is likely to be its immediate context, whether rural or urban. In rural and unspoilt country areas, connections with the landscape and with seasonal changes are most obviously seen and felt; and although the country garden may have to contend with problems of wind and weather, here, at least, it has the invaluable advantage of a setting in which it plays a harmonious part. The larger the garden, the greater the opportunities for creating areas of different styles and moods. Formality and informality, if skilfully blended, can co-exist quite happily, and produce effects which are both dramatic and visually satisfying, as many gardens show. But too much artifice, or planting which is out of scale or sympathy with the surroundings, may be discordant and inappropriate.

Unfortunately, the large country garden with uninterrupted vistas is only available to the few and, in any case, the encroachment of roads, overhead cables, and buildings is now an established fact of life in many previously unspoilt areas of countryside. As buildings spread, gardens become smaller.

These obstructions tend to make it more and more of a necessity for the garden to turn in on itself in order to attain some sense of seclusion and tranquillity. This is most apparent in the city garden, which is inhibited physically and visually by buildings, hard surfaces and vertical lines whose presence interrupts and excludes the reference point of the horizon. Gardens in an urban environment are frequently artificial, in the most extreme sense, because they have to be made in spaces left over from buildings; they are overshadowed, overlooked, and all too often, built on ground which contains more building rubble than soil. Harmony and restfulness, if they do not come from outside, have to be created by more deliberate means.

Planting and microclimate

Nevertheless, every situation has its advantages, and what the suburban or small city garden lacks in physical space and visual opportunity, it often makes up for in the type of protected environment it can offer plants. Of course, if we were to have in our gardens only those plants which would grow there naturally or easily, then gardening would be a simple enough process. But as it is, we garden to get rid of natural colonizers and invaders, cultivate the ground, and even change the composition of the soil, in order to grow plants from different regions and different soil types. Many of the plants we desire to grow are cultivated garden plants which originate from warmer or cooler regions. Plants respond to gentle conditions, shelter from strong winds, and not too great heat or prolonged periods of cold. Of the hardier plants which tolerate lower temperatures, wind exposure, shade and imperfect soil, almost all will do better in more benign conditions. As a result, the gardens which are most interestingly planted, as well as being most pleasant to sit and work in, are those which are in some way sheltered against extremes of weather.

A garden may be protected naturally by virtue of geographical location and favourable situation, or quite incidentally, by its proximity to other gardens and large trees. The effect of this protection is to create a secondary and benevolent microclimate inside the garden. Walls and adjacent buildings will absorb and reflect additional warmth, and have a similarly protective though more limited influence.

Gardens in exposed situations on high and open ground and on the windward side of steep hills are, in all respects, shaped and weathered by their situation. They are likely to need some form of constructed shelter, and possibly terracing, to deflect the wind and reduce the risk of soil erosion. The most effective protection against high wind exposure is a deliberately planned windbreak of suitable trees, such as conifers and coastal natives, all of which are very hardy. These should be planted in staggered rows, if extra protective depth is needed. In smaller and less exposed gardens, a sturdy hedge will give shelter within its lee, of up to 10 times the hedge height. A solid wall is not a suitable barrier, for although the small area immediately on its inner lee side will be both warm and sheltered, the wind's impact is not dispersed, as it would be through a semi-permeable barrier, but rather hurled over the top, where it rises to create a greater turbulence within a few feet of the other side. This problem is a very real one in the areas around and between high-rise city buildings, where planted shelters are not a possibility.

The scale of planting needs to be related to the space, and the type of plants chosen will help to establish the general mood of the garden. Here, the trees and evergreens set the tone, and are balanced by sweeps of herbaceous planting in the misty colours of an impressionist painting.

Aspect

Closely related to the microclimate of the garden is its aspect, and relative amounts of sun and shade received will strongly influence how each part of the garden is used, and help to provide a basis for a working plan. In temperate climates where the sun's duration and strength vary considerably throughout the year, the best aspects are those which are in full sun or receive the rays of the afternoon sun, for these aspects receive the greatest amounts of continuous sunshine and are, consequently, the warmest. A shaded aspect is essentially a cool one, and can be rather gloomy if the garden is also enclosed and heavily overshadowed. Open gardens in partial sun are rather more congenial, since they will benefit from morning and afternoon sun during the summer months. It can be tricky if the garden is exposed – the wind can often be bitingly cold in late winter, and may shrivel and carry off spring blossom. It is not altogether a safe spot for tender and evergreen plants either, for if the ground is heavily frosted at night, too rapid thawing from the early morning sun while the ground is still cold, can damage young growth or even kill outright.

If you live in an area which is frost-prone it is a good idea to take the precaution of laying straw or sacking around the roots of young and tender plants in late winter, and to leave the planting of new evergreens until after the last danger of frost has passed in spring. Plants in the shelter of a house or garden wall, are generally safer than those in the open. Gardens on slopes are at an advantage in this respect, for the even distribution of any available sun across the slope, and the movement of air will help to prevent frosts from settling. The larger the garden, the greater will be the variation across the site in relative amounts of sun and shade, giving opportunities for a diversity of planting. A small garden with high walls, or one that is overhung by neighbouring trees, will be sheltered, but may be in shade for a large part of the day, irrespective of the direction it faces. If this is the case, it is better to accept the fact, and to grow those plants which tolerate shade. The areas under deciduous trees can be used for spring bulbs and the early-flowering shrubs which come into flower before the tree canopy is formed.

Walls provide a protected environment for plants, but also cast shade. These two successful and quite different interpretations of the courtyard garden prove that if shade limits the use of colourful planting, year-round interest can be provided by the thoughtful choice of interesting forms and textures in a wealth of materials, both paved and planted.

EXISTING FEATURES

The visual character of a garden comes directly under the influence of its immediate surroundings, and if the views are open, the smallest garden will have a sense of spaciousness about it. Lack of confinement is very pleasing, provided there is a point of focus beyond the garden – a group of trees, or simply undulating countryside, for example.

The eye has a tendency to seek a reference point within its field of vision, the most comfortable being one which is at or around the point of middle distance; if this is absent, the result can be curiously unsettling. A garden which opens outwards and lacks any particular features outside its confines, can seem, at best, bland. If this is the case, it needs to be defined by a boundary or by a series of focal points which draw the eye progressively towards the outer limits of vision. It is even possible to use a good view or a single focal point to make a link between the garden and its surroundings. If the point of focus is at some distance, it can be emphasized by a gap left in the planting, through which it can be glimpsed. The whole design of a garden can be made to centre around a wider view, and planting used to echo the sweep, and bring the eye to rest at this point of resolution. In many ways, a garden in such a setting ought not to attempt to compete with the view, and planting is best kept relatively simple, without too much distracting foreground detail.

When the view is an eyesore, or the garden dominated by buildings, however, the opposite is true. Here all your skills must be directed at drawing attention into the garden itself. Often camouflage will be your most useful tool – buildings below a certain height, for instance, can be effectively screened by trellis or well-placed trees. But often such problems are not only immutable, they also cannot be disguised so easily. The key then is to transform the offending object or view by using tricks of scale and perspective.

Existing features can become positive focal points for a design. Here, the interesting shape of a mature tree is given emphasis with complementary paving and planting at its base.

Relationship of house to garden

The character of the house itself may well suggest the style of design and planting. Profusion of informal planting and a minmum of paving will suit a cottage garden, but might also, in a different context, be the way to deal with awkward proportions of indifferent architecture. Fine architecture itself will be an asset to the garden.

If the garden is large enough to allow a long vista back, stretches of paving should be in proportion to the house and planting used boldly and sculpturally, with the result that both house and garden are balanced visually. Where boundaries follow the orientation of the house, a certain formality may be unavoidable; but this often suits the lines of a well-proportioned period or very modern house. If boundaries extend at an angle from the house, the orientation may be displaced, and the design must work in two directions at once, in order to satisfy the spatial requirements of the ground plan, without confusing the views from the central axis of the house.

Features of the garden

Further influences on the garden plan will be any fixed elements *inside* the boundaries, such as garden buildings and large trees. In a small garden these elements can be very intrusive and if, for structural reasons, you are unable to get rid of them, the design may have to centre around them in such a way as to screen them effectively or use them as positive features. Large trees in small areas can cast a great deal of shadow, and create areas of dry shade around them which are difficult to plant. In towns, large trees are often protected by law and cannot be removed. If this is the case, you might consider the possibility of paving around them, as closely as the roots will allow, and making a circular bed around the trunk for shallow-rooting and shade-tolerant ground-cover plants, and miniature spring bulbs. Trees around the perimeter, if they block out too much light, might be pollarded or pleached; if done properly, this can make an attractive and unusual formal screen.

Soil

The growing medium in the garden is of crucial importance to the plants that grow there. Even if the garden is new to you, you can tell a great deal about the soil conditions from the type of plants already growing there and their general state of health – areas to look out for are those where plants are growing poorly or not at all. But it is well worth your while to have the soil professionally analyzed.

A soil type may be predominantly acid or alkaline because of the underlying geology, but it is most likely to be somewhere in between, and to vary slightly over the garden. In a sense, it is not the relative acidity or alkalinity

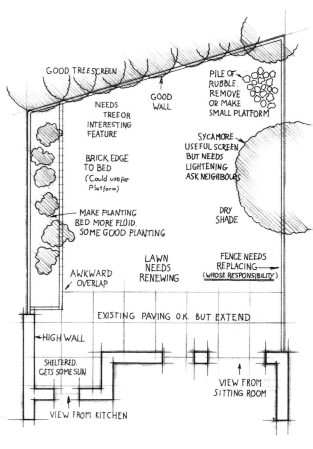

of the soil that is most important (though a high facto either way may affect planting choice) but its compositio and structure.

A soil may contain all the essential nutrients, but b unable to support plant growth properly because it heavily compacted and badly drained. Good drainage o sticky clays is essential, otherwise waterlogging an extreme acidity result, a condition signalled by poor an sickly growth, and the appearance of green and moss patches on the soil surface. In severe conditions, structura drains may have to be laid; but it will also help to open u the soil, break up hard, compacted areas, and dig in plent of bulky and strawy manure, along with sand, grit and pea to facilitate drainage.

Light and sandy soils drain quickly, with the result tha nutrients are easily washed out by heavy rains. Th depletion of essential nutrients means that such soils wi become exhausted unless regular dressings or manure an garden compost are given to maintain fertility.

A common feature of town gardens is the dry dust stuff that passes for soil, but probably owes more of it composition to building rubble. While this is not, in itsel without nutritional value, it needs large dressings c organic material to give it body and improve the texture Also, the addition of peat to the soil will help t counteract the tendency to dryness, which may be problem alongside walls, and under large trees.

PLANNING YOUR GARDEN: MAKING CHOICES

How the Garden is to be used

O **Mainly for relaxation:**
- paving
- seating
- barbeque
- low-maintenance shrubs
- some perennials
- ground cover

O **Time to spare – the flower garden:**
- lawn
- ornamental shrubs
- beds for herbaceous perennials
- roses
- shed for tools
- area for compost
- incinerator

O **Produce – the Working garden:**
- vegetable plot
- fruit trees
- greenhouse and/or frame
- work area to be screened from house
- path for access

O **Allowing open space for children:**
- bikes
- climbing frame
- sandpit
- swing
- tree-house
- room for adults' sitting area

Later, paving can be reduced to increase planting room, sunken sandpit might be converted to pool

O **Elderly or Disabled:**
- raised beds and clear space around
- even hard surface instead of lawn
- small working greenhouse
- colour and interest from low-maintenance shrubs and evergreens

O If starting from scratch, paving/construction costs and labour will be the areas of greatest expenditure, but are worth doing well – mistakes can be costly and permanent.

O Become familiar with the garden if it is new to you. Spend time in it before tearing out existing trees or feature planting – they are often there for a good reason.

O If the existing layout is satisfactory in terms of use of space and materials, transformations can be achieved by planting alone. Save any good planting; move evergreens in spring, deciduous shrubs in autumn. Move carefully to prepared bed, taking care not to damage too much root growth, and water regularly until fully established and showing signs of new growth.

O Neglected gardens can often be restored by thorough clearing, weed elimination and professional pruning of overgrown or badly-shaped trees and shrubs. Treasures are sometimes revealed beneath vigorous climbers, so cut back carefully initially, and wait until spring before disturbing too much ground – there may be dormant perennials and bulbs which are worth keeping.

Garden elements and features

O Consider how the important elements can be arranged to make best use of the garden's shape, size and general aspect; restrain the urge to include too many features all at once. Give thought to the finish of constructed work and garden beds, particularly where new edges and junctions are created.

O **Constructed and Functional:**
- Boundaries
- *fences/walls*
- Hard paving
  brick
  stone
  concrete
- Soft floor
  gravel
- Path
  solid/stepping stones
- *Shed/Greenhouse*
- *Steps and Terraces*
- *Raised Beds/retaining walls*
- *Pergolas/Arches*
- *Vegetable Plot*
- *Lighting*
- Water
  formal pool/fountain
  informal water with planting
- Constructed screens
  woven
  wattle
  split bambo
  trellis (light)
  timber
  concrete
  "honeycomb" wall
- *blocks (dense)*
  Service area/Compost/
- Incinerator
- Barbeque
- Climbing Frame/Sandpit

O **Planted:**
- *Lawn*
- *Hedges*
  Deciduous/Evergreen
  Flowering/Foliage
- Wall Climbers
- Ground-cover
- Borders
  mixed
  herbaceous
- Island Beds
- Aquatic and waterside
- Trees
- Tall background shrubs
- Medium-height planting
- Small and detailed planting
- Rock garden/Alpine
- Areas under trees
- Wild corner
- *Herb Garden*
- Peat Beds
- Patio Planting
  tubs and pots

FINDING
THE
DESIGN

A plan enables you to explore various ways of using your available space effectively. It demonstrates, to scale, how the different areas and elements of the garden will relate to one another. What it cannot do, however, is give any tangible idea of the relative heights and depths which give the garden substance. It is important to consider carefully how any changes that you make will immediately and eventually affect the "feel" as well as the look of the garden. Structures and planting of various heights should be visualized in proportion to flat stretches of lawn or paving, as well as in relation to each other.

The even proportions of this town garden are given character and fluidity with a beautifully laid-out path of stone setts. The fine form of the apple tree makes a central focus, and adds another dimension by creating hidden corners behind.

The framework

The outline framework of the garden will begin to emerge as you consider most suitable positions for siting a working area, a paved place for seating, tall background planting, feature planting, and so on.

The limitations imposed on you by size and shape need practical consideration, so that too many disparate elements are not jostling one another for space; the whole garden should have a coherent unity, rather than being a patchwork of applied styles and ideas. It helps to keep the flow between one area and another if visual links are made with thematic planting, and the junctions masked at points where vertical surfaces meet – staggering the line of paving where it butts against a lawn, for instance, will play down the division and give a pleasanter sense of continuity than a straight edge. The smaller the space, the more important it is to balance the scale of the design with the proportions of the garden: overstatement and excessive detail will tend to be distracting and unharmonious.

The permanent framework of the garden will be composed of structures, paving, lawn, trees and evergreen planting, and needs to be sufficiently well-defined to sustain interest throughout the year. Strong groups of evergreen shrubs will help to balance the effect of hard surfaces and lines, and counteract the visual drabness of too much concrete. But a predominance of unchanging elements presents a static picture, which needs to be lifted with the finer lines of graceful deciduous shrubs and splashes of colour here and there. A mature garden with a good framework of established trees can take its interest solely from their outline shapes in winter, and there is a great delight in watching the well-planted deciduous garden gradually unfold and renew itself each year.

This aspect of change and of surprise lies at the heart of our continual fascination with the garden in all its forms. Constant and imperceptible movement make it at once always familiar, yet always different. Variations of light and shade across the garden introduce depth by bringing certain areas into focus, making others apparently recede, at different times of day and different times of year. You can play with the visual depth by positioning the bright colours where they will catch the light, and break the denser areas of shade with pale greens, whites and yellows.

Areas of dappled shade and fragmented light have a particular quality that can be captured and momentarily held by the thoughtful choice of surfaces on which the light comes to rest – textured paving, water, faceted leaf forms and the patterns of bark on a tree trunk.

These small details are in every way as vital as the larger considerations of how to use the space, for it is these details that help to enrich the fabric of the garden and breathe life into the design.

Enclosures

The elusive "third dimension" of the garden is not defined by its boundaries, but will always exist in those areas where the smallest details of form and colour combine magically with the light, to create an atmosphere which is somehow outside time. Luxuriant planting, tall and arching forms, or the more formal lines of a clipped hedge, can be used to make a small and intimate space within a space, which is totally or partially hidden from view of the house and the rest of the garden. These small enclosures are often an essential part of the design in city gardens, for a space which is dominated by tall buildings, or heavily overlooked, is seldom an attractive or relaxing place to sit. Very small gardens in this situation are up against a problem, for there will be little chance to distance yourself from the world, when it is very much in evidence around you. You may come to feel that light is less of a priority than privacy. One solution would be a

simple frame of timber slats extending just above the back wall and over part of the garden, which could be used to support climbers and take a canopy of foliage. Although this will make planting underneath more difficult, the climbers themselves will benefit from the downward light – the whole space could even be given a romantic touch by the addition of a small, shady pool or elegant statue.

Very small gardens

Designing within strict limitations can be pretty challenging and demands both imagination and ingenuity because the characteristics of the garden and any particular oddities tend to be exaggerated by smallness – much of the space in shade cast by neighbouring trees, or boundary walls and fences, may be causing you to rely on diversity of plant form and variegation to make up for the lack of colour. As a substitute for lawn, paving laid informally to allow small carpeting plants to creep in between, or gravel

in which many plants will happily grow and seed themselves, will make a garden room which is at all times pleasant to look upon. Small walled gardens with a warm and open aspect can often become wonderful sun traps; the wall space can be used to the maximum for tender climbers and wall shrubs, or hanging pots filled with colourful perennials and annuals, leaving the central space free for a table and chairs.

Tiered planting creates a clearing in a tiny shaded garden and makes full use of all the space. Every detail contributes to the effect, from the irregular stone slabs and carefully placed objects, to the diversity of plant forms, and all is scaled to create a rich environment in miniature.

The vertical element

Using the vertical space to the full in a small garden is not only practical in terms of space, it also helps to break up and soften the effect of too many hard lines and of walls which are disproportionate to the scale of the garden. A raised bed will help to reduce the effect and distance of a boundary slightly; but since it introduces another vertical line, the bed should be kept low and the edges and corners masked with planting.

With gardens on a slope, you will be much concerned with using the vertical plane – terracing is often the best solution if the gradient is steep. A slope, particularly if it climbs upwards from the house, will tend to foreshorten the view, and a series of shallow platforms built in to the slope will both counterbalance this effect and increase the amount of usable space. In small gardens, a change of level may have to be made more abruptly, and this should be kept as close to the house as possible, without making the steps too steep and possibly dangerous. At the far end, a shallow grassed or paved platform, laid at an angle to the rest of the garden, will add visual interest and complete a steep transition in a gentle way.

Garden styles

A garden's "style" may come into being in any number of different ways. Quite often it is the more or less accidental result of arranging the layout in a certain way because of the garden shape, or because of the need for screening and enclosure. Occasionally, it is the more deliberate result of an emphatic design which turns upon a single feature such as an especially good view or a large tree. Sometimes a particular kind of planting has to be used because of the soil type or because of poor light condition, and the plants themselves will lend their own character to the garden. Curiously enough, when choice is limited by these physical restraints, it concentrates the imagination wonderfully, and some of the most successful and original schemes arise from the most apparently unpromising situations.

Less easy to deal with are gardens which have few, if any, distinctive features, and therefore a lack of either positives or negatives from which to start. Gardens on new housing developments or suburban plots with entirely regular lines will lack the fine patina or time that mature planting and long usage bring. If designing from scratch, it is often tempting to fill up all the space at once. But a more satisfying shape can be realized, if you phase the work gradually over a period of time, allowing the framework to develop. Give careful thought to the choice of materials, so that the scheme does not look brand new, and choose a variety of plants – some slow- and some fast-growing – so that you can enjoy a sense of the garden's having evolved, rather than of its having been "installed".

In theoretical terms, there are two distinctive schools of garden style: the first, which takes its model from nature, permits the plants to make their own impact, and "abhors a straight line"; and the second, which contains the natural forms within the structural framework of a carefully projected design. Most often lack of space prohibits an uncompromising design in either direction. At one extreme, the formal garden implies the grand gesture, and planning on a regal scale; while at the other, the true wild garden needs space and an appropriate context to be entirely convincing.

Visiting gardens on view to the public is always a wonderful way of finding inspiration and new ideas, but it has its dangers. A garden should always be primarily an expression of its owner's personal tastes and preferences, and not a compendium of ideas reproduced out of scale and out of context. What is most of value is some idea of the essence of what makes these gardens great in their use of space and planting, and this can be used as a springboard for ideas which are appropriate to your needs and the particular character of your garden.

Formal gardens

A formal design will use strong forms and symmetry to make its impact and this is often already present in gardens of a particular shape, especially when the boundaries are clearly defined. A formal structure, such as a pergola or well-constructed terrace may be used to make the most of length or width in a garden; or, where features are lacking, to give definition to a large and open area. However, no element of the garden should ever seem "stranded" and it is important that if you are going to include a pergola or distinct path, it should appear to have a definite purpose and a direction – even if one does not exist in reality.

Tricks of scale and perspective can be used in various ways to create different spatial illusions. A distinctive

The romantic garden suggests profusion and mystery. Here, rich planting which is controlled but not restrained leads enticingly to a doorway that is concealed by climbers.

feature, such as a raised pool or statue for example, placed towards the foreground will draw attention to that area, and by foreshortening the nearer view, create a greater sense of depth behind.

The long vista framed in a series of gracefully adorned arches is, unfortunately, not a feature of many gardens, but the device itself can still be used to great effect in a long garden, and a garden seat or fine pot placed at the far end. A focal point placed centrally, or to one side and about halfway down a long path, will help to halt attention and thus slow movement down.

A path which is made to narrow gradually towards the end of a garden will intensify the effect of elongation, and the visual trick will gain more credibility if planting is also subtly scaled, so that strong forms and colours in the foreground merge progressively with mass foliage and paler colours towards the back. A false door on the back wall glimpsed through the planting, might be used to add further intrigue to the mystery. Obviously such blatant artifice is not intended to be taken seriously, and must be handled with flair, and a certain amount of humour if it is to succeed.

In a very tiny space, there is much to be said for the principle of emphasizing rather than attempting to play down the size. A striking effect might be created by the use of a *trompe l'oeuil* design on the back wall or, alternatively, the perspective trellis arches which are available ready made.

The deliberate use of strangeness is a less orthodox way of creating an effect in a small garden, with outsized plants, pots and unexpected ornaments arranged to make a modern folly. But the ultimate success of any such scheme lies entirely in its originality – an assorted jumble of curios and odds and ends can never be made to work unless these are the underlying factors of inspiration and a strong sense of the desired effect.

Informal gardens
A good way of dressing an uninspiring space, and at the same time making a virtue out of necessity, is to apply the principles of the romantic garden, with luxuriant planting, rambling and tumbling forms. This begins to approach the informality of the wild garden, but still uses structural lines to keep planting somewhat in check. The deliberately unkempt garden has enormous appeal, and even if you are not fortunate enough to have a gothic ruin in your back garden, you can still bring magic and mystery to a dark corner by framing it with an arch which is planted with ramblers, and partly hidden by taller planting in front.

It is perhaps not that surprising that the wild or semi-wild garden has been taken up with such enthusiasm by so many city gardeners. After all, creating a planted oasis in the wilderness has always been a strong theme in the history of gardening, it is just that our concept of wilderness has changed. One of the great advantages of the natural garden is that rampant planting can be used to give privacy and, at the same time, hide a multitude of sins. An ugly boundary wall or unromantic fence can be festooned with climbers, and even a scruffy patch of paving can acquire charm if partly lost among a profusion of foliage and flowers. The informal garden must, none-theless, never provide an excuse for outright neglect; for unless you exercise some restraint over the more vigorous plants, the smaller details will be lost under a welter of tangled shapes. Neither will a mass of uniform planting, however luxuriant, be particularly interesting to look at, and the natural garden needs careful planning in the sense that it ought to be an interesting visual experience. Different colours and forms can be used together, but associations which are complementary rather than com-petitive will give the most pleasing results.

Architectural gardens
At quite the other end of the stylistic scale is the architectural garden which is rigorously formal in its approach to gardening, and allows for little that is accidental in its evolution. These kind of gardens rely strongly on simplicity of effect and economy of form, so that they tend to look best when conceived as an outside extension to a well-designed modern building.

The architectural design emerges strongly from the garden plan and uses bold geometric shapes in a series of interlocking patterns. Playing with shapes within the plan is, in any case, a useful way of working out the dynamics of the space. Carried to its conclusion, the blocks and circles become paved or planted enclosures for sitting, water and so on, according to the areas of light and shade. This type of scheme will only be really effective if combined with strong planting forms, well-chosen materials, and excellent craftsmanship. A variety of textures and surfaces is needed to prevent monotony; and the design should be carefully thought out in terms of how the different surfaces will relate to each other, and how they will appear

Garden design is three-dimensional, and vertical planning can do much to enhance the overall impression. A functional path can be made mysterious by being enclosed with tall and climbing plants. In this long garden, one area has been screened from another, while still giving the impression of glimpses throught the whole vista.

in both light and shade. One of the possible drawbacks of this kind of block planning, is the extent to which it relies for success on a continually high standard of performance from the planting. If plants look weak or straggly or fail to fill the allotted space, the results will tend to be visible immediately – regular maintenance is needed to keep plants in health and the garden looking at its best.

Shapes

In all but the largest country gardens, the house is likely to define one of the main boundary lines, and the garden extend itself in some shape outwards from the line of the house. Each shape has its advantages and disadvantages, and there will be endless permutations of size and aspect which make one arrangement rather than another more suitable for a particular garden.

Long and narrow

The long narrow garden is a familiar enough shape, and characteristic of many town or city gardens. These sites pose particular problems of layout but have strong visual potential in their depth. There are many different ways of dressing the shape, but all are based on the idea of dividing the garden into two or more areas across its width, so as to avoid a corridor effect. A formal division can be made with clipped hedging, trellis or other constructed screen, which either extends across two-thirds of the width, or allows a central passage through to the area behind. Any solid or constructed division is most effective if kept toward the back, where it will not overwhelm.

Alternatively, different areas can be suggested or semi-enclosed by planting alone, using different heights and forms to create hidden niches and corners behind. Any division, suggested or otherwise, should slow movement down, while at the same time inviting you on, and the area about two-thirds of the way along the length makes a good stationary point before the end of the garden is discovered.

A repeated pattern of brick circles makes a design that is both visually satisfying and functional in its use of space. Here, both hard and soft materials combine with ease, and the balance is maintained by generous and bold planting. Close-carpeting plants like *Stachys*, *Vinca* and *Epimedium*, made excellent and rapidly effective ground cover - and constrast well with the neat shape of *Hebe* and the strikingly dramatic *Euphorbia*.

Where the width is insufficient for a generous curve, geometric divisions can be made by a path or paving pattern which runs from side to side. If the sunniest part of the garden is at the back, there may be a case for turning the design on its head, and having a small paved area or a lawn there. You can create an access to this area which is both direct and unobtrusive by running a pergola or planted pathway along the length, and to one side of the garden.

Rectangles

The evenly proportioned rectangle has greater flexibility in its central space, and is a more gracious shape. It has an air of formality which suggests – and in the smaller spaces tends to enforce – a symmetrical layout. The simplest arrangement of perimeter planting which leaves the centre open for lawn or paving, is pleasing even if unexciting, but useful if space is needed for play or seating areas. Since the central axis is inevitably emphasized by planting on either side, a less rigid effect can be achieved if the line of lawn or paving is deregularized, and planting is allowed to spill out and naturally soften the edges. Focal planting introduced at key points on either side breaks the monotony of a highly symmetrical arrangement, and helps to lift the attention away from the centre. In larger gardens, generous sweeps of planting can be made to curve quite closely in towards the centre and make a circular enclosure there. By turning the axis to make a diagonal layout, you can maximize the length from corner to furthest corner, and this makes sense if you want to catch a favourable aspect or make the most of a strong focal point at the far corner. Where a rectangular garden lies sideways on to the house, the view is abruptly foreshortened, and dense planting in the corners will help increase the illusion of depth, but makes a rather formal arrangement. Shifting the emphasis diagonally, so that there is a feature in one corner, such as a small raised terrace, water or simply a specimen tree, will make best use of the length and distract from the lack of depth. This is also the best way of unifying the different parts of an upside-down L-shape, where one leg of the garden disappears around the side of the house.

Other shapes

It quite often happens that a garden shape does not obligingly line up along the house axis, and some confusion of orientation occurs. The triangular or tapering garden may lie at almost any angle to the house. These shapes are often the result of land having been bought and added on to neighbouring gardens in the past; they are often, unfortunately, also very small. The design must work hard in two directions at once: to deal with the fact that the eye is drawn inexorably towards the narrowest point, and to balance that by bringing interest into the foreground. By cutting off a smaller triangle in that corner, you can create a small planted enclosure or sunken area which adds interest in itself. The broader base line will also make a more acceptable shape in the main body of the garden.

Squares

The even proportions of the square give enormous flexibility in the central space, and a feeling of spaciousness. The exact square is a garden shape most often found in cities and towns where it has been artifically or deliberately created as a space between or central to other buildings. Emphasis will always come to rest in the centre and some circular resolution is needed in small gardens, to avoid the box-in-box effect which is the result of running planting beds around the edge, thus reinforcing the shape. Where the proportions are already strongly emphasized by good boundary walls, the balanced effect is very restful. You could not do better than to take inspiration from Mediterranean courtyard gardens with their paved surfaces, plants in pots and central fountains or pools – all of which contribute to a feeling of beauty and serenity.

Deep curved beds in the corner, narrow beds at the back and sides, will frame the central space of a small garden, leaving it free for lawn or interesting paving, with a focal point provided by an island bed or single tree. Using the diagonal axis will make the most of a sunny corner and the same bed shape can be used instead for paving. To avoid an awkward junction where paving would otherwise meet planting and cut the garden in two separate halves, you will need to break up the paving with planting or else stagger the line on either side.

A pleasant and open outlook can be retained in a larger space by keeping the perimeter only lightly planted. An informal group of deciduous trees in the centre will bring in pattern and colour, as well as introducing a sense of enclosure without obscuring light or views.

Every garden dictates its own plan, to some extent, simply by its shape. The shape should never be thought of as a rigid element, however, for within its confines it can be as plastic as you wish. A rectangular shape, or one that is too long can be divided into smaller sections, by altering the points of focus – or creating new ones. An awkward shape can be modified by clever use of hard landscaping devices, such as walls, statuary and trellises.

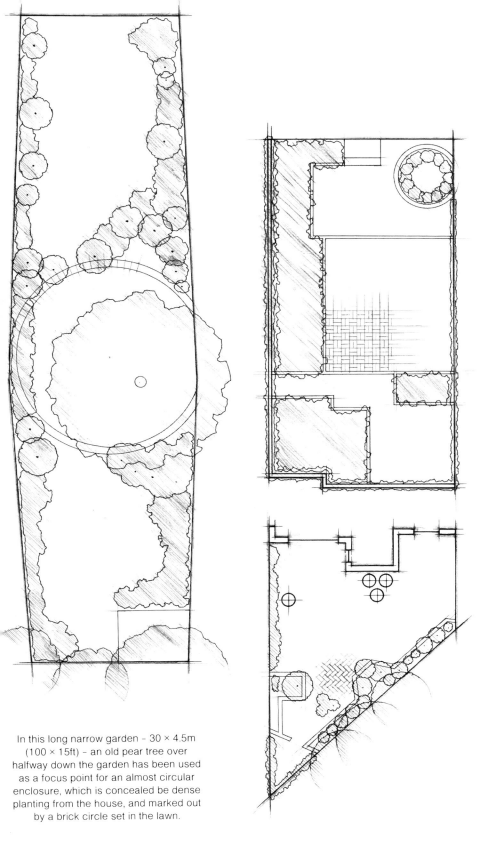

A rectangular garden – 9m (30ft) – formally divided into three, using brick and gravel flooring. Since the garden is in light shade for most of the day planning has been chosen for form and foliage.

In this long narrow garden – 30 × 4.5m (100 × 15ft) – an old pear tree over halfway down the garden has been used as a focus point for an almost circular enclosure, which is concealed be dense planting from the house, and marked out by a brick circle set in the lawn.

A tiny triangular garden with awkward orientation, high surrounding walls and very little direct sunlight. A small trellis pavilion is built into the apex of the triangle and the paving is brick, laid in a herringbone pattern. The planting bed is positioned to distract the eye from the shape and take maximum advantage of the light.

GARDEN ELEMENTS

The arrangement of all the structural elements in a garden will determine the way the space is used and influence the style. The extent of this influence, however, depends on the overall design of the garden, and will thus vary from the architectural or minimalist garden (with their total reliance on structure for design affect) to the wild, or natural, planted garden.

The effectiveness of any hard landscaping will rely on the use of sympathetic materials. Their texture and shape are major elements of design and when selected should complement the period and style of the house, the size of garden and its setting. Similarly, any structure should be scaled to suit the size of space. Simple uncomplicated structures built in one style will create a unity between the house and garden and visually enlarge the space; too many imposing elements will merely distract the eye and destroy a harmonious atmosphere, which no amount of subtle planting will ever overcome.

Occasionally the character of a space appears simple as a magical and happy coincidence of light and colour. The charm of this small garden room lies in its simplicity – an apparently artless composition which seems always to have been there. Stone ornament and a canopy of *Bougainvillea* are held in the strong patterns of light and shade cast on the brick floor.

Paving

The wide range of paving materials ensures that there is at least one that will evoke the particular atmosphere that you wish to achieve in a garden. In the small, walled, town garden the attraction of wall-to-wall brick, with planting pockets is undeniable. The scale is ideal for the space, and it may be laid – either on-edge or flat, in numerous configurations – to form the perfect floor. Equally desirable and far less costly, is gravel, with softer tread, and high light reflection qualities, which will usefully brighten up the dullest area.

On a larger scale are pebbles and river stones which may be arranged in patterns and imbedded in concrete to create interesting detail. Attractive effects may also be achieved by combining two materials. The contrast in shape and form of granite river stones, arranged in groups, among stone slabs, will provide interest and relief in larger areas. The varied shapes and sizes of pre-cast concrete or simulated-stone pavers, which ensure a suitable scale and pattern for any size garden, also look particularly good when set off by bricks, or, when left "floating" as stepping stones, on a gravel surround (they are best kept away from natural stone, however, for they will never wear in the same way or complement them).

Natural or sandstone slabs, with their old, mellowing qualities, instantly create a mature-garden "look". Tightly butted together they make a solid, formal base for garden furniture and when slightly-spaced provide planting pockets for the softening forms of tiny creeping plants. Randomly laid to form crazy paving, they will enhance the more relaxed planting design – especially in areas where the natural choice of timber might prove too dangerous: for although timber slabs or raised decking will usefully "lift" the most informal atmosphere, use is better restricted to dry sunny areas where the growth of slime-inducing algae will be discouraged.

Paved areas, such as patios, terraces and main pathways, which are likely to carry "heavy traffic", should always be laid on strong, levelled foundations and have a slight gradient, or slope, away from any building or towards a drain. This is unnecessary for raised decking, where the slightly spaced boards rest on a supporting structure built around the shape of the land.

Terraces

The incorporation of a patio or terrace in the garden is always pleasant because it provides a fixed base for outside living and enhances the overall design by its interesting use of space.

In less clement climes, the ideal place to site this feature is the area which receives the most sun, and this will depend on the aspect. Gardens in full sun will enjoy the maximum light. But if the garden faces away from sun then the garden area immediately next to the house will be in shadow for a large part of the day. In this case, the patio is better sited towards the middle of the garden. These areas away from the building are inevitably more secluded and have a certain charm of their own, especially when surrounded by interesting planting.

Entertaining and outside eating are made easier if the terrace is adjacent to the house, but even here you might leave some pockets for growing shrubs and climbers to soften the impact of the house walls. A group of thoughtfully arranged plants in attractive containers will distract the eye and focus attention towards the garden.

Paving need never be restricted to one particular area. Small areas of loosely laid flagstones or bricks make attractive pockets around the larger "country style" garden imaginatively breaking up planting to create tranquil seating areas or a setting for an arbour. Circles of brick paving, placed slightly away from the trunk of a mature tree, will provide interesting focal detail where little vegetation would flourish – and the curved outline will naturally soften outwards into the planting beyond. Nor should paving be finished in the same way, for the edge of a paved area will add to its overall effect. A staggered edge will merge into an adjoining area, and informally soften, while a strongly defined straight edge will positively contain and separate it.

Pathways

In most informal gardens, pathways are essential to provide practical access to the service area, but long routes can be avoided by siting it near the house, and creating an attractive screen around it – a position which will not ruin the view down the garden, and also make for more convenient access.

The design of a pathway affects the way an area is walked through and how it is viewed. It may be dark and narrow – suddenly opening out to increase the sense of space beyond; or, wide and curving to enhance the depth of a parallel flower bed. The spatial atmosphere is also increased if the entire route is not obvious from the house – an obscured path brings a sense of mystery to a garden inviting closer inspection, and the interest is sustained as the views are slowly unfolded. This is most easily achieved by planting, but the shape of the paving material is also important because it will affect the apparent size of a path. Bricks laid across the width, for example, will widen

Here the problem of a rectangular garden on a steep slope is resolved by terracing that follows the lines of the house and the use of strong plant forms.

and shorten, but laid lengthwise they will seemingly increase the length of the shortest path. The size of the paving will also influence the pace through the area – large stepping stones are rapidly passed over, but small detailed textures are slowly absorbed, creating intrinsic visual interest when the affect of many more obvious features have long since been absorbed and accepted.

Paths which are in constant use need "hard" materials, such as paving slabs, brick, stone or well-seasoned, timber; but for lightly used routes, bark-chippings, gravel and grass are all suitable. If they continue from a terrace, they are generally better constructed in the same material, to ensure continuity. But a different texture can be mixed with it to gradually introduce a change in atmosphere. The paving of a terrace when continued along a path will be softened if surrounded by gravel; timber rounds and bark-chipping might lead away from decking, through wilder more overgrown planting.

Boundary walls
The shape of a garden is defined by its boundary walls and, as such, their effect is fixed. However, much may be done to soften their impact before any planting is introduced. Small areas of ugly coloured or badly repaired brick walls can be covered with a coat of white paint, which will disguise the imperfections and also increase light reflection in the darkest corner. The use of a muted pastel shade will unify and enhance the style of an outside living space. Larger expanses of wall and structurally sound but gloomy fences are quickly improved by fixing trellis panels along their length, creating a neat, harmonious backdrop along which to train wall shrubs and climbers. (It is well worth checking the condition of any existing fence and, if necessary, replacing it before attaching anything – there is little point in establishing a plant on a support that is likely to collapse.)

A simple, well-constructed, unobtrusive boundary will not interrupt the flow of planting in any garden. A normally "strong" feature, such as a wall, as long as it is in sympathy with the overall design (paving, for example), will enhance the style of more architectural areas of the garden. Its height will determine the view beyond the garden – in large gardens a subtle variation would be to incorporate or exclude external features. An open aspect may be visually included in any size garden when solid barriers are replaced by open fencing.

A highly architectural interpretation of the garden wall makes an impressive entrance, and the finely crafted brickwork is a feature in its own right. Evergreen planting and gravel add variations of colour and texture.

Walls and steps

A garden on a slope presents an exciting opportunity to introduce steps and retaining walls to create changes of level. In large areas, their structure may be used to effect in order to influence the atmosphere in the garden. Their impact can be minimized with masses of softening plant forms; but, generally, in small spaces, the degree of impact will be controlled by the gradient and the size of the garden, for these will dictate the number and height of steps.

Steps with low risers and long tread will enforce a leisurely pace through an area. Steep steps are better restricted to short bursts when their use is unavoidable – as it frequently is in these small areas – in order to create at least one, sufficiently large, level living area.

When the design is not so restricted by size it may allow for a grand feature, such as a gracious sweep of generously proportioned stone steps or a formal series of steps arranged in a semicircle often seen in large gardens. In a country-style garden, informal naturalistic steps can be cut into a bank, and supported by pegged planks, leaving the slope free for sprawling ground-cover plants.

The necessity for retaining walls in small areas means a more formal atmosphere, but this can always be lightened by clever use of the contained areas of soil they provide. For here it is possible to mix lime-loving and hating plants to create imaginative hanging gardens and fully exploit the potential of the vertical space of the walls.

A sloping garden is not a prerequisite for raised beds for, in fact, gardens will benefit from a positive structural break to relieve horizontal lines. In the tiniest areas this will be most simply achieved by making a low shelf along a wall or creating a shallow change of level, where pots may be arranged. In larger spaces, a more ambitious arrangement of raised beds with several changes of level can be incorporated without disturbing the harmony or visually encroaching upon the space.

Structures

Another way of heightening the vertical interest in a garden is with a climber-clad pergola. When houses have an L-shaped extension, a simple, "Mediterranean" construction of stretched wires between house and party wall will brighten up what is frequently a dead space and integrate it with the rest of the garden. Alternatively, a simple pergola, designed to suit the house style, may be built along the back of the house to create a frame for the garden view.

An overhead structure promotes a feeling of privacy within the garden and this feeling is always increased in proportion to its distance from the house. A simple gazebo, with trellis side panels – or more ornate, more expensive latticework panels, if you prefer – makes a splendid shaded retreat which usefully doubles as an

Depending on the severity of the slope, steps can be dramatic (above), the design deliberately emphasizing the change in level, or, on a gentle incline (right), steps can be suggested simply by the arrangement of paving.

overnight storage area for garden furniture during the summer months. An arbour, constructed over a seat in the garden, creates an attractive and effective focal point at the end of a pergola.

Trellis always makes an attractive screening material in the garden. It can be lightly covered with deciduous climbers, to allow a view through to another area, or planted solidly with evergreens to screen an unwanted view of a "service area". Left unadorned, it will serve as a striking feature in its own right. The many shapes and designs of prefabricated panels now available means that the ambitious home handyman will find enough choice to achieve a harmonious effect.

Sometimes in gardens it is possible to distract the eye from an unwanted view by emphasizing a focal point elsewhere. This may be a particularly arresting arrangement of plants, or a statue, fountain or pool, which when framed will tunnel the vision in its direction. This is much easier to achieve in larger gardens, where shrubs, trees, a pergola or an arch can be set back from the house and subtly draw attention. In small spaces where everything is obvious, a screen is frequently essential, but an arch nearer to the house will enclose a feature sufficiently to create a focal point.

Water

The tranquil effect of water will always make it a desirable feature in a garden and it need never be excluded through lack of space. Small wall-fixed fountains, or a simple spout, will charmingly set off the smallest shady corner. You could even design a miniature courtyard around a large pool, with wide, raised, seating edges.

The simpler, less-complicated shapes, in sympathy with the overall design, are ideal because they do not detract from the effect of the water itself. Symmetrically shaped ponds with fountains fit perfectly into paved areas and, depending on the choice of fountain – from the very formal centrepiece to the lowest single jet – evoke a variety of atmospheres. Further away from the building, for instance, a round or oval shape will harmonize with the softer surroundings, where it may even be set among moisture-loving plants in order to enhance a more naturalistic area. (The selection and arrangement of aquatic plants and fountain will also heighten its affect, but sometimes, a still, empty pond simply reflecting the life around it, is most appropriate.)

A serene arrangement which centres on a gentle change of levels. Mossy brick and the softening influence of water suggest that shade, too, has design qualities of great value.

PLANTING

What could be more captivating – or indeed, more satisfying – than the sight of a fully planted garden in flower, where colour and shape are created by planting alone, and the whole is set against a well-kept lawn. The trees, shrubs, herbaceous perennials and the flowering annuals and bulbs, in all their myriad forms and colours, make up the living element of the garden; and unlike the hard, fixed elements, they may be used to create an ever-changing mood throughout the year.

A slowly unwinding pattern which has been established with generous sweeps of planting of similar forms will gently draw the eye around its shape and beyond. Against this backdrop, stronger or more detailed shapes and colours, will arrest the eye by providing vital points of interest. The apparent ease with which such beautiful gardens unfold themselves always conceals a great deal of careful and very deliberate planning.

Plants must be chosen for their ability to complement and contribute to the general effect. Unsympathetic or overly dominant elements that threaten to upset the balance may need to be removed; but plants will often behave with quite disarming individuality, and there should always be room for those delightful accidents of association which frequently occur in the face of the most rigorous planning.

A sense of style and purpose combined with practical horticultural knowledge are needed to create effective designs. When using plants as a form of soft landscaping, success depends on absolutely the right choice of plant for a particular position.

Types of planting

These planted "tapestries" rely on strong groups of herbaceous planting to weave colour in and out of the design, but they also need an outline framework of trees and shrubs to hold the shape together through the winter months.

Evergreen plants are useful for giving definition, and will create a certain amount of year-round continuity, but their visual value is limited. It is most frequently the ephemeral deciduous shrubs which provide dramatic seasonal interest and the elements of change, the many winter-flowering shrubs which will brighten any garden, during what can be a dreary time, often provide little interest throughout the rest of the year, and need to be balanced with leaf and colour from the summer-flowering plants and bulbs.

Lawns

A smooth, bright-green, and immaculately kept lawn at the height of summer conjures up one of the most potent images of the ideal garden. It creates a strong focal point in a garden and provides the perfect foil for a rich variety of plant forms. But it is more flexible than the still, dreamy image suggests, because the very shape and size of the lawn itself may be used to evoke a variety of atmospheres and effects.

A precisely laid lawn makes a perfect backdrop for the plants and ornaments of the formal garden, especially when it is confined within the straight lines of brick or stone paving – a subtle divider between the lawn and the soft herbaceous foliage, where it may gently flop over.

Green in its many shades is restful and pleasing. Smooth lawns and well-kept hedges make a calm backdrop for brightly coloured flowers (right) and give a garden form; while the foliage of many perennial plants (above) retains its shape and beauty long after the flowering season is over, so the garden need never be bare or lack visual interest.

without disturbing the symmetry. The softer, curved edges of an informally shaped lawn are less austere and merge with the plants, gently outlining their shapes and occasionally forming a ground cover under spreading forms.

A clear positive shape provides a pleasant area conducive relaxation, and at the same time creates harmony in the garden by effectively strengthening its design; fragmented, ribbon-like shapes dotted with flowerbeds interrupt the flow and are always better avoided. If, however, a wild or natural lawn is appropriate, the planting and grass are obviously inseparable, and the lawn becomes the flower garden.

Groups of planting

In the paved area, courtyard garden or the small garden where a lawn is impractical, plants may be arranged in conveniently planned pockets among the paving, their hummock-shaped, sometimes spiky, forms heightening the interest with subtle shade variations and contrasting textures. The evergreens, Rue, Santolina, lavender and low-growing *Hebe pinquifolia* "Pagei", will provide shape and clarity throughout the year and might be set off in the summer by Alchemillas, self-seeding forget-me-nots, and many of the silver-leaved and feathery plants which will thrive in sunny positions. In seating areas, fragrant, ground-hugging thymes and creeping mint will draw the groups of planting together without interrupting the use of space, while away from the main routes, an occasional upright spike will distract from the house, stop the eye and introduce vertical interest. The tall, sun-loving Verbascums and Euphorbias will flourish in the additional heat reflected off the paving; in a shadier spot foxgloves may be introduced, and grown with Hostas, Heuchera and lower growing ferns.

In some gardens, these groups would provide sufficient interest, especially if the walls were clad with flowering climbers, but they might also be incorporated into the paved area of a larger garden to soften the influence of the house walls and gradually introduce taller planting in another area. Repetition of form or colour will help to maintain the flow between one part of the garden and another, so that, for instance, the grey-blue of small

Regular trimming and maintenance is needed to maintain the sculptural shape of planting in this kind of design. Full sun, good drainage, and additional warmth reflected off the paving make an ideal situation for shapely evergreen plants like Lavender, *Hebes* and *Santolina*, and the many aromatic flowering Thymes.

shrubby plants like Caryoteris and Perovskia, might be picked up further on by a slender Eucalyptus or the silvery foliage of the Moroccan Broom (*Cytisus battandiere*).

The larger the space, the greater will be the opportunities for introducing an element of drama with a distinctive tree shape or a group of large-leaved shrubs or tall grasses. The Pampas grass makes a splendid feature plant, but is seldom at its best unless it can be viewed from a distance, with plenty of space around it. The effect of any such focal points needs to be carefully thought out in terms of the impact on the space around it. In small areas, or in a very detailed planting arrangement, the intricate form of *Acer palmatum* "Dissectum" or the stripy leaves of a clump of Phalaris will be all that is needed to create on accent.

Although an abrupt change of planting will tend to work against the unity of a design, this does not mean that planting in a small space has to be bland or boring, but simply that concentration on a specific theme or single style will be most effective. An architectural garden or a simplified interpretation of a medieval knot garden, with prettily clipped box hedges enclosing a variety of herbs and the more ornamental vegetables, both make a strong

designs in a small space. By contrast, haphazard arrangement of closely planted native species – hawthorn dog roses, mallow with a montana clematis or old man's beard – scrambling through, creates a delightfully natural garden style which is rapidly established on the poor soil conditions which are frequently inherited – after building work, on a new site, for instance.

Colour

It is a matter of personal preference whether the use of colour in a garden is carefully controlled or allowed to run riot. Deliberate colour grouping can be used to great effect, and often suits the restrained lines of a formal design. Cool blues with palest yellows and creams will seem to enlarge a space, as will a scheme which uses shades

Good colour sense is important in garden planning, though how it is applied is naturally a matter of personal choice. A group of *Alstroemeria* (right) picks up the colour of the formal red brick path; a more lavish palette is in keeping with the informal character of the open country garden (above).

of white and pale pink with soft grey-green foliage. A forceful but essentially cool colour like purple can be blended with the warmer shades from the same spectrum – mauves, lilacs and pale blues and pinks – to give a soft and hazy effect. Combined with colours from the opposite ends of the spectrum – the acid and lime greens – it will add sharpness. The hot reds, oranges and yellows tend to jump out in a design and, therefore, in small spaces, they are best kept in the foreground. A brilliant group of flames and reds will be given extra depth if it also includes the paler oranges, creams and yellows, and fewer plants do this as gloriously as rhododendrons and azaleas, provided they can be grown in a lime-free soil.

Of course, colour does not have space for a plant to retire gracefully after its season is over, it is better to

Visual emphasis can be created by imposing something, such as a statue (above), or simply by using the rich colour nature provides (left).

choose plants which have other features which are interesting, aside from their flowers, for although the flowering season is limited the effect of form and foliage will continue to draw attention over a considerably longer period.

Strongly defined shapes among informal planning create points of interest and lift the uniformity of the fluid forms. There is hardly a garden that will not benefit from the inclusion of at least one deciduous tree in the design, and if there is not room for the larger-growing varieties, a single small flowering cherry, or the ornamental weeping pear, *Pyrus salicifolia*, will lift the emphasis away from small-scale planting and add another tier of interest.

The naturally controlled shapes of conifers can be used to provide a permanent vertical or horizontal emphasis, and look well in strong

to be organized in this way, and the association of colours in a natural habitat provides as good a palette as any from which to choose. An almost complete range of colours may be found in a wildflower meadow, but the effect is never garish because they are contained and held in relief by the surrounding to create their own effect. Nothing evokes the spirit of a shaded woodland area more effectively than a group of arching ferns, or the feeling of water, than bamboo growing in a gravel bed.

There are also many shrubs with colourful foliage – the white-almost-green of *Cornus alba* "Aurea", yellow-green of *Philadelphus coronarius*, "Aureus", cream-pink of *Fuchsia magellanica* "Versicolor" and the deep red Acers, making it possible for virtually every area, whether in full sun or semi-shade, to have colour at times when herbaceous plants are not in flower. These plants are invaluable for the interest they provide in low-maintenance shrub gardens, where little herbaceous planting is required, and in the smaller garden where there is not enough of it to sustain a continuous display of flowers.

Form and foliage
The period of little colour, after the main herbaceous season, is most likely to be a problem of small gardens, where unsightly gaps and uninteresting clumps of leaves will be immediately apparent. Unless there is sufficient

linear designs. Clipped box or a small yew evokes a formal atmosphere, and makes a good accompaniment to low and colourful planting, as will the strong fan shape of the architectural Yucca with its erectly held and spiky leaves. The arching shape of shrubs like the deciduous Amelanchier, or the open habit of *Ceanothus* x "Gloire de Versailles", are less decisive, but provide the perfect growing conditions for the lower-growing and shade-loving herbaceous plants, Solomon's Seal, ferns and hostas, which may be interplanted with bulbs to flower in succession from late winter through to early summer.

Many herbaceous plants, like the spiky Irises, have striking leaf shapes which give an edge to groups of soft planting. *Acanthus spinosus* has deeply lobed, shining dark green leaves and stands out strongly in a dark corner. The large grey-blue foliage of the tall plume poppy, *Macleaya cordata* has the gratifying habit of plunging forward from the back of the border to mingle with other plants.

The leaves of some plants, particularly the glossy and silver, will tend to always catch the eye because they reflect the light so well. You can use this quality to achieve a variety of effects, depending on the mood you want to capture. The silvery Artemisias, seen from a distance, appear as a soft feathery haze – noticeable, but not intrusive, quite unlike the brilliantly eye-stopping effect of the green and gold splashed leaves of *Eleagnus pungens* 'Maculata'.

GARDEN DESIGN PROJECTS

Whether pocket-size or a large garden surrounded by open vistas, there are innumerable ideas you can apply to either transform your whole garden or adapt a small area of it.

Each of the garden ideas which follows is meant to inspire, to hint at the potential that can be achieved by combining the principles of garden design with a little practical application. Within every garden feature or idea are details of a number of individual projects – to show you how they are done and, should you wish, give you the guidance to carry them out yourself.

SETTING FOR A WATER GARDEN

A well-stocked herbaceous border is one of the glories of a summer garden. The hardy perennials with which it is planted become familiar friends, delighting with their rich colours and varied forms. They are as irresistible to the human eye as they are to butterflies and bees.

In this example the border forms the backdrop for a pool, occupying a sunny corner of a walled garden. To allow air to circulate, a space has been left between the back of the border and the wall.

Soil removed from the pool area has been added to the border to provide a gentle upward slope to the rear, ensuring an even more striking display. Because of the gradient one looks directly at the mass of flowering stems rather than over their tops.

When transferring soil in this way it is important to keep the topsoil and the less fertile subsoil at their natural levels, never mixing them.

As well as mirroring the border behind it, the pool offers its own display of flowers. These include nymphaea (water-lilies), which are rooted in containers placed on the floor of the pool, as well as shallow-water plants set on shelving around the edge.

As a finishing touch, allowing this tranquil beauty to be enjoyed at leisure, a garden bench is provided within a rose-clad arbour. Where better to relax and enjoy the sunshine on a summer's day?

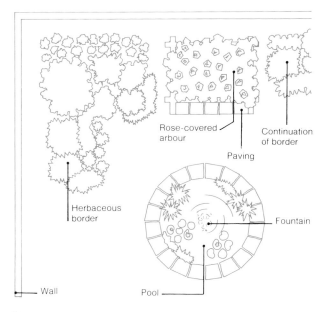

Rose-covered arbour

Continuation of border

Paving

Herbaceous border

Fountain

Wall

Pool

Planning The Border

The herbaceous plants that are the mainstay of such a border die down each autumn, emerging again after the winter. This means that the bed will appear virtually empty for a good part of each year. This can be avoided, if you wish, by planting a few winter-flowering shrubs to brighten the scene during the gloomier months. Position them before planting the herbaceous perennials.

Size
Many herbaceous perennials make substantial growth. They need space to develop if they are to look their best. The bed illustrated has a minimum front-to-back measurement of 1.8m (6ft) – by no means overgenerous. Length is less critical, depending on the space available, but a narrow strip of border invariably looks inadequate.

Position
Full sunshine and well-drained soil are the ideals, providing the right conditions for most herbaceous plants. Even so, there are a number of species suited to open shade or fairly damp soil.

Open shade, as opposed to the gloom cast by overhanging trees, is to be found on the side of a fence or wall away from the sun. "Damp soil" refers to heavy, moisture-retentive loam rather than the sour, sticky mess that results from lack of drainage. The latter requires fundamental improvement, by improving the soil and installing a drainage channel or drainage pipes.

Choosing plants
Whether you raise plants from seed or buy them at a nursery or garden centre, choice should be governed by size, flowering season, colour and the qualities of the foliage. Assuming that you would prefer an extended period of bloom, choose and position the plants accordingly so that there

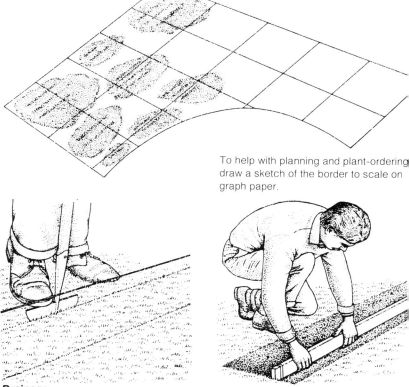

To help with planning and plant-ordering draw a sketch of the border to scale on graph paper.

Drainage
1 First mark out the run with string, then remove a strip of turf and about 23cm (9in) of soil.

2 Lay the Land Drainer strip along one side of the trench, then replace the soil and the turf.

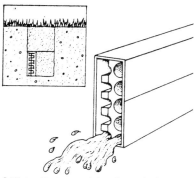

3 Water that percolates through the outer covering flows through the plastic core to the outlet.

Simple Drainage Method
A Land Drainer consists of a plastic core, shaped to allow a free flow of water, surrounded by a tough filter fabric. This allows water to seep through but keeps soil particles out.

If the land does not have a natural slope, dig the trench with a slight fall towards the outlet. Ideally, this should be a ditch or an existing drain but, failing this, it is not difficult to construct a soakaway. On cultivated ground, lay the drainer so its top is below spade depth. It need not be so deep under a lawn.

Planting

1 Measure the correct distance between planting holes, forming these with a trowel.

2 Cut one side of the plastic container to release the rootball. Take care not to damage the roots.

3 Use a rule or stick to check that the top of the rootball is level with the surrounding soil.

4 Replace the soil around the rootball, firming it with your fingertips. Water the soil if dry.

Planting

Container-grown perennials, as sold at most garden centres, may be planted at any time of year, provided the soil is neither sticky nor frozen. Plants raised in a nursery bed in open ground are best moved during late autumn or early spring, while they are dormant.

Prepare the bed by digging in well-rotted garden compost or manure, removing the roots of any perennial weeds. Do this a month before planting, leaving the ground rough, then break down the surface with a fork or pronged cultivator just before planting. Finally, rake in a dressing of general fertilizer.

Dig the planting holes with a trowel – or a border spade for especially large roots – spacing the holes to suit the plants' eventual spread. After ensuring that the compost is moist, remove the plastic from container-grown plants, place the rootball in the hole and gently tease out any roots that seem awkwardly placed. Replace the soil around the rootball, firming it gently with your foot.

The treatment for bare-rooted plants is much the same, except that all the roots should be spread out evenly before the soil is replaced. If the soil is at all dry, water thoroughly before planting.

Supporting

Many of the taller perennials need support at flowering time, otherwise they would collapse under their own weight. This applies also to some of the shorter plants which have slender stems. The time to act is *before* any damage is done, ideally, therefore, the supports should be accommodated when you plan the layout of your border. Canes are best for the stems of delphiniums and the like, tying the plants with soft string. Twiggy sticks are a better choice for bushier plants, such as cornflowers.

will be a balanced area of colour from spring to autumn. Just what these colours are is very much a personal choice, though there are obvious clashes to avoid.

Height plays a major part in determining position, the taller kinds providing a background for more compact growth. Bear in mind, though, that some plants attain maximum size for a few weeks only while in bloom. The width or spread of plants determines their spacing.

For maximum effect, position plants in blocks or drifts of the same kind rather than planting them singly, which may give your border an air of casual untidiness and detract from its impact.

As this suggests, some sort of sketch plan is needed before you buy plants and set them in place. It needs to be precise, but even a drawing that is only roughly to scale will help you to avoid waste and ensure a pleasing overall result.

Making a pool

Butyl rubber sheeting is the best material for constructing a substantial pool, with laminated PVC the runner-up. Pools moulded from plastic or fibre-glass are too small to provide a major garden feature. Polythene sheeting is too flimsy and short-lived. Butyl lasts for longer than PVC – 50 years or more – and, unlike concrete, is not liable to crack and leak. Moreover, it is a simple matter to lay it.

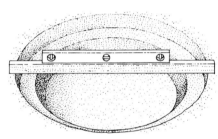

Check carefully with a spirit level, that the opposite edges of the pool are level.

Shape, size and site

Aim for a minimum surface area of 4sq m (about 5sq yd) – more if possible. The temperature fluctuations in very small pools provide less stable conditions for plants and fish. For the setting illustrated, an area of at least 7sq m (8sq yd) would be appropriate, the actual size depending on the scale of the border.

Note the regular shape. Though oval and kidney-shaped pools are equally satisfactory, narrow channels and other complicated outlines make it more difficult to lay the liner neatly and evenly.

To calculate the size of liner needed, add twice the pool's depth to both the length and the width, plus another 60cm (2ft) in each case to allow for tucking under the paving

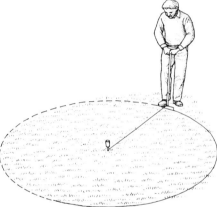

Making the pool

1 A peg, string and half-moon edger provide the easiest means of cutting turf for a circular pool.

2 First strip the soil from within the circle, then dig out the soil. A sharp spade is the best tool.

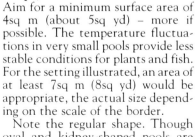

3 Leave shelves around at least part of the edge for growing marginal (shallow-water) plants.

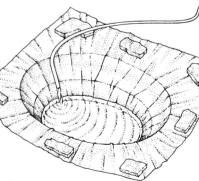

4 Before filling, place stones or bricks on the liner so that the water stretches it into place.

Tuck the surplus liner into neat folds ather than leaving it to bunch and retch unevenly.

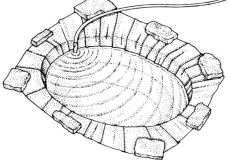

6 Now complete the filling. As the water rises, ease the stones to avoid over-stretching the liner.

When full, trim the liner to leave a flap everal inches wide around the edge of e pool.

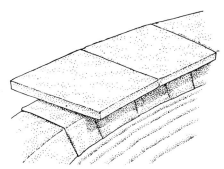

8 Lay paving all around the pool edge, placing it so that it will both protect and conceal the liner.

and remove any turf. The pool will be edged with paving, overhanging the water by about 5cm (2in) to conceal the lining, so remove a strip of soil to a depth that will allow the slabs to lie flush with the turf.

When digging the sides of the pool slope them quite sharply inwards. For water lilies the base needs to be about 45cm (18in) deep. For growing "marginal" plants, which require only shallow water, leave a shelf 23cm (9in) from the surface round part of the perimeter. This needs to be about 30cm (1 ft) wide. A second shelf, nearer to the surface of the pool, may also be formed.

At this stage make sure that the edges of the pool, where the paving will be laid, are quite level. A spirit level placed on a plank provides a sure guide. Shave off surplus soil as necessary, otherwise part of the liner will be exposed when the pool is eventually filled.

On stony soil spread sand, thick plastic sheeting or even newspapers over the sides and base of the exca-vation. This will reduce the risk of damage to the liner. Now lay the liner over the hole, with bricks or stones placed near its edge to hold the material as flat as possible. Make sure that it overhangs the edge evenly all around because it will be impossible to make adjustments once the water presses it into place.

Fill with water from a hose, easing and removing the weights gradually as the liner stretches and moulds into place. At the same time make any necessary pleats and tucks as neatly and unobtrusively as possible.

Trim off surplus material from around the edge, leaving enough to place under the paving. Lay the slabs in position on a cement-mortar bedding, with the inner edge over-hanging the water by up to 5cm (2in). As well as concealing the liner from view, this will prevent its degradation by sunlight.

urround. Take, for example, a pool m (10ft) long, 1.5m (5ft) wide and 5cm (1½ft) deep. The length of the ner will need to be 4.5m (15ft), nade up of 3m (10ft) plus 90cm (3ft) lus 60cm (2ft). The width of the ner will be 3m (10ft), made up of .5m (5ft) plus 90cm (3ft) plus 60cm 2ft). For a circular pool the length nd width are, of course, the same.

A sunny position, well clear of verhanging trees, is needed. Plants nd fish will thrive in such condi-

tions, while a build-up of fallen leaves in autumn results in a soggy, stifling blanket. Though sunlight promotes the growth of algae, causing the water to become green, condi-tions will right themselves naturally as the leaves of water lilies and other plants spread and shade the surface (see also Care of Pools.)

Construction
Mark the shape with a hosepipe or length of rope, then cut the outline

Installing a fountain

Stocking with plants and fish

The catalogues of water garden specialists describe what is available and give much useful advice as well. For the pool itself you will need oxygenating plants to help keep the water clear and will also be offered a choice of deep-water aquatics – principally water lilies – along with marginal plants for shallow water. Some of the latter need to be fully submerged. Others need only 2.5cm (1 in) or so of water. There are also floating plants that help to prevent the water becoming green and to suppress the uncontrolled growth of blanket weed.

Late spring is the ideal time for planting a garden pool. As explained on p.177, the plants are better grown in containers rather than in soil placed on the pool bottom. This makes subsequent care easier and keeps vigorous species within bounds.

Fish

Suitable fish for garden pools include goldfish, shubunkins, walking fish and koi carp. As a rough guide to the stocking rate, a minimum of 30cm sq (1 sq ft) of surface is needed for each 5cm (2in) length of fish. Overstocking may result in oxygen starvation, leading to deaths.

Installing a fountain

A fountain can hardly be classed as a natural feature and on this account may not find favour with every gardener. Yet the sight and sound of moving water have obvious attractions. The splashing helps to oxygenate the pool, which can be an advantage to any fish in it during sultry weather.

Fountains are easy to install. A submersible pump is placed on a plinth – a few bricks, for example – on the pool bottom with the jet just clear of the surface. The electric cable is taken up under the pool edging to a point where it can be

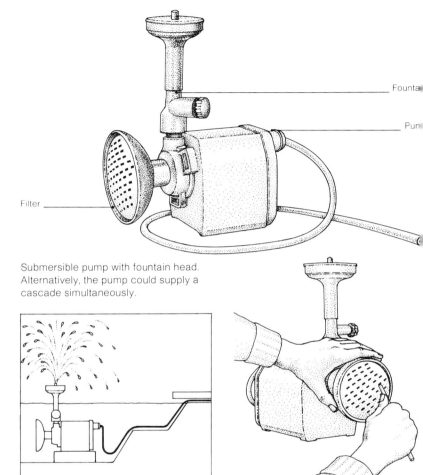

Founta

Pum

Filter

Submersible pump with fountain head. Alternatively, the pump could supply a cascade simultaneously.

1 A brick plinth raises the fountain just above the water. The paving edge conceals the cable.

2 The pump filter must be cleared at intervals to ensure that the flow of water is uninterrupted.

joined, by means of a waterproof connector, to the mains lead. For safety, employ a professional for fixed wiring and have the circuit protected by a core balance circuit breaker (core balance relay).

As well as mains-voltage pumps there are low-voltage models that operate, through a transformer, at a safe 24 volts.

Water garden specialists offer a variety of pumps and fountain jets. The more elaborate the jet, the

more powerful the pump needed. On most pumps a flow adjuster enables the height and spread of the jets to be matched to the capacity of the pool.

Another possibility is to supply both a fountain and a waterfall from the same pump. This puts greater demands on the unit so check that the pump can deliver sufficient water to the required level while the fountain is in action (see p. 86 for details of waterfall construction).

rose-clad arbour

Charming to look at, the cladding
of scented roses also makes this a
delightful place to sit. Ramblers are
ideal for training over such a
structure, though their period of
blooming is relatively short.
"Albertine" has richly-scented
pink flowers. Those of "Polyantha
Grandiflora" are small, single and
white in colour.

The alternative would be one of
the less-vigorous but repeat-
flowering climbers, such as
"Casino" (yellow), "Handel" (rose-
tipped white) or "Pink Perpetue".

The structure in this instance is
of wrought iron, one of a number
of commercially available types. Its
delicate appearance, at variance
with its true strength, is part of the
appeal. An arbour can also be
made with rustic poles, secured
with galvanized nails.

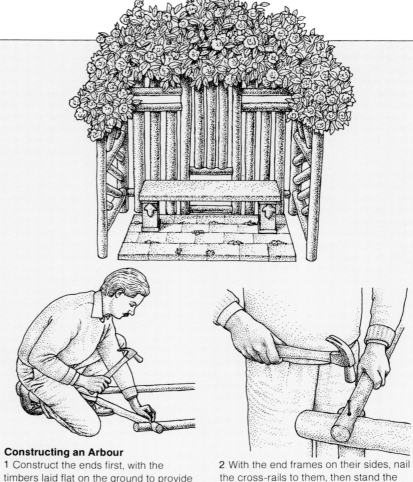

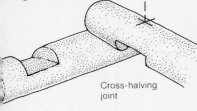

Cross-halving
joint

Constructing an Arbour
1 Construct the ends first, with the
timbers laid flat on the ground to provide
even support.

2 With the end frames on their sides, nail
the cross-rails to them, then stand the
structure upright.

Construct the sides on the flat,
then erect them and add the back
and top rails. To extend the life of
the uprights, first stand the bottom
60cm (2ft) of each pole in creosote
for 24 hours. Place them 45cm
(18in) deep in the soil.

As a finishing touch, a number of
chamomile plants (*Anthemis
nobilis*) have been set between the
irregular pieces of paving laid
under and in front of the seat.
They emit a pleasing aroma when
stepped upon, though they will not
withstand continuous wear.
See also p. 117 for suggestions on
benches suitable for arbours.

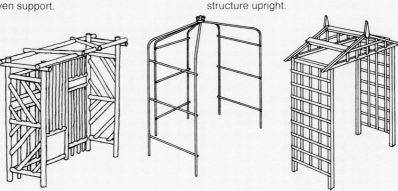

Though rustic timber is ideal for the
purpose, there are other forms of arbour.
Metal structures can be bought ready-

made, while sawn timber with a trellis
cladding lends itself to DIY construction.

A PLACE IN THE SUN

Most patios are built close to the house, where they provide a convenient place for relaxing and for enjoying outdoor meals. This assumes, though, that the area gets plenty of sunshine for much of the day throughout the warmer months of the year. If shaded, whether by the house or by trees, its use will be severely restricted.

In this event it is better to build the sitting area in a sunnier spot. Study the pattern of sunlight and shade in your garden, taking account of the longer shadows cast during spring and autumn. Mark out the chosen site and consider what else will be needed for privacy and shelter. A firm, all-weather access path is essential.

The screen in the illustration protects the paved area from. Bearing in mind this rural setting, panels of local reed were chosen instead of the usual lapped or woven fencing. They provide a sympathetic background for climbing plants.

A hired mechanical vibrator made light and speedy work of laying the paved surface. Consisting of paving slabs, each 40 × 20cm (16 × 8in), the paving was compacted into a bed of sand. This is a job that most people could tackle, especially since it does not involve mixing or carrying concrete.

The pool built in one corner adds interest and a restful note. Though with a rather small surface area, it has vertical sides to ensure a maximum volume of water. The sunny position is an aid to plant growth, which in turn helps to keep the water clear.

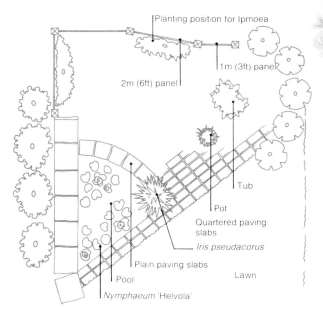

Planting position for Ipmoea

1m (3ft) panel

2m (6ft) panel

Tub

Pot

Quartered paving slabs

Iris pseudacorus

Plain paving slabs

Lawn

Pool

Nymphaeum 'Helvola'

Preparing the site

Mark out the area with a line and pegs, setting the line a few inches beyond the proposed edge of the paving. Skim any weeds and rubbish from the surface, together with protruding roots, but loosen it as little as possible. Rake the soil even, if necessary first removing some top-soil to ensure that the surface of the paving will be at the required level.

On normal soil allow for the thickness of the slabs and for about 5cm (2in) of bedding sand. However, on clay or peaty soils, which are less stable, remove a further 10cm (4in) of soil and replace this with a layer of broken stone or hard core to provide a firm foundation.

If such a foundation layer is needed, tamp it firmly into place with the end of a pole or beam or else with the vibrator that will be used later to settle the paving into the sand. It is better not to use builder's rubble that has resulted from demolition work as it is difficult to achieve a firm base with this.

Where there is no risk of tree roots being harmed, a total weedkiller, such as sodium chlorate, may be applied to the under layer before the sub-base of stone is laid.

Erecting a screen

In this instance the panels are of reed but the general method of erection is the same for other types of fencing panel.

The posts are the most vulnerable part of any fence, the timber at and below ground level being vulnerable to rot. Brushing with creosote will provide a little temporary protection but a better method by far is vacuum/pressure treatment, forcing the preservative deep into the timber. This process is carried out by the supplier.

Posts preserved by this method will last for many years when set in earth or concrete. A post hole-borer, which can generally be hired,

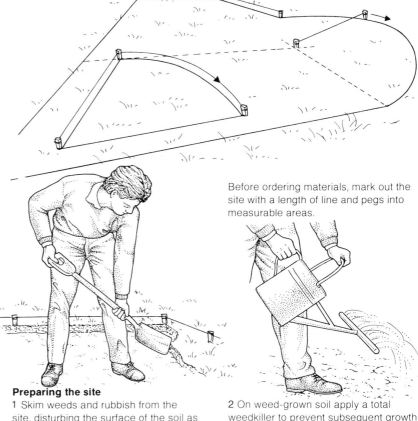

Before ordering materials, mark out the site with a length of line and pegs into measurable areas.

Preparing the site
1 Skim weeds and rubbish from the site, disturbing the surface of the soil as little as possible.

2 On weed-grown soil apply a total weedkiller to prevent subsequent growth between paving.

The metal dolly is placed in the socket while hammering.

is a help when digging holes. These should be up to 60cm (2ft) deep for a tall fence, 45cm (1½ft) for one of medium height.

The alternative, used here, is to insert the end of each post in a metal socket. The socket is mounted on a tapered spike which is driven into the ground with a sledgehammer. These fittings cost more than concreting, but the posts need not be so long and the risk of the wood rotting is much reduced.

Erecting a screen
When using a post-hole auger, pull it out at intervals in order to remove the loosened soil.

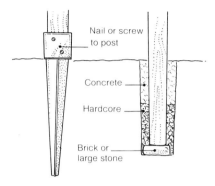

Nail or screw to post

Concrete

Hardcore

Brick or large stone

2 Sockets are best on firm ground. On soft soil, make a hole and case the post in concrete.

Check at intervals that the posts are vertical while driving in a metal support.

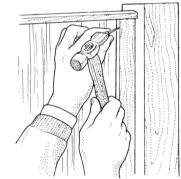

4 Lightweight panels can be secured by driving nails through the side frames into the posts.

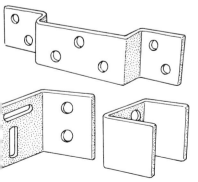

Brackets of various shapes are available for fixing fence panels to the support posts.

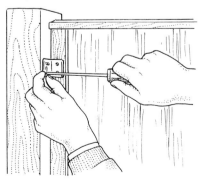

6 Fastened with brackets and screws, heavy panels are both more secure and more easily removed.

To erect a screen by this means, first mark out the line of the fence, then drive in a spike and socket at one end. Insert a post in the socket – some types have a tightening bolt – then attach a panel to it. This will provide a guide to positioning the next spike. There are various types of metal fittings, obtainable from fencing suppliers, for securing panels to posts.

While driving the spike into the ground it is essential to keep it both upright and square-on. To check that it is upright, place a spirit level against the sides of the socket from time to time. Ease the spike to either side as necessary.

To keep the socket square-on to the line of fencing there is a tool incorporating a lever bar that enables the post to be twisted if necessary.

Posts for panel fences should be 8 × 8cm (3 × 3in) in section. When ordering, remember that you will need one more post than the number of panels. When calculating the number of panels, which generally come in 1.8m (6ft) widths, allow for the 8cm (3in) width of each post.

Climbers against a fence
As well as softening the outline of fencing, climbing plants can provide an eye-catching splash of colour. Most need supports for tendrils to twine around or for stems to be secured. Green, plastic-covered wire will do the job unobtrusively. Staple it to the posts at 30cm (1 ft) intervals, starting 60cm (2ft) above the ground.

For a sunny, sheltered spot, one of the smaller varieties of Bougainvillea or jasmine. It could be grown in a substantial container or in a planting pocket left in the paving. Do not plant out until the late spring.

For the side panel, facing east in this instance, consider a honeysuckle (*Lonicera brownii* 'Firecracker'). This species produces scented flowers throughout the summer.

Laying paving

There are two principle methods of laying paving slabs and blocks. One, suitable when fairly large slabs are laid on a firm surface, is to bed them on blobs of mortar. This makes for easy levelling as described on p. 116.

The second method, especially suitable for concrete blocks and bricks, is to bed them on a layer of sand. This method, described here, requires a mechanical vibrator. These machines can be hired from plant-hire firms or, sometimes, from their DIY equivalents.

Bedding on a continuous layer of mortar is seldom required in gardens. Even for a driveway it should be sufficient to lay a 10cm (4in) sub-base of crushed stone before placing the sand. An exception is crazy paving, which does need a mortar base (see p. 72).

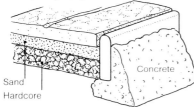

Sand
Hardcore
Concrete

Supporting the edge

A firm edge is needed to prevent the blocks or slabs moving sideways under pressure. Position opposing edges as accurately as possible to correspond with the size of the paving units, otherwise a good deal of awkward cutting may be needed during the later stages of laying.

Use pre-cast concrete edging pieces for the kerb, bedding them in concrete with their upper edges flush with, or a little above, the eventual level of the paving. Use taut lines and a spirit level as a guide.

Let the concrete harden for a few days before laying the paving.

Placing the sand

Check again that the base is level and firm. Use a rake to spread sharp

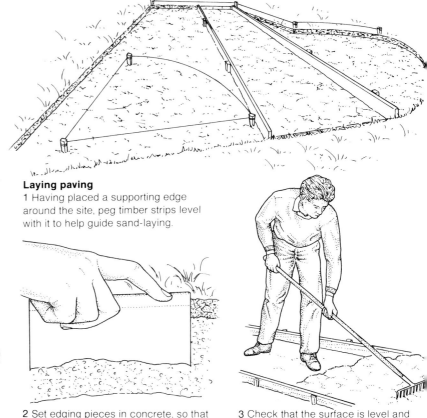

Laying paving
1 Having placed a supporting edge around the site, peg timber strips level with it to help guide sand-laying.

2 Set edging pieces in concrete, so that their tops are flush with the eventual level of the paving.

3 Check that the surface is level and firm, then spread sharp sand over it using a rake.

sand about 6cm (2½in) deep over an area extending 3m (10ft) or so from the side that you propose to start working. For convenience, this should be the side on which the sand is stacked.

With a helper, draw a straight-edged plank over the sand to level the surface. If the plank will straddle the patio from kerb to kerb, so much the better. Simply notch its ends so that it projects downwards somewhat less than the thickness of the paving.

For example, for 4cm (1½in) slab the sand should be 3cm (1¼in below the level of the kerb.

If the patio is too wide to allow this, peg a strip of timber in position halfway across, its top level with the kerb, to serve as a temporary guide.

Laying the paving

Now start to lay the slabs or blocks placing them tight against each other. When it becomes necessar to walk on the newly-laid blocks

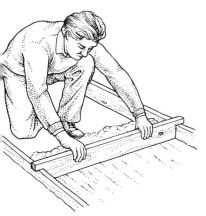

Level the sand between the timber strips, using a board notched to the thickness of the paving.

Firm the blocks into the sand with a mechanical vibrator. Two or three passes are needed.

Use a bolster and heavy hammer to cut slabs. For safety, wear goggles while doing so.

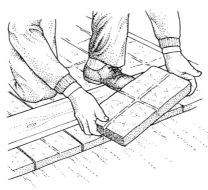

5 Start laying the blocks against one of the raised edges. Make sure that they are tightly butted.

7 Instead of using a vibrator the blocks may be tapped into place. They will not be quite so secure.

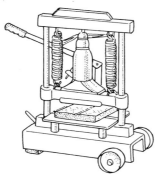

9 A hydraulic stone-splitter not only saves work but also makes for more accurate cutting.

first place planks to spread your weight. Where part blocks are needed to complete the edges, use a hammer and bolster to first form a groove on both sides and then complete the cut with a sharp blow. For a large patio it may be worth hiring a hydraulic stone-splitter or a brick saw with diamond blade.

There may be small, irregular spaces that are difficult to deal with. These can be filled later with cement-mortar, placing pieces of the paving in the surface to minimize the change in colour.

When most of the sanded area has been covered it is time to vibrate the blocks into place. Make two or three passes with the machine but go no closer than 1m (1 yd) from the unsupported edge. Complete the compacted area by spreading more sand over the paving, using a brush and the vibrator to work this between the blocks.

Continue with a further band of sand and paving, still with planks laid across the area that has yet to be consolidated. When the far side is reached it is important that the pieces of paving fit the space exactly. This will call for very careful cutting unless your original planning and marking-out was accurate.

The vibrated blocks can be walked on immediately. There is no need to insert mortar between the joints.

Repairs

If blocks become cracked or stained, or have to be lifted for any other purpose, the damaged area is easily lifted by breaking a block with a hammer, removing the pieces and then lifting those around it.

Rather than hire a vibrator for replacing a small area, first dampen the sand and then tamp it level and compact. Tap the slabs or blocks into it, placing a block of wood on the surface of the paving and striking it with a hammer.

Making a pool with masonry

For the majority of garden pools, especially fairly large ones with an informal shape, a flexible liner is the most satisfactory means of construction. Compact or angular designs are a possible exception as they involve much folding of the material.

The alternatives are either pre-fabricated pools made from fibre-glass or semi-rigid plastic or else a pool built in situ from concrete blocks. (Though the former require less work it can be quite tricky to dig a hole that exactly matches the moulding of the pool.)

Concrete was chosen in the present instance because there was no

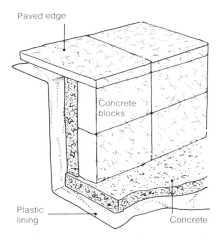

Paved edge — Concrete blocks — Plastic lining — Concrete

Making the pool
1 Dig the hole, allowing for both the thickness of the blocks and the outer concrete filling.

2 After removing protruding stones, line the hole with a piece of medium-grade plastic sheeting.

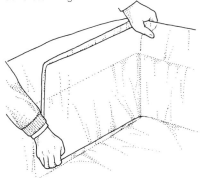

3 Trim the top edges, and cut the corners, to give a flap that will be covered by the paving.

4 Fold the pleats against the side walls. Take care not to pierce or rupture the plastic sheet.

prefabricated design of the required shape and size. Also, the vertical sides of a concrete pool allow a greater water content reducing harmful fluctuations in temperature. The water is 45cm (18in) deep.

Perhaps the chief point to note is that the pool is lined with water-proof material. Unlined concrete pools are notorious for developing disastrous leaks.

Digging the hole
As the cross-sectional view shows, the excavation has to be sufficiently deep and broad to allow for a base

and double side walls. The base is a 10cm (4in) slab of concrete, laid in situ and broad enough to support the walls. The sides consist of concrete facing blocks, 9 or 10cm (3½ or 4in) thick, with a backing of 10cm (4in) of concrete added after the walls are built.

The base therefore needs to be some 40cm (16in) longer and wider than the proposed internal dimensions of the pool.

After digging the hole, line it with

medium-heavy plastic sheeting. Being buried, this will not be harmed by ultra-violet rays. But make sure that there are no protruding stones to damage it. Fold the plastic back at the corners.

Using a 1:5 mix of cement and combined sand/stone aggregates, cover the base with a 10cm (4in) layer of concrete, again taking care not to damage the plastic sheeting. Use a board to achieve a smooth and reasonably level surface. As the

5 Cover the base with a layer of concrete. Lay this gently over the plastic lining and tamp it level.

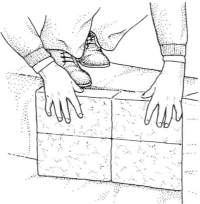

6 Wait for the concrete to set before building the walls. Leave a space for the concrete infilling.

7 Back-fill with concrete, tamping each layer gently to eliminate the chance of air pockets.

8 Place paving slabs over the flap of plastic and the tops of the walls. No need for an overhang.

concrete starts to set, roughen the edges slightly where the walls and backfill will stand.

Build the sides a couple of days later, leaving a gap for backfilling behind the blocks. Lay the blocks with a mortar made from 1 part sand to 3½ parts masonry cement, filling and smoothing the joints carefully.

Two days later, back-fill with a similar mix to that used for the base. Keep the work covered with a sheet of plastic for a further three days, then fill the pool with water and keep it topped up for another similar period. After this, the paving surround may be laid.

Finally, change the water and leave it to stand for at least a week before introducing any plants. If you wish to include marginal plants, which need shallow water, set the containers on plinths close to the edge. Should you favour a miniature water lily, this, too, will need relatively shallow planting.

Planting roses

Though not central to this scheme, bush roses will provide long-lasting colour during the months when the patio is in frequent use. For some, the relaxed, free-flowering habit of floribundas will be first choice. Others may prefer the more individual beauty of hybrid tea roses.

Either way, beds of a single variety have the most telling effect. Both kinds are planted in the same way, practically any time of year being suitable for those supplied in plastic containers. Winter is the best period for planting roses with bare roots, but very early spring can be suitable.

Dig the soil a month or so in advance so that it will have time to settle. While doing so, work in a generous dressing of well-rotted manure or garden compost. Work the surface to a finer tilth just

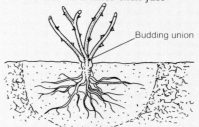

Budding union

before planting.

Dig the planting holes 45cm (18in) apart and deep enough to allow the budding union, seen as a bulge at the base of the stem, to be about level with or just under the surface. Spread compost, around the roots or rootballs to give the plants a good start.

Planting a hedge

Allow 75cm (2½ft) between escallonia plants, setting them about 45cm (1½ft) from the edge of the paving. For alternative suggestions, see pp. 151–153.

A FOOD GROWER'S GARDEN

Functional gardens, with the emphasis on fruit and vegetables, need not lack style. A degree of planning also makes for easier working. In winter, for instance, good access to all areas keeps mud and compacted soil to a minimum. Close grouping of activities reduces the amount of walking and carrying.

In this typically elongated suburban garden the productive area has been set at one end, defined and to some extent concealed by a honeycomb brick wall. Its separate components are linked by crazy paving, a functional yet decorative surface that is easily laid around the interlocking shapes of greenhouse, vegetable plot and so on.

The greenhouse, fittingly, is the centrepiece, a hexagonal model that combines good looks with effective performance. With the staging removed, tomatoes and cucumbers occupy much of the interior during the summer. These are raised from seed during the spring, along with such hardy crops as marrows, melons and squash.

Close by is a cold frame, valuable for hardening off seedlings and for raising early salad and brassica plants. There is, too, a separate herb bed.

With no space for bush fruit trees, two espalier apples, chosen for mutual pollination, are planted alongisde the fence at the back of the vegetable plot. The cage is given over to soft fruits.

The remainder of the garden is of no consequence here, except for one feature worth special note. This is the children's play area, a sunken sandpit. Easily constructed, it will provide hours of pleasure for a very modest outlay and small amount of effort.

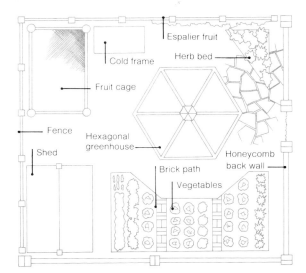

Espalier fruit

Cold frame

Herb bed

Fruit cage

Fence

Hexagonal greenhouse

Shed

Honeycomb back wall

Brick path

Vegetables

Laying crazy paving

Once weathered, crazy paving forms an attractive surface for paths and patios. Curving outlines are no problem and the finished result has more individuality than ready-made slabs. The random-shaped stones are available from builders' merchants and from some garden centres, a tonne of stone being sufficient for about 7.5sq m (9sq yds).

A drawback is that crazy paving needs to be laid on a solid concrete base. Without this, the smaller pieces of stone are unlikely to remain level. A bedding layer of mortar goes on top of the concrete.

Forming the base

Set out the path with pegs and string on each side. The strings are to mark the level of the path as well as its edges, so check by placing a board and spirit level across them. About 75cm (2½ft) is the minimum satisfactory width.

Next, remove sufficient soil to allow for 5–8cm (2–3in) of concrete, 13mm (½in) of mortar and the thickness of the stones. On soft soil, dig out another 8cm (3in) for a layer of crushed stone; consolidate this layer over the base after tamping the soil firm.

A 1:5 mix of cement and aggregates (mixed sand and stone) is suitable for the foundation layer. Tamp this firm with a board the same width as the path, then cover with plastic sheeting to prevent too-rapid drying. Leave it for at least two days before going on to the next stage.

Laying the paving

For the bedding layer of mortar mix one part cement with five parts of sharp sand. Only a thin layer is needed, enough to allow the pieces of stone to be tapped level and to hold them secure. Mix and lay a metre (about a yard) at a time.

Use straight-edged stones for the edges, filling in with a balanced,

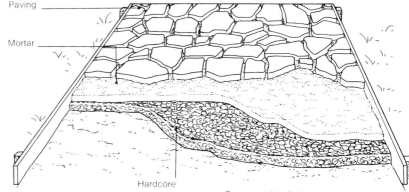

Paving

Mortar

Hardcore

Crazy paving is both strong and attractive, but laying it in position involves a good deal of hard work.

Laying crazy paving
1 After setting the path out with pegs and string, check the level with a board and spirit level.

2 Remove enough soil to allow for the concrete sub-base, the mortar and the pieces of stone.

interlocking mix of small and large pieces. Check the level constantly with a board placed across the surface to join the string markers on each side.

Finally, after a further two days, fill in between the stones with a 1:4 mix of cement and sand. Keep this mixture fairly dry to reduce the risk of staining the surface of the stones. This lapse of time allows the stones to settle down into the layer of mortar.

3 Tap the stones into a thin layer of mortar which has been placed on the hardened concrete base.

Check frequently that each piece of stone is level, otherwise puddles will remain after rain.

Tap down uneven slabs with a mallet. In warm weather cover newly-laid paving with plastic.

Fill between slabs with a fairly dry mortar mix. Smooth this mortar with the trowel blade.

Erecting screens

There is something to be said for separating the fruit and vegetable department of a garden from its ornamental area. Each, after all, has a quite different purpose and appearance. The division can be a simple boundary marker, such as a low hedge, or take a more positive form.

The wall chosen in this instance is of honeycomb design, a subtle means of dividing without completely shutting off. The shed and fruit cage, neither of them especially beautiful, are concealed, but the hexagonal greenhouse may be seen through the entry opening. A wall of this sort needs solid foundations, with strengthening piers at intervals for added stability.

For a simpler and less expensive alternative, a trellis structure supporting sweet peas will form a colourful screen in summer and remain partially effective in winter.

Concrete screen blocks may appear rather stark unless their angular form is softened with plant growth. Nevertheless, they are easy to erect and are by no means out of place in an urban setting.

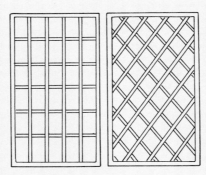

Trellis, bought or home-made, is most often used as an attractive support for climbing plants.

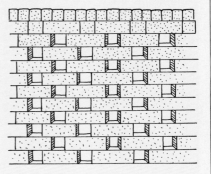

A honeycomb brick wall screens effectively and filters the wind. Building is uncomplicated.

Concrete screen blocks come in a number of patterns. Precast pier blocks are available, too.

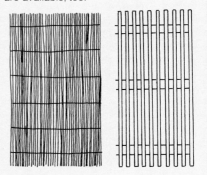

Screens made of bamboo or slatted timber can be used for dividing panels attached to posts.

Planning the food garden

Trained fruit trees – cordons or espaliers – make good use of limited space in small gardens. Soft fruits, such as raspberries and currants, can give remarkable yields for the ground they occupy.

In the vegetable garden give priority to salad crops, which are so much more enjoyable when freshly picked, together with any delicacies that may be in short supply and difficult to find in the shops.

It goes without saying that plenty of sun is needed. This, and well-nourished soil, will go a long way to ensuring successful crops.

Beds for vegetables

Instead of growing their vegetables in well-spaced rows, some gardeners now concentrate them in beds a little over 1 metre (about a yard) wide. Here, the sowings or plantings are much closer, with many more plants packed into a given area, and they are tended from narrow paths left between the beds.

Overall, this results in greater output. As well as making better use of space, the bed system reduces or eliminates the need to walk on cultivated ground. The soil can be manured, forked over and hoed from the paths; this will result in markedly improved soil structure – especially on heavy ground.

As a broad rule, allow as much space *between* rows as you would normally leave between plants *in* the row. Such heavy cropping demands generous feeding with nourishing organic matter.

Fruit cages

Unless protected with netting, soft fruit crops provide a feast for birds and squirrels. A cage is the answer, either a ready-made structure made of metal or plastic tubing or a home-made timber frame. The cost of the former is not unreasonable and is worthwhile in the long run.

Vegetables grown in beds, with small paths between, may be planted more closely than in open ground.

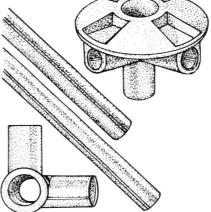

1 Patent plastic fittings such as these allow easy construction of a netting-covered fruit cage.

2 When pushed into the corner sockets, the plastic tubing fits snugly to form uprights and supports.

During the summer, use 19mm (3/4in) netting for both the sides and the top. For the winter, replace the roof with 10cm or 15cm (4in or 6in) mesh. This narrower gauge will keep not only pigeons out but also prevent a damaging build-up of snow.

Trained fruit trees

Classed as "restricted" trees, both cordons and espaliers are trained to a series of supporting wires. Plant cordons 75–90cm. (2½–3ft) apart,

espaliers 3–4.5m (10 ft–15 ft), depending on the vigour of their rootstocks. You should ask the supplier for full details about this and check also that the varieties which you have chosen, if not self-fertile, are able to cross-pollinate.

He may also explain how to prune and train the trees. Otherwise, you will need a book that covers the subject in detail to consult – you might consider buying one, it is an excellent investment.

Base for a greenhouse

A firm, level base is needed. Subsidence will distort the frame, resulting in broken panes. Some greenhouses are supplied with a sturdy base and need no additional foundations. Failing this, you will have to make your own.

A combination of brick and concrete is suitable for either aluminium or timber greenhouses. The concrete is a strip 15cm (6in) wide and 8cm (3in) deep laid in a trench, its top level with the surrounding soil. For a rectangular house, ensure that the corners are right angles by checking that the diagonal measurements are equal.

Having given the concrete a couple of days to harden, lay a single course of bricks on a mortar bed, with mortar joints between. Ideally, the outer edge of the bricks should allow the greenhouse frame to overhang very slightly, shedding any rainwater.

A strip of damp-proof course or roofing felt placed on the bricks is a further aid to preserving the condition of a timber frame.

Base for a shed

The timber floor supplied with most sheds must be placed on a solid base. The choice rests between paving slabs and concrete laid in situ.

If you choose paving slabs, remove an inch or two of soil, ram the base firm and lay the slabs on blobs of mortar (see p. 116.) Alternatively, tap them into a bed of sharp sand.

To lay a slab of concrete, first remove 5cm (2in) of soil from the area. Peg 8 × 1.3cm (3 × ½in) formwork around the edges, its top 2.5cm (1 in) above the adjacent ground. Check that the corners are "square" by ensuring that the diagonal measurements are equal.

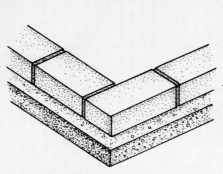

Laying greenhouse base
1 For a greenhouse base, first lay a strip of concrete. On top of this lay a single course of bricks.

2 If a greenhouse is timber-framed, lay a strip of damp-proof felt on top of the brick base.

3 A shed needs a concrete base, so remove 5cm (2in) of soil and peg formwork around the edges.

4 Use a plank to compact and level the concrete, removing any surplus by drawing it backwards.

Use a spirit level placed on a plank to check that the opposite sides of the framework are level.

Using a 1:4 mix of cement and combined aggregates (sand and stones), lay an 8cm (3in) slab of concrete within the formwork. Level the surface with the top of the surround, first tamping it with the edge of a plank.

Place 8 × 5cm (3 × 2in) joists on the hardened concrete to support the wooden floor.

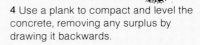

For a larger base – a garage, for instance – divide the whole area into sections which are more manageable.

WAYS WITH TREES

Tree planting is not an everyday job. For most of us it occurs only periodically during the making of a garden, so all the more reason to approach it thoughtfully.

Positioning a tree needs as much care as its choice. In a small garden it is often the focal point around which all else revolves. It deserves, therefore, to be a planning priority rather than an afterthought, carefully schemed to draw the eye by reason of its form and foliage – perhaps also its flowers or berries.

Functionally, trees offer much else. Shade, screening and shelter from wind are three possible gains, depending on the species chosen. If nothing else, a tree will provide a restful backdrop to beds and borders or draw attention across a green spread of lawn.

The illustrations suggest only a few of the many possibilities. They show, also, how a tree can be complemented by its setting or with selective underplanting. For further inspiration one has only to walk around some of the many gardens open to the public – the smaller ones for preference.

1. *Acer japonicum* 'Aureum'
2. *Betula pendula* 'Youngii'
3. *Malus* 'John Downie'
4. *Prunus subhirtella* 'Pendula'
5. *Cornus nuttallii*
6. *Picea pungens* 'Glauca'

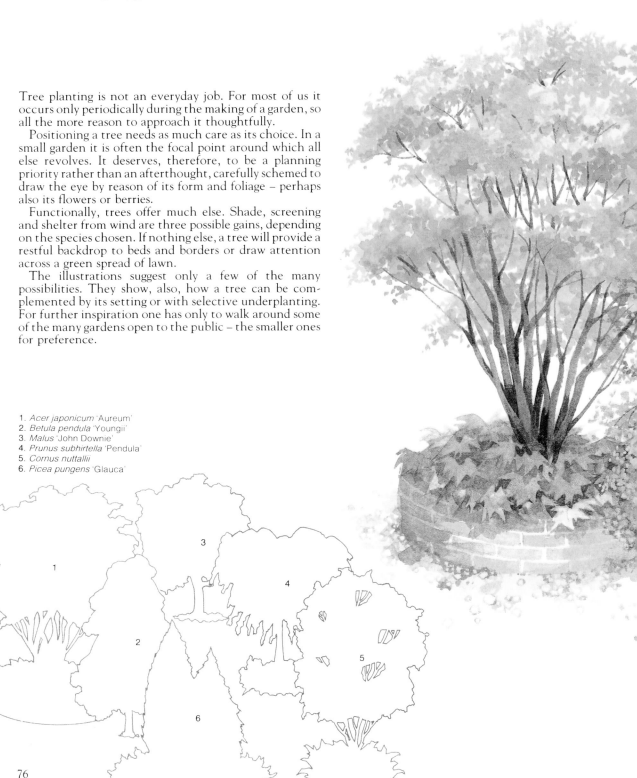

Choosing and planting trees

First of all be clear about your object. Is it functional – to gain shade, shelter, a screen – or aesthetic? Even when, as generally happens, motives are mixed, there are still likely to be priorities.

For shade you will need a tree with a spreading habit, such as *Acer negundo*. As a fast-growing windbreak, there remain few equals to the ubiquitous Leyland cypress. Screening is more difficult to pin down, size being the chief factor. Keep in mind the value of evergreens, such as variegated hollies.

Size means *eventual* height and spread, for many a charming sapling develops into a brooding giant. In this context think of your neighbours' gardens as well as your own, too-dominant trees being a common cause of friction. This may involve root growth as well as foliage, because a large, densely-leaved tree will starve nearby soil of both moisture and essential nutriments.

Where to plant

Trees are better kept at a distance from the house. Planted too close (less than perhaps 7.5m (8yd), depending on size) the more vigorous kinds will darken rooms and may even damage the structure. Roots, particularly those of willows, are capable of penetrating the drains and damaging foundations.

Deciding what to plant and where to plant it is a joint exercise. It comes down to doing your homework indoors – principally, browsing through books and catalogues for ideas – and then, armed with knowledge, moving into the garden. A plan mapped out on paper is not much help, for the vertical dimension is all-important.

In particular, consider shape in relation to position – columnar, spreading, weeping, round-headed . . . The right choice will set the scene for everything around.

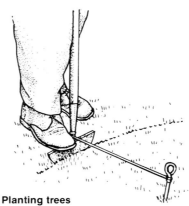

Planting trees

1 In turf, use a peg and string as a guide to cutting a circle with a half-moon edger.

2 Place the earth that you dig out from the hole on a large sheet of plastic laid alongside.

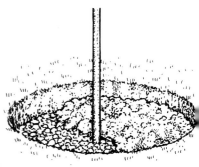

3 Hammer in a supporting stake, if one is needed, before placing the tree in its final position.

4 Loosen the soil in the bottom of the hole, mixing in some organic matter such as garden compost.

Particular species have their special needs. Overall, most require reasonably free-draining soil and a good share of sunshine, but some insist on either acid or alkaline conditions, a relatively frost-free site or one sheltered from strong winds. Checking these needs is all part of the necessary homework.

When to plant

As with shrubs, young trees sold in plastic containers may be planted at any time of year when the soil is neither parched, saturated nor frozen. The easiest way is to buy them when convenient and then wait, if necessary, for the right conditions. Best time of all is a period of mild, damp weather.

Bare-rooted trees, sold by some nurseries, are available during the dormant months of late autumn to early spring. But avoid periods when the temperature is freezing or the soil saturated.

Trim off any damaged roots, then spread the rest of the roots evenly over the prepared base.

6 Place the soil mixture around the roots, shaking the stem to settle it, then level hold line with a fork.

Use a batten to check that the soil mark on the stem aligns with the soil level of the ground soil.

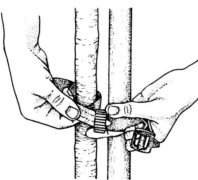

8 A plastic tie is ideal for securing the stem of the newly planted tree to the supporting stake.

Fasten the strap so that the buffer piece stops the stem from rubbing against the stake.

10 Adjust the fastening from time to time as the tree grows, so preventing undue pressure.

Broad-leaved evergreens are best planted in autumn or spring. For conifers, spring is the ideal time. Because neither is ever fully dormant, they are sold in containers. The more tender evergreens are best planted in spring.

Planting and supporting
It really is worth going to a little trouble, bearing in mind the tree's likely life span. Dig out a planting hole deep and broad enough to take the soil-ball or the spread-out roots, with some room to spare. When settled, the young tree will need to be at its previous depth, as judged by the soil mark on the stem of bare-rooted saplings or the surface of the compost of container-grown plants.

With a fork, loosen the soil at the bottom of the hole and mix in some peat, garden compost or rotted manure. This will give a boost to the developing roots. With the same object, mix some organic material with the soil dug out of the hole.

Where needed, hammer in a supporting stake. If this is left until after planting you may damage the roots. Now plant the young tree, firming the enriched soil mixture over the bare-roots or around the soil-ball.

Secure the trunk to the stake with a couple of plastic ties. These adjust to allow for growth and will not damage bark. Give soil over roots a soaking to settle it.

Inexpensive tree guards will protect the young bark. Should you think you might need them, any cost involved could be money well spent.

If you plant in spring or summer, take care that the soil around the tree does not dry out. Conifers and other evergreens are particularly at risk, so keep the ground moist and spray the foliage with water once or twice a day during dry spells.

A ROCK GARDEN AND WATERFALL

Constructing a convincing rock garden can be quite a challenge. After all, what is a patch of mountain terrain doing in a green and level setting? Yet the effort is abundantly worthwhile, for alpine plants have the appeal of all miniature things, with brilliantly-coloured flowers and exquisitely delicate form. A sunny aspect is essential, well away from overhanging trees.

The construction seen here started with an advantage. It is built on and into an existing bank, avoiding the currant-bun effect one sometimes encounters on flat ground. The aim, whatever the contours, should be to simulate a rocky outcrop. A further aid was the backing of trees and shrubs and the scope for ground-cover planting, each of these helping to create a natural setting.

At one end, where the bank levels out, the rock garden merges into a scree bed. In nature, such a collection of chippings and small stones would be found beneath a steep slope or cliff. Needless to say, the plants growing in such a mixture are adapted to sharp drainage.

As a finishing touch a miniature cascade tumbles down the slope between the plants, ending in a slate-edged pool. The onlooker has no clue that the water is circulated from here to the top of the bank by means of a submerged pump and buried piping.

It should be mentioned that alpines are easy to grow even where space and other considerations rule out a true rock garden. Sinks and raised beds are equally suitable so long as the compost or soil is gritty and free-draining.

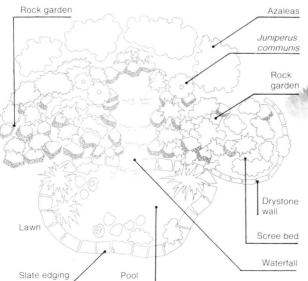

Rock garden

Azaleas

Juniperus communis

Rock garden

Drystone wall

Scree bed

Waterfall

Lawn

Slate edging

Pool

Constructing a rock garden

The pieces of rock must seem to project from the soil, not to rest upon it. That is the key to a successful rock garden. It should appear as an outcrop, exposed because the overlying material has been eroded away. Most important of all, the soil around the rocks must be free-draining, though capable of retaining moisture during dry weather.

When building into a bank, where drainage is generally good, there should be few problems. If the soil is heavy, though, or the bank takes water from the area behind, it may be necessary to dig part of it away and place a drainage layer before replacing the soil and building the rock garden.

In this event, and always on flat ground, start by removing and stacking the topsoil, then spread a good layer of crushed stone or hardcore in the excavation. If you dug up part of the lawn in the first instance, replace the turves, inverting them over the drainage layer.

At this stage try to remove every trace of perennial weeds. This means roots as well as leaves and stems. If left until the rock garden has been built and planted, careful use of selective weedkillers will be the only effective way to tackle them.

Buying stone

Choose a local stone if there is one. It is more likely to look "right" and ought to be cheaper than others carried from a greater distance. Go for substantial pieces, bearing in mind that up to two thirds of their mass needs to be buried. Weathered rocks with detectable strata are the most effective.

Placing the stones

Start with one of the biggest pieces. With a projecting corner facing forwards, scoop a hole large enough to contain about half its mass. Place it so that any clear strata lines are

Built into a bank, the aim of a rock garden is to simulate a natural outcrop.

Constructing a rock garden

1 To ensure really sharp drainage, remove the topsoil to one side and spread a layer of broken stones over the soil exposed. If turves were cut from the surface, invert these to cover this drainage layer.

nearly horizontal, though with the upper face of the stone tilted back a little. The idea is to direct rainwater towards the slope of the rock garden, not outwards and away from it.

This first stage applies whether you are building on flat ground or into a bank. But from then on there

are differences. On flat ground, se additional stones on each side at th same level, placing them a littl further back. Strata lines must alig with those of the first piece. Th effect might be compared with tha of a ship with a blunt bow.

On a bank, the side stones wi

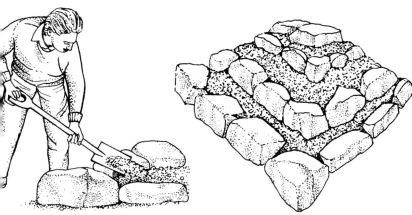

Choose a large slab as a cornerstone.
ill in behind this slab with a free-
raining soil mixture.

3 Position each piece of rock so that its
upper face will tilt back slightly into the
slope itself.

have to be roughly in line with the one laid first, but make maximum use of the different sizes and contours to vary their height and projection. Leave only small spaces between stones – fissures rather than gaps.

When building on flat ground, especially, the soil around and behind rocks needs firming into place. A blunt-ended rammer – a stick with a rounded end about 4cm (1½in) across – is handy for the purpose. To raise the overall level, as for an outcrop, and to bury the upper parts of the rocks you will need a gritty, moisture-retaining compost.

For this, mix the excavated topsoil with peat and either coarse sand or grit. The ideal mix depends on the nature of the soil, but on average add one part of peat and another of sharp sand or grit to each two parts of topsoil.

Heavy soil needs rather more sand or grit to aid drainage. Light soil requires extra peat for moisture retention. In both cases work in a good sprinkling of blood and bone.

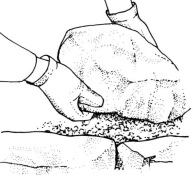

Use a blunt-ended ramming stick to
rm the gritty soil mixture around the
labs of rock.

5 When placing subsequent layers of
rock, straddle the joints that were formed
in the course beneath.

With the foundation layer in position, add a second one, the faces of the rocks a little further back than those beneath. It will help if some of the stones, like bricks in a wall, straddle the joints in the lower layer. This will minimize soil erosion through the crevices.

While building this and subsequent tiers, set the roots of trailing or rosette-forming plants in some of the fissures. Firm the soil around them and water gently. Among the many suitable kinds are saxifrages, sempervivums, gypsophilas, sedums and several species of dianthus.

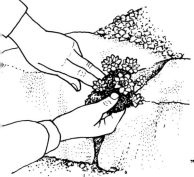

6 While building, set the roots of trailing
r rosette-forming plants in some of the
ssures between the rocks.

7 Complete the main planting after the
soil has settled, first spreading a layer of
rock chippings.

These apart, give the soil a little time to settle before completing the main planting. Before you do this, cover the whole rock garden with a 13mm (½in) layer of rock chippings. This will help to keep the soil moist, deter slugs and prevent mud splashes on the low-growing plants.

Making a scree bed

A scree bed goes naturally alongside a rock garden, and is a home for some truly delightful plants.

The purpose of these beds is to provide the right conditions for plants adapted to a singularly spartan way of life. As already mentioned, they will be found under natural conditions at the base of mountains and steep slopes where fragments of rocks have accumulated over the centuries. Beneath, and mixed with the stones, there will be eroded soil, providing nourishment and a source of moisture for these tough little plants.

Many kinds of plants will thrive in a scree. Some of them are particularly suitable, though, among them various natives, campanulas, limoniums and ranunculus, each needing impeccable drainage and a cool, stone-covered run to accommodate their roots.

It follows that a successful scree bed will have even sharper drainage than an ordinary rock garden. Nevertheless, it must be capable of retaining moisture during the warmer months. The key to these seemingly contradictory needs lies in the way it is constructed.

On heavy soil the bed must be raised above the surrounding ground. This can be achieved with a low dry wall (see p. 128). The need is not so great on light, free-draining soil, though a slightly raised level is an advantage in this instance.

Place a 15cm (6in) layer of rubble or broken stone about 45cm (18in) under the eventual surface, covering this with a layer of inverted turves. Over these place the main filling, a mix of 10 parts stone chippings, 1 part loam, 1 part peat and 1 part sharp sand. Secure the loam from elsewhere if your own soil is sticky or lumpy in texture.

Insert small rocks in the surface for appearance as much as anything, and scatter more grit around and under the plants to fill any gaps between them and the rocks.

Making a scree bed

1 Having removed turves and about 45cm (18in) of soil, lay rubble or broken stones over the base.

2 A low retaining wall made of flat stones will help to ensure that the bed is raised and free-draining.

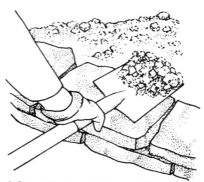

3 Cover the inverted turves with a mix of stone chippings, gritty soil, peat and sharp sand.

4 Bed small rocks in the surface of the scree. Scatter chippings around and under the plants.

Planting and caring for alpines

Almost always sold in pots, alpines may be planted at any time of year except during frosty spells. Water the compost an hour before planting. Draw the dressing of rock chippings to one side, then use a trowel to form a planting hole broad and deep enough to accommodate the rootball.

Match each point to its setting. Those with a prostrate habit look well beside a rock over which they can spread their foliage. Those forming rosettes, liable to damage from water collecting in them, benefit from the protection of a crevice. Do not overlook the ability of upright, miniature conifers to enhance the overall effect of the bed.

After firming the soil around the rootball, replace the chippings under and around the foliage. Make sure that the soil around the plants does not dry out until the roots have grown into it from the compost, which will take several weeks. Left dry, the roots will remain confined to the original soil ball and the plant may well die.

Watering

Once plants are established, water rock gardens and screes only during prolonged dry weather. Use a sprinkler to give a gentle soaking that will penetrate well into the soil and under the rocks.

Top-dressing

Renew the surface layer each spring with a fresh dressing of chippings, mixing this with equal parts of loam and peat. To each bucketful of the mix add a good handful of blood and bone and fish-based fertilizer if available.

Winter protection

In autumn and early winter

Having moved the chippings aside, plant the unbroken rootball and firm the soil around it.

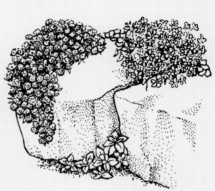

The habit of each plant – compact or prostrate – suggests where on the rock garden it will look best.

If water is needed at all, be sure to give enough to penetrate well into the soil.

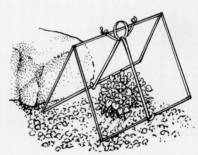

A small cloche, or glass supported by wires, is needed to protect some plants from winter wet.

remove any leaves from the scree. The wet covering can be fatal to plants and encourage slugs.

There are a few alpines, including some dianthus, lewisias and origanums, that succumb to winter wet. Cover them with a small sheet of glass supported on wire struts. Plants with leaves that have a woolly or hairy covering are particularly at risk.

Planting ground-cover

Ground-cover plants have certain qualities in common. Most are low-growing, tough, spreading species that will look after themselves and suppress weeds. It is still necessary to get rid of perennial weeds before planting them.

Many are suitable for growing under trees and shrubs, including roses. Another asset is their ability to thrive on steep banks. It comes almost as a bonus that many are most attractive.

Details of some popular ground-cover plants are on p. 139.

Constructing a waterfall

There are several possible ways to set about this. For a rock garden waterfall, as here, one will be aiming for a natural effect. This is more challenging than a formal cascade created with ornamental pieces.

Choosing the pump
The flow is provided by an electric pump, submerged in the pool, feeding a length of piping buried in the bank. This means the pool water is circulated continuously. The outlet, at the head of the waterfall, can be hidden by means of foliage or an overhanging rock.

The quantity of water tumbling down the cascade is governed principally by the capacity of the pump and the fall's height. The higher the outlet, the smaller the flow.

In the present instance the head of the fall is about 75cm (2½ft) above pool level. Even a small pump will deliver nearly 1500 litres of water an hour to this height, sufficient to provide a continuous stream some 15cm (6in) wide. For a livelier cascade or a higher outlet there are submersible pumps with a substantially more powerful performance.

Avoid being too ambitious, though. Plants growing in the pool do not like too much disturbance. Ideally, the hourly turnover rate should not exceed the volume of water in the pool. Even then, it is as well to position the pump close to the base of the fall, minimizing cross-currents.

Stand the pump on bricks, clear of any sediment. Use 25mm (1 in) PVC hose to carry the water, burying this out of sight beneath the pool surround. Do the same with the electric cable, taking this to a point where it can be joined, with a waterproof connector, to the mains supply by an electrician.

Forming the watercourse
The easiest way, if not necessarily the best, is to buy a ready-formed

The waterfall is fed, through a hidden pipe, by a small pump that it submerged in the pool itself.

Constructing a waterfall
1 Use a butyl liner to form a leak-proof watercourse. If necessary, lay overlapping strips.

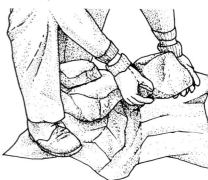

2 Disguise the liner with the aid of cement-bedded stones. Overhanging plants help, too.

fibreglass or moulded plastic watercourse which simply needs setting in the ground. Two or more of these, each with a paving lip, can be combined to form a series of cascades.

These ready-made units are stone-coloured and have a rough finish. Even so, unless further disguised with rocks and plants their artificial nature remains fairly apparent.

It might be thought that a watercourse formed from concrete laid in situ would be the simplest method.

Unfortunately, this is almost bound to develop leaks, resulting in a gradual emptying of the pool.

The answer is to lay a length of waterproof pool liner first, then to cover this with stones bedded in cement. With careful placing of the stones you can make the stream alter course, check its flow and create miniature pools.

All the necessary materials and equipment are obtainable from water garden specialists.

Pool management

Green water is a common phenomenon with all new pools soon after planting. As explained in p.60, the water in a pool will normally clear of its own accord after about a month or six weeks as plants take up excess mineral salts. In small pools the trouble may sometimes persist. The answer then is to install a pool filter or treat the water with an algicide.

Spring
Every four or five years thin out plants that have grown too large, dividing them to increase your stock if you wish.
Start to feed fish with floating pellets, giving no more than they will take in three or four minutes. Fed each morning, they soon become hand-tame.
If excessive blanket weed forms, remove it by thrusting a cane into a clump and twisting it around.

Summer
Top-up the pool occasionally to make up for evaporation. To help the fish, raise the oxygen level during hot, sultry weather by operating the fountain or waterfall daily or spraying the surface with a hose. Continue daily feeding until late summer.

Autumn
Remove the foliage of marginal plants as it starts to die. Stretch netting over the surface to catch falling leaves.
In cold areas float a pool heater on the surface to maintain an ice-free patch. This will allow gases, harmful to fish, to escape. Breaking the ice may harm them.

An electric pool-heater will maintain an ice-free patch, through which gases harmful to fish can escape.

Placing a pump on a low plinth keeps the inlet clear of sediment on the bottom of the pool.

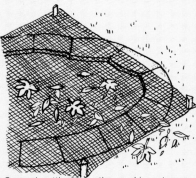
Spread netting over the pool in autumn to stop leaves falling into the water and decomposing.

Remove blanket weed by pushing a bamboo cane into the mass, twirling it around and then removing it.

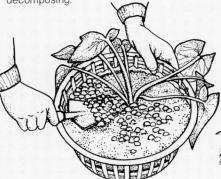
When planting in containers, place gravel on the compost to prevent fish from disturbing it.

Immerse new lilies over a period of weeks, standing them on bricks and removing these progressively.

A SCENTED WALK

Variations on this theme would suit a great many gardens, even where space is more restricted. It is the elements that count – an enticing path straddled by a rustic pergola, the latter framing a distinctive ornament at the further end.

The pergola is clad with roses, one to each upright, delighting with their colour and scent during high summer. The beds on either side are planted with lavender, which all remain in flower for weeks on end. Rosemary and other herbs would be an alternative should one prefer to avoid such a heady mix of perfumes.

The theme is easily varied, because paths do not have to be straight nor to end quite so dramatically. A pergola is no less eye-catching when constructed across a curving path in a smaller, narrower garden. It can be made from sawn timbers, if preferred, and there are easily-assembled kits sold for the purpose.

With ornaments, too, the changes may be rung. A stone owl peering from a tangle of shrubs is no less effective than a sculpture positioned as a focal point.

A well-laid lawn provides the setting for so many enticing garden designs. We shall be discussing how to get instant results by laying turves. Also considered are points that go to make a successful shrub border, which here provides a background to the formal walkway.

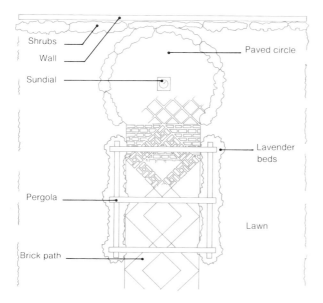

Shrubs
Wall
Sundial
Pergola
Brick path
Paved circle
Lavender beds
Lawn

Constructing a pergola

Treated pine poles are suitable if a rustic pergola is preferred. Use 10cm (4in) dia. poles for the uprights, 8cm (3in) dia. timber for the side-rails (parallel with the path) and 5–8cm (2–3in) poles for straddling the path.

Overall dimensions are not all that critical, but they should not be far removed from the following: a minimum height of 2–2.1m (6½–7ft) is advisable, bearing in mind that rose stems will be trained along the cross-rails. The width may be a little less – say, 1.7–1.8m (5½–6ft). If narrower than this the structure may look distinctly out of balance. Lengthwise – along the path – allow 2–2.4m (6½–8ft) between uprights, with the cross-rails secured every 1–1.2m (3–4ft).

Soak the bottom 60cm (2ft) of the uprights in creosote if untreated. It is best to buy them in advance and store them under cover to dry out. Dig post holes 45cm (18in) deep and fill in around the timber with concrete, checking with a spirit level to ensure that they are vertical.

Lay the remainder of the poles on the ground to correspond with their planned positions, with the side-rails underneath. Meanwhile, take careful measurements to see exactly where the joints need to be cut. Side-rails will have to be joined immediately above uprights, with adjacent ends cut at 45 degrees.

Position cross-rails clear of the side-rail joints, cutting a simple halving joint in each member with a saw and chisel. Treat all cut ends with creosote. Secure the cross-rails to the side-rails with galvanised nails, driving in some at an angle. Then lift each completed section onto the uprights and nail them in place.

Angled struts jointed and fastened between the uprights and side-rails make the structure more robust and improve its appearance. They are better screwed into place through pre-drilled holes.

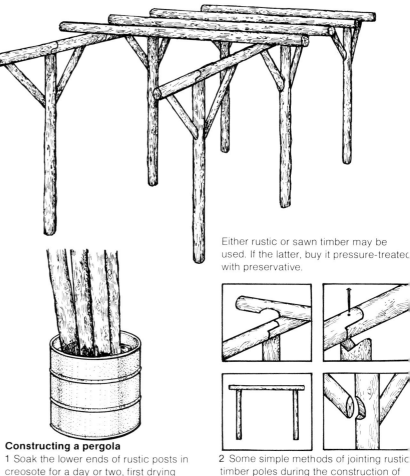

Constructing a pergola

1 Soak the lower ends of rustic posts in creosote for a day or two, first drying them if possible.

Either rustic or sawn timber may be used. If the latter, buy it pressure-treated with preservative.

2 Some simple methods of jointing rustic timber poles during the construction of pergola.

3 Side view of a completed pergola. If constructed with simple poles, use 10cm (4in) diameter for the uprights, slightly smaller timbers for side and cross rails. Secure with galvanized nails.

Garden ornaments

In the present instance an eye-catching sculpture has been placed to draw the eye along the path and through the pergola – to provide a focal point, in short. It is a common enough motive for introducing an ornament, though not the only one.

In a different way, an owl or a woodland animal that blends with its background can be just as effective, perhaps introducing an element of surprise as it peers through foliage. As with more prominent ornaments, position is all-important and deserves advance planning.

Scale and style need thought, too. The effect may be ruined by too small or too large an object, the former a particular risk in spacious, open surroundings. Like positioning, the matter needs considering on the spot, before visiting suppliers, so that you can gauge the size and type of ornament needed.

Style is partly a matter of setting, partly of individual taste. Mellow, expansive surroundings complement classic designs, whether of containers or statuary. The latter looks particularly well in a garden planned on formal lines.

In small gardens there is a risk of seeming pretentious if too large or too grand an ornament is chosen. Fortunately, there are plenty of nice, small pieces around.

It is, of course, personal taste, that is the final arbiter, when it comes to choosing ornamentation for your garden. Some tastes may even decide to admit plaster garden gnomes to the scene. Everyone may not like them, but it is difficult to deny that they have a certain affinity with sharply-coloured annuals grown in soldier-like rows. And why not – if a garden exists at all, its prime reason for doing so should be to satisfy its owner, rather than to impress or cater to the prejudices of other people!

Bear in mind that bowls and urns, if planted, will need as much attention as other containers.

Choose statues with some care. A sundial might prove a wiser choice for the average garden.

Bird and animal sculptures gain much from a natural setting, even if partly concealed.

Roses for a Pergola

The option rests between ramblers and climbers, both suitable for the purpose. Ramblers do particularly well in an open position and their supple stems are fairly easy to train along the horizontals. But the flowering period is rather brief compared to that of climbers.

Though the stems of climbing roses tend to be stiffer, all but the most vigorous varieties can be trained on a pergola. Choose a repeat-flowering variety.

On balance, these free-flowering climbers probably give the best value for money and space. Yet there remains a nostalgic charm about some of the long-established ramblers, such as "Albertine", "Dorothy Perkins" or "Sander's White", that is hard to ignore.

Keep the stems tied loosely to the uprights. Regular training of main shoots is essential.

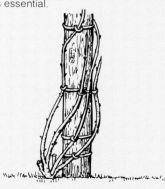

The supple stems of a rambler are fairly easy to train to both vertical and horizontal poles.

Laying turf

Turves cost more than grass seed and their quality varies a good deal. It certainly pays to buy from a reputable supplier. That said, they offer the means of an "instant" lawn and without the risk of damage from hungry birds.

Lay turves between early autumn and late winter or even in early spring if you are prepared to water during subsequent dry weather. Naturally, avoid times when the ground is frozen or waterlogged.

Site preparation

This follows much the same lines whether you are planning to sow seeds (see p.123) or lay turves. Start well in advance – several months ahead, if possible – to give the ground time to settle. In the case of seeded lawns this is a particular help in reducing the competition from annual weed seeds.

Start by clearing the site, including destroying any perennial weeds with a weedkiller such as glyphosate. Two or three weeks later fork out the dead stems and roots.

Level any obvious high points or hollows, using a rake if these are slight. Fill substantial hollows with commercial topsoil or with soil moved from another part of the garden. To level a hillock, first dig out the topsoil and place it to one side. Then dig out and dispose of the appropriate amount of subsoil, finally replacing the topsoil.

Consider drainage at this stage. Badly-drained soil, subject to waterlogging, will never sustain a satisfactory lawn. Digging may be sufficient in some cases, otherwise a system of pipes, leading to a ditch or soakaway, may be needed.

Agricultural-type drainage pipes are effective but are a considerable labour to lay. Easier to lay in a fairly shallow trench is the special plastic land drainage pipe made for this kind of work.

Turfing a lawn

1 First clear the site by digging out large weeds and unwanted plants, then apply a weedkiller.

2 Level small bumps with a rake. If removing hillocks, ensure that the layer of topsoil remains.

3 After digging, and spreading fertilizer, firm the soil evenly by treading all over.

4 A final raking will fill any small hollows and also provide a fine tilth in which roots can grow.

Now dig over the whole site, adding organic matter such as compost, peat or manure if the soil is poor. Leave the ground to settle for a few weeks, then break down surface lumps with a fork or pronged cultivator. For a large area, a motor cultivator may be hired instead of undertaking such hard digging.

Before sowing a lawn it is an advantage to leave the site untouched for a while, then to hoe it or apply weedkiller. This will help to get rid of annual weeds. There is less point in doing so if you are turfing.

In both cases the final stage of preparation starts with sprinkling a general fertilizer, such as HPK about 5:7:4, over the soil 60 gr per sq m (oz per sq yd). Next, rake it evenly then tread it with a shuffling action to firm the soil and reveal any soft spots. Give a final raking to achieve a fine, level tilth.

Lay the turves in a bonded pattern, just .e brickwork, pressing them firmly into ace. Work from a plank placed on the

turves to avoid uneven pressure or pushing them out of place.

Sprinkle a mixture of soil and peat to any gaps between the turves. Brush it as you go.

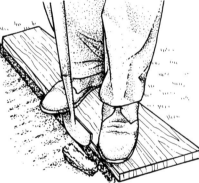

7 When laying is completed, trim the edges of the lawn to shape with a half-moon edging iron.

Some months later – in spring if the rves were laid in autumn – apply a wn fertilizer.

9 If the turf is shaggy, rake gently before the first cut in spring. Set the blades of the mower high.

Laying turves

Mark the outline of the lawn with pegs and string. Have the turves stacked at the side from which you propose laying them. Make a "tamper" by fastening a broom handle to one or more squares of thick board. This will be used for pressing the turves into place.

Start by laying a line of turves along one side, their edges protruding just beyond the string if you will need to cut a fresh edge later – around a curved border, for instance.

Press each turf gently but firmly into place, if necessary adding or removing soil from beneath to make up for uneven thickness. Butt adjacent turves firmly together.

Working from a plank placed on the first row, lay the second row of turves. Cut the first piece in half so that this second row bridges the joints in the first, like bricks in a wall. Carry a bucket of sifted soil and peat with you to fill any obvious gaps, and brush more into the joints. If preferred, this may be left until all the turves have been laid.

Continue laying the turves in this fashion, always working from a board and with one or more additional boards to give access and freedom of movement. After the whole lawn has been laid, cut the edges with a half-moon edging iron.

After-care

A lawn laid during the cool weather will need little further attention. Rolling is sometimes advised but should not normally be necessary. If grass is very shaggy, a light trim with a hover mower would do no harm.

As grass grows, set the blades high for the first mowing or two, gradually lowering them as the season advances. Apply a lawn fertilizer in late spring to help sustain growth during the summer. Take particular care that the turf does not dry out, by watering with a sprinkler.

Some paving alternatives

Despite the ingenuity of manufacturers it is seldom difficult to recognize factory-made paving. There is a predictability about some of the patterns, while even the most skilful addition of different pigments may not conceal that concrete is the basic material.

For something a little more individual one has either to look for different materials – natural, for preference – or else to lay standard paving in a more original way. Taking the latter point first, even rectangular slabs assume new interest if different shapes and sizes are intermingled, perhaps with some projecting to form an irregular edge to the side of a path.

Bricks remain one of the most popular forms of paving. Old, weathered bricks, if obtainable, are a delight; brand-new pavers can be laid in a variety of patterns – stretcher bond, herringbone, parquet, basket weave and so on.

Cobbles set in a bed of mortar form an immensely durable surface – better, though, for a path than for a patio where furniture may need to be placed. Random-shaped natural stone is another possibility, provided the pieces are sufficiently smooth.

Sandstone slabs are a singularly attractive form of paving, though by no means cheap. In this instance there is a factory-made alternative which offers close rivalry at an affordable price.

The solution in some cases may be to mix materials and patterns. Plain slabs become less dreary if cobbles or crazy paving are laid in alternate spaces. The same will happen if there is a brick edging on either side. The hard outline of an undistinguished path can be softened by overhanging foliage and flowers.

Overall, the appearance of paving is almost as important as its function. Choosing it deserves thorough thought and care.

1 Random-shaped stones, set in mortar, form an interesting though rather uneven surface.

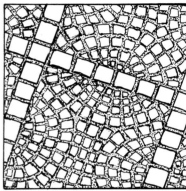

4 Some quarry tiles are made in this hexagonal pattern. A mixture of colours adds to the interest.

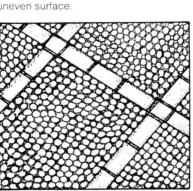

2 Stone setts laid in a regular pattern will form a handsome terrace or patio.

3 Cobbles set in mortar are durable and attractive but the surface is a little irregular.

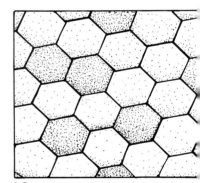

5 Crazy paving, making use of random-shaped stones, is suitable for paths and broader areas.

6 With their rounded edges, these stone slabs would not make for very comfortable walking.

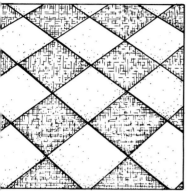

Concrete paving looks less dull if slabs ~~wi~~th different textures and finishes are ~~m~~ixed with them.

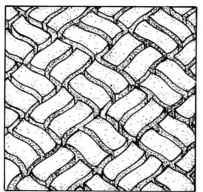

8 Though expensive, shaped clay pavers are among the most attractive forms of garden paving.

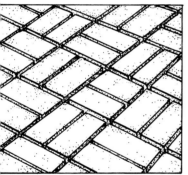

A basket-weave pattern is just one of ~~s~~everal methods of laying paving bricks.

10 Herringbone-pattern brickwork. Though eye-catching, many of the edging bricks have to be cut.

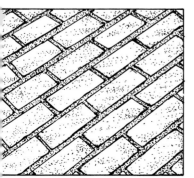

~~I~~ Paths laid with coursed bricks need ~~th~~e least cutting. Avoid soft types, which ~~cr~~umble in the frost.

12 An unusual brick pattern, with each group centred around a half brick which has been placed on end.

Planning a Shrub Border

Among the most diverse of plants, shrubs are also some of the easiest to grow. Most will prosper from year to year, requiring a minimum of feeding and other attention and with annual pruning, if needed, based on easily mastered principles.

There are species which flower in every month of the year – even during the depths of winter. Some are grown principally for their foliage, including a number with brilliant autumn tints. Others are noted for the beauty of their form.

With such a wealth from which to choose, selection becomes all the more critical in a small garden. Start by shortlisting those that most take your fancy, noting their main display season. You must then decide whether to go for interest right through the year or to concentrate on the months of spring and summer.

Size is critical, for there must be space for the shrubs to develop without growing into one another. Better a loose planting for a year or two than to end with a jungle, so consider the eventual spread of plants and not just their height.

Next, satisfy yourself that the soil and available light are suitable for the species you favour. Some need acid soil, many require plenty of sun. It's unwise to ignore their natural conditions.

Finally, consider how they will look together. It is at this stage that you will need a sheet of paper, with a scaled plan of the planting site, in order to play around with the possibilities. Bear in mind the value of evergreens, the appeal of shrubs with variegated foliage. Take account of other garden features, which may need concealing or softening and bit by bit the plan will take shape.

LIVING BOUNDARIES

To some, the word "hedge" conjures up an image of dour privet or funereal yew. Common privet has proved invasive, but there are many other plants for hedging. Flowers, attractive foliage and berries can all be enjoyed for no extra trouble or expense.

A limitation, though, is the incompatability of a free-flowering habit with close clipping. For a truly geometrical outline a hedge needs to be chosen for foliage quality alone. This is because flowers are often carried in loose sprays, which must be allowed to develop unchecked. Such a hedge needs lighter, less frequent trimming.

The deciding point is generally the position and purpose of the hedge. Flat clipping can be an advantage where space is at a premium – in a suburban front garden, perhaps. Elsewhere, the laxer habit of a flowering hedge will be amply repaid by its annual display. Consider planting one when screens or dividers are being considered, not only for boundary markers.

A word of caution, though. Just like a wall, a substantial hedge of any type may put adjacent ground in shade. It will also extract moisture and nutrients from the soil on *both* sides, creating a band where plants will not thrive so readily. Extra watering and feeding, and even a degree of root restriction, may be needed.

Subject to this, make the most of hedging in your garden. A living colourful boundary has so much more going for it than a featureless fence.

1. *Taxus baccata* (Yew)
2. Rose hedge
3. *Fagus sylvatica* 'purpurea' (Purple beech)
4. *Pyracantha watereri*
5. *Chamaecyparis lawsoniana* (Cypress)
6. English lavender
7. *Berberis thunbergii Atropurpurea*
(Deciduous barberries)
8. Box

Planting and shaping a hedge

Hedging plants bought in plastic containers may be put in the ground at any time of year, given reasonable soil conditions. If they are bare-rooted – lifted straight from the nursery bed – then late autumn until early spring is the right season for deciduous species, earlier in the autumn or a little later in the spring for evergreens.

Mark out the proposed line with a string and pegs, allowing sufficient space for growth on the boundary side. If the ground is not already cultivated, dig a strip about 60cm (2ft) wide, working in some organic matter such as rotted manure, compost or peat. Sprinkle superphosphate over the surface, two handfuls to each metre or yard run, and leave the soil to settle for a week or two.

Small, well-branched hedging plants are the best. Avoid tall plants with bare stems. Use a border spade to dig the holes, spacing them to suit the species, and make sure that they are broad enough to take the spread-out roots. Mix some sieved compost or commercial planting mixture with the soil before firming it back round the roots. The soil mark on the stem should be level with the surface of the surrounding soil.

Check container-grown plants for ingrowing or excessively cramped roots. Having loosened these, leaving the rest of the compost undisturbed, set the rootball in the hole and firm the planting mix around it. The top of the rootball should be level with the surface.

Watering the plants in will help to settle the soil around their roots. This apart, it is vital to keep the soil moist around spring-planted evergreens and all container-grown hedges planted during the drier months. Continue until new roots have developed, which will take at least a couple of months. If possible, shelter newly-planted evergreens from drying winds.

Planting hedges
1 Plant against a pegged line and be sure to allow space for growth on the boundary side.

2 Use a batten to check that container-grown plants are set level with the surrounding soil.

3 Use a foot to firm the soil or planting mixture evenly around the rootball.

Shaping

Left to themselves, many hedging plants will develop bare stems and fairly sparse shoots. The natural habit of a beech, for instance, is to grow a spread of well-spaced branches on top of a massive trunk.

The solution is to cut back the shoots of most species by between a third and a half immediately after planting. This will encourage tight, bushy growth and a stem that produces shoots from near ground level.

Exceptions include conifers, laurel holly and yew, the top shoots of which should not be touched and the remainder only lightly trimmed.

Continue this clipping back, where appropriate, each year until the plants have reached the required height. Overall trimming to shape may then begin.

Clipping and trimming

Use shears or a mechanical trimmer to clip formal hedges, doing this a

A powered trimmer gives formal edges a neat cut. For safety, pass the cord over your shoulder.

A pair of secateurs is the tool for cutting an informal hedge, such as escallonia or rose.

...ast twice a year, or more often ...an that should it be necessary. For ...bsolute perfection, you should take ...re when trimming to slope each ...de of the hedge slightly inwards ...wards the top.

Secateurs are a better tool than ...ears or mechanical trimmers when ...imming lax, informal hedges. The ...st time to remove over-long shoots ... order to maintain the hedge's ...verall shape and size is immediately ...ter flowering.

A Box-edged Herb Garden

This is an idea for gardeners not short of time, a traditional means of edging and separating herb beds. Such an attractive feature cannot fail to become a talking point.

The edging of box (*Buxus sempervirens*) is of a very special dwarf variety, "Suffruticosa", which grows only about 30cm (1 ft) high. The little plants are spaced 23cm (9in) apart. Fortunately, they are readily available and will grow in most soils.

The design of the bed needs to be formal, in keeping with the clipped edging, and of a size that

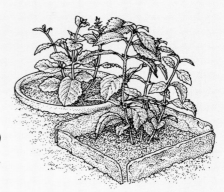

To curb the roots of mint, contain them either by planting in pots or else inserting slates around the plants.

will suit the quantity of herbs that will be grown. It is as well not to be over-ambitious or to make the compartments too fussy or unnecessarily cramped.

When choosing which herbs to grow, and where to plant them, bear in mind that some are rampant growers. Mint and tarragon are prime examples, so edge their compartments with slates buried vertically.

Height is critical, too. For a

formal, box-edged herb garden it would be better to concentrate on low-growing kinds. Giants such as fennel and angelica are better grown elsewhere, perhaps with other perennials in the border.

Among the most suitable kinds for such a scheme are chives, coriander, pot marjoram, mint, parsley, sage, summer and winter savory, sorrel and thyme. Of these, all but coriander, parsley and summer savory are perennials.

A TINY, SHADED YARD

Cramped surroundings and rationed sunlight place harsh restrictions on anyone creating a garden. How, in such an unpromising situation, are plants to be grown and the spirit cheered? Remarkably, there are examples galore of tiny havens rich with colour and greenery. The ingredients, it seems, are a mix of determination and imagination. There are also a few guidelines worth noting.

The side passage of this town house receives practically no sunlight. Yet rather than abandon it to dustbins the owner has chosen to grow ferns there, a rich segment of the plant world ideal for landscaping in shade.

Behind the house, emphasis on the vertical has helped to disguise just how small an area it is. The walls, painted white to reflect available light, support climbing plants and a number of suspended pots. The trellis on which the climbers are trained has to be easily removable so that the surface can receive an occasional freshening coat.

Across the far end is a raised bed, providing another change of levels. Trailing plants are set along part of its edge, making use of even this small vertical space.

The surface of the yard is paved with bricks, no great extravagance for such a small area. Laid in a basket-weave pattern, they give a touch of added character. In the sunniest spot, against a wall in full sun, a sink garden bright with alpines greets anyone emerging from the side passage. On the other side, where shade is prevalent, fuchsias and foxgloves are planted in tubs to flower a little later in the year.

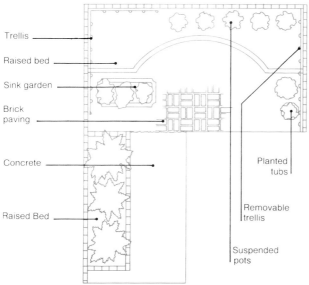

Trellis

Raised bed

Sink garden

Brick paving

Concrete

Raised Bed

Planted tubs

Removable trellis

Suspended pots

Laying brick paving

It is vital to buy the right sort of bricks. Many of those used for building walls are too soft and porous. Laid as paving, they quickly become saturated and will then split and crumble during frosty weather.

Instead, choose only the sort of bricks which are dense and hard, or else pavers specially made for the purpose. The latter are ideal, being thinner than other bricks and with a smooth face on each side. It is sometimes possible to buy old, weathered pavers. Like new ones, they are among the more expensive types of paving.

When laying bricks for a patio or yard, as here, allow a gentle fall away from the house for drainage. Where the surface joins the house the bricks must be at least 15cm (6in) below the damp-proof course.

Laying on sand

The method of laying depends on the firmness of the site. Provided it is well compacted, with no risk of subsidence, the easiest method is to place them on sand, as described for concrete blocks on p.66. Instead of a plate vibrator, they can, if you prefer, be tapped into the sand with a mallet. A hammer may be used instead if a piece of wood is first placed over the paver.

Laying on mortar

On soft ground lay a sub-base of concrete (1 part cement, 5 parts mixed sand and stones). When removing soil during site preparation allow for a slab 5–8cm (2–3in) thick, together with 13mm ($\frac{1}{2}$in) of mortar and the thickness of the bricks. Tamp or tread the surface as firm as possible before laying the concrete.

After two or three days, when the concrete will have hardened, place the bricks on a bed of mortar, spreading a small area at a time. Tap each brick into place, using a straight edge and level to ensure a

Laying brick paving
1 On soft ground first lay a concrete slab. Set the bricks on mortar, a few rows at a time.

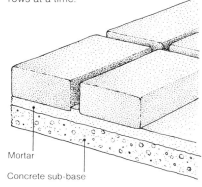

Mortar
Concrete sub-base

3 The finished path, made up of three separate layers, will be immensely strong.

---

true, even surface. The bricks may either be butted against each other or else laid so that there are even spacings between for subsequent filling with mortar.

As shown, bricks may be laid in a number of patterns, each with certain repeat characteristics. When calculating how many will be needed to cover the area, you should first check the size of the available pavers. These vary in surface area as well as in thickness.

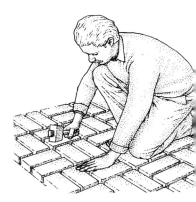

2 Tap the bricks into place with a mallet either butted together or with equal spaces between.

4 Check constantly that the surface is level, using a spirit level placed on a straight batten.

5 Use the handle of the trowel instead of the mallet for any minor adjustments to the level of the paving.

Sink Gardens

Not everyone has space or a suitable site for a rock garden. Fortunately, this need not prevent alpines from being grown. A stone trough, if you can get one, makes a perfect setting. So does an ordinary glazed sink, with or without a little camouflage on the outside. Raised beds and hollow walls prove equally suitable.

The essentials, as in a rock garden, are sound drainage and a gritty, open, growing medium. If a sink or trough is used, cover the drain hole with pieces of crock from a broken clay pot, then place a layer of stones or similar drainage material over the base. This may be restricted to the area around and over the crocks if the sink is too shallow.

In a raised bed mix peat and grit with the soil to combine moisture-holding with free drainage. Fill sinks and troughs with a high grade potting compost to which has been added half its bulk of grit or sharp sand. Before doing so, move the container to its final position, placing it on bricks so that the drain hole is free from any obstruction.

Covering a glazed sink

To improve the appearance of a glazed sink, first score the outside, the rim and the upper inch or two of the inside with a coarse hacksaw blade, then coat this area with PVA adhesive. When this is nearly dry, cover it with a 13mm (½in) layer of two parts damp peat, one part sharp sand and one part cement. Mix these ingredients together dry before adding water to produce a mortar-like paste.

Apply this covering with a brick-laying trowel, leaving the surface rough. Cover with a sheet of plastic immediately afterwards to

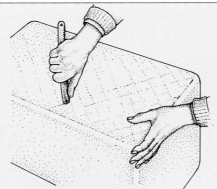

Making a sink garden
1 First score the outside of the old sink to provide a better foundation for the covering material.

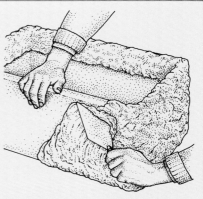

2 Coat the sides with PVA adhesive, then cover this with the peat, cement and sand mix.

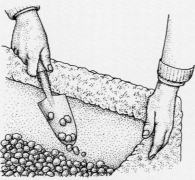

3 Place a curved crock over the plug-hole, then cover the base with a layer of small stones.

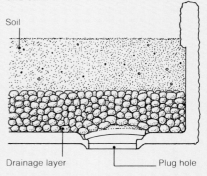

Soil

Drainage layer   Plug hole

4 Cross-section of the prepared sink, ready for planting. Support it so that it stands clear of the ground.

prevent over-rapid drying. Leave for a couple of weeks before removing the plastic and introducing the plants.

If you wish, set small rocks in the surface of raised beds and troughs. Cover the surface with gravel or chippings after planting. Troughs and sinks, especially shallow ones, need fairly frequent watering during dry weather because their ability to retain moisture is limited.

Retaining walls and trellis

Some beds are freestanding, with two exposed sides. This one is built against an existing wall, so only a single retaining wall is needed in the front. For this, concrete walling blocks have been chosen. They have a rough finish to simulate stone. Bricks, if preferred, would be laid in the same way.

Foundations

Though the wall is only 60cm (2ft) high, a concrete foundation is required. This needs to be at least 10cm (4in) thick and laid on an 8cm (3in) layer of broken stone or rubble. Make the foundations three times wider than the thickness of the wall.

For a straight wall mark the edge of the foundation trench with pegs and string. For a curving outline, as here, lay out a hosepipe or thick rope and mark along its edge with a sharp spade. Dig the trench deep enough for the foundations, plus one course of blocks or three courses of bricks.

Laying the blocks

Allow two or three days for the concrete to harden before starting to build on the foundations, then place a 13mm (½in) layer of mortar, the same width as the blocks or bricks, on top of the concrete. Tap the first block (brick) into position at one end.

Before placing the second block, "butter" the upper and lower corners of its end face with mortar, then tap it into place. The horizontal and vertical joints should be of equal thickness, about 10mm (⅜in). Use a spirit level to check the horizontal and vertical faces. Trim off any excess mortar, but wait until the filling is just beginning to harden before smoothing the joint with an offcut of tubing or hosepipe.

Lay subsequent courses of blocks or bricks with their vertical joints mid-way between those of the course beneath. This gives the wall much

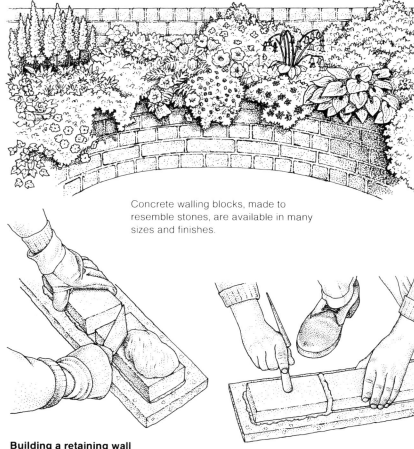

Concrete walling blocks, made to resemble stones, are available in many sizes and finishes.

Building a retaining wall

1 Lay the first course on a secure foundation. Without this the wall may tilt after a while.

2 Using the handle of the trowel, tap each block firmly into place on the mortar course.

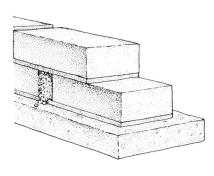

3 Leave occasional open joints in the lower courses to allow rainwater to drain from behind.

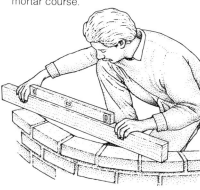

4 Check levels frequently, using a plank, if necessary, to straddle a curving wall.

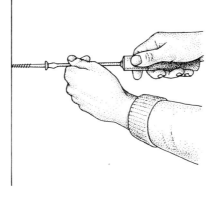

the latter. The task will be that much easier if neither piece is more than 75cm (2½ft) deep and if climbers with lax stems are chosen.

Sections of trellis generally have reinforced edges strong enough to allow them to be suspended. Round-headed screws, 10- or 12-gauge and with a rust-proof finish, are suitable for the purpose. Drive them into wall plugs inserted in pre-drilled holes. The inner, vertical face of the screw head, which has been left protruding, will hold the trellis securely in place.

Supporting trellis
For supporting the trellis, first drill holes take 10- or 12-gauge screws and matching wall plugs.

2 Insert the screws, first greasing them so that they turn more easily when inserted in the plugs.

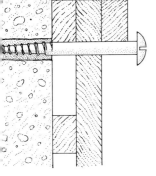

Cross-section showing how the top ame of the trellis is supported by the und-headed screws.

4 After loosening the plant ties it is easy to remove the trellis for redecorating the garden wall.

Growing Ferns

Too often overlooked as "boring", ferns are, in fact, a most diverse race of plants. They are of great antiquity, evolving long before any of the flowering plants to which we generally give pride of place.

One of their special values is that they thrive in shade, especially when clear of dripping trees. They do best in a slightly acid soil that is moist but never becomes waterlogged. They should be protected from excessive wind.

Ferns may be grown on their own or with other shade-lovers such as hostas, wood anemones, alchemillas and epimediums.

There are both evergreen and deciduous kinds. Of the former, hartstongue (*Asplenium scolopendrium*) is a familiar wild plant. Shield ferns (Polystichum) also keep their attractive foliage through the winter, as does the compact *Polypodium vulgare*.

One of the most beautiful deciduous species is the lady fern (*Athyrium filix-femina*), closely rivalled by the maidenhair fern (*Adiantum pedatum*).

Study a specialist catalogue for a full account of the many species.

reater strength. Where the ends of he wall butt into an existing wall, nk them with wire or strip-metal all ties embedded in the mortar, rst chiselling out a recess in the xisting wall.

Leave occasional unmortared joints above-ground courses to allow xcess water to drain away. This is specially important in the course osest to ground level.

Removable Trellis
White-painted walls, even when partly covered with climbing plants, will help to transform an enclosed, shaded yard. Inevitably, though, the cement-wash gradually becomes dirty and dulled, demanding a fresh coat. This is virtually impossible if the plants have been trained on wires or other permanently-fixed supports.

Probably the simplest solution is to erect a removable trellis made up of separate upper and lower units. When re-painting is due, lower the upper one first, hinging it downwards over the lower one, then unhook

VARIETY IN PLANT CONTAINERS

Containers are the key to growing plants on walls, paving and windowsills – anywhere and everywhere that an extra splash of colour could help to brighten the scene. This applies especially to small gardens, which appear so much larger when full use is made of vertical space.

Containers are valuable, too, in gardens where the soil is inhospitable. Chalk-lovers and lime-hunters are equally easy to cater for, not to mention the multitude of ordinary plants that will sulk if their roots are thrust into sticky clay.

Ground-level containers are as varied as their uses. Practically anything may be pressed into service, always provided it has a drainage outlet and is not so small that it will dry out rapidly. Tubs, troughs, pots, bowls and urns are all in the running. Chimney pots and old wooden wheelbarrows are among the offbeat possibilities. So even are chamber pots, provided drainage holes can be drilled.

The larger the container, the more important it is to position it before filling with compost. Bear in mind, too, the not inconsiderable cost of this filling when deciding how many containers are wanted, and how large. The need for frequent, often daily, watering should be considered.

Bedding plants are only one of the planting possibilities. Bulbs are another, along with shrubs and miniature trees. Given reasonable root space, an annual top-dressing will keep the latter going for years. In this category come a number of shrubby climbers for which there may not be a convenient planting space.

And so to windowboxes, hanging baskets and wall pots. Here, cascading plants look especially well, a veritable kaleidoscope of colour tumbling down the walls for fully half the year. The remarkable thing is how easy such containers are to plant and tend. A beginner could do worse than make them his first venture.

1. Bay (centre); *Impatiens*/Busy Lizzie (bottom of container)
2. Fuchsias with white geraniums
3. Ivy-leaf geranium, *Lobelia* (dark red), *Helichrysum* (trailing)
4. Green and variegated ivies; *Lysimachia*/Creeping Jenny
5. *Hydrangea* (Lace cap)
6. *Yucca* and petunias
7. Herbs
8. Miniature narcissi
9. Nasturtium

Choosing and planting containers

Whichever material you favour – wood, plastic, terracotta, fibreglass – choose containers that go with the style of your house and garden. Though a half barrel looks well almost anywhere, a concrete bowl may sit uneasily on the mellow bricks of a period terrace. Plastic moulded to a classical design has an unfortunate habit of looking exactly what it is. An ornate stone urn may appear pretentious in a starkly modern setting. In short, with man-made materials it is the extremes of design that call for special caution.

Most container-grown plants need a position that gets plenty of sun. Just as important, avoid places under the drip of trees, even if they are open to the south.

Remember the chore of watering when considering windowboxes and wall-hung containers. If in doubt, experiment with a can full of water to see whether you can cope.

Take particular care that windowboxes are secure. Anchor each end of the box to the window-frame with a long gate hook and eye.

Composts for container plants

The choice is between a soil-type compost – one based on a John Innes formula – and commercial types consisting principally of peat. Both can give good results but a compost made with soil is better for shrubs and other long-term plants.

It has an advantage, too, even for annuals. Peat allowed to become over-dry may be difficult to get back to its original, moisture-holding texture. Against this, peat composts are lighter to handle. Weight is especially important for roof gardens and some windowsills.

If you choose a soil-based compost use one recommended for annuals and other short-term plants; check also that you have a suitable mix for the shrubs or trees chosen.

Planting in containers
1 If the container lacks drainage outlets, either drill or bore a number of holes in the base.

2 Place a layer of drainage material, such as broken stones, over the bottom of the container.

3 Fill to near the rim of the tub with a commercial potting compost, either peat-based or soil-based.

Planting

Treat the timber with a non-toxic preservative before filling and planting windowboxes, tubs and other wooden containers. Where necessary, rest containers on bricks to ensure free drainage.

Place a layer of stones or other drainage material on the bottom of the container, with one or more large pieces straddling the drain hole. Curved pieces of broken plant pot are ideal as they will allow water to escape while preventing smaller stones from being washed through.

Now fill with compost to within about 2cm (¾in) of the rim. Use a trowel for planting, firming the compost around each rootball. When planting annuals, remember that trailing species are best placed around the rim. In a mixed planting of bulbs and spring bedding, put the plants in first, or you may damage the bulbs. Water the container thoroughly after planting.

Hanging baskets

There are baskets, rather like plastic dishes, that simply have to be filled with compost and planted. True baskets, made with wire, must be lined in order to prevent the compost from falling out.

The material that looks best is sphagnum moss, obtainable from a garden centre or nursery. Paper-bark is a good liner. Choose high quality compost.

Rest the basket on a bucket while lining and filling. Place a layer of moss in the bottom, then some compost. Now insert one or two trailing plants through the

4 Firm a peat-based compost gently but evenly as you fill the container. Add more if needed.

5 Plant with a trowel, afterwards firming the soil and compost around the root-ball with your fingertips.

6 Water the plants, taking care to keep them well-watered while they make fresh roots.

Planting in hanging baskets
1 With the basket resting on a bucket, line it with moss and then fill it with potting compost.

2 Insert plant roots through the moss into the compost as you fill, then plant more in the surface.

the summer, checking the compost at least daily. A twice-daily check may be needed for hanging baskets and small, heavily-planted containers. It is particularly important not to let peat-based composts dry out.

frame, firming the soil over their roots. Continue building up the mossy lining and compost filling, adding occasional trailing plants as you do so.

Take the moss up to the rim of the basket but finish with the compost at least 25mm (1 in) lower. This space will help when watering. Set some upright or bushy plants into the surface of the compost.

After-care
Watering is the prime task during

About a month after planting in peat-based composts start a fortnightly feeding routine with liquid fertilizer. Plants in a soil-based compost will need similar feeding two months after planting. Stop feeding in the autumn.

Shrubs and trees need top-dressing every spring. Replace the top 5–8cm (2–3in) of soil with new fertile compost.

Finally, remember to remove dead flowers before they have a chance to form seed. This will help to prolong the period of bloom.

A WILD CORNER

Most of us pay lip service to conservation, though feeling that it is largely out of our control. So why not form an oasis in one's own garden, where wildflowers can flourish along with a variety of insects, small mammals and other creatures? Even a tiny patch is worthwhile, especially where there are like-minded neighbours.

There is more to it, of course, than "do-gooding". A patch of wild garden, interfered with as little as possible, brings enormous satisfaction. There will be things to look *for* as well as to look *at*, especially if water plays a part in the scheme. Frogs and toads will find their way there, along with dragonflies and damsel flies. There may be visitors from the plant world, too, carried on the wind or by birds and able to take root in this haven where the hoe is unknown.

Wilderness it may be, but nature welcomes a helping hand. A planting of typical hedgerow species – hawthorn, wild rose, sloe – forms the most sympathetic background. It needs keeping within bounds by occasional pruning rather than clipping. A bog garden linked to the pool extends the possibilities and the attraction to wildlife.

Drifts of bulbs are an obvious choice, thrusting through the shaggy grass when there is as yet little colour elsewhere. To follow, what better than an assortment of native wildflowers, once so plentiful in meadows and hedgerows? Seeds are readily obtainable and quite easy to propagate.

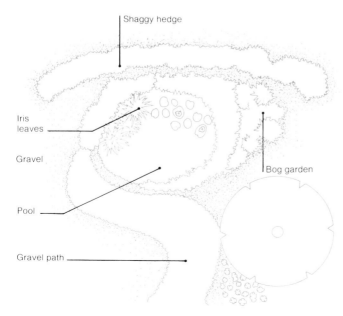

Shaggy hedge

Iris leaves

Gravel

Pool

Bog garden

Gravel path

Making a wild garden

Some preparatory work is needed on most sites if a "wild" garden is to be really effective. This may seem a contradiction but one is trying, after all, to achieve a varied habitat in a limited space. Once established, little further work is required.

Choose a predominantly open patch of garden, even if part of it is tree-shaded. A pool needs plenty of sunshine, as do the grasses and wild-flowers that are native to meadow-land. Plant bulbs in the shadier spots, choosing species for both spring and autumn flowering.

Whether there is existing turf or you have to sow afresh, avoid enriching the ground with manure or fertilizers. Most wild plants perform all the better without them. If you feel that the soil is exceptionally poor, use an organic fertilizer, such as blood, bone and fishmeal, which will have a better long-term effect on soil structure.

Wildflowers, just like cultivated species, fall under the standard headings of annual, biennial and perennial. All are hardy, of course, and some are self-seeding. Seed catalogues offer them for sale separately and in mixtures.

Sow biennials and perennials in the autumn or spring in pots or pans of seed compost, placing these outdoors but covered with glass. Some require periodic freezing during the winter to "unlock" their germination mechanism. Prick the seedlings out into pots and grow them on until large enough for planting out.

Sow hardy annuals in the spring, preferably directly into the turf after first trimming it and then tearing the surface with a pronged cultivator.

Pools and bog gardens

Instructions for making a pool will be found on p.68. A liner is essential, even though the aim is for a completely natural effect. With this in mind, the edging of paving stones

Pool and bog garden blend naturally, th latter formed by an extension of the pool's synthetic rubber liner.

Laying the path

1 Clear a strip for the approach path and pool edging. Lay rubble or concrete to check the weeds.

2 Spread gravel over the hard base. Overhanging grass will conceal the edges in due course.

should be omitted and the turf taken up to and just over the edge of the liner. Leave only a hand's-width of the pool liner protruding beyond the water.

Rather than trample a path around the pool, lay gravel over the area most likely to be used. This serves the purpose without looking out of place. It is important, though, to provide a generous sub-base of stones or rubble, or even an inch or two of concrete, to prevent the

gravel becoming submerged by pla growth. Herbicides are taboo in wild garden.

A bog garden to one side of t pool will provide an even mo varied habitat, together with sc for growing waterside plants. make one, dig out a further ar 30cm (1 ft) deep alongside the p and extend the liner over this, wi the edges turned up to ground lev The meeting point of pool and b garden should be just below wat

uilding the bog garden

Dig out a hollow for the bog garden.
e butyl liner should overlap that of
e pool.

2 Fill the bog garden by mixing some
peat with the soil that you dug out from
the area.

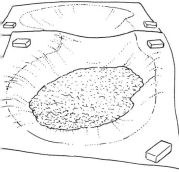

Punch a few holes in the sides of the
g garden liner. Fill with the mix to form
aised bed.

4 Place stones or turves around the
edge of the bog garden to conceal the
lining material.

imming the grass

Trim the grass twice at the height of
mmer and again during the second
f of autumn.

2 Rake off the cut grass to allow new
growth to emerge. Mix it with straw for
the compost heap.

level, allowing the pool to spill over.

Mix peat with the topsoil that you
excavated from the bog garden area.
Replace this mixture to form a bed
slightly higher than its surroundings.
To add a bog garden to an existing
pool, use a pool repair kit and a strip
of butyl to join the two liners.

Bulbs to choose

Spring bulbs are a key part of the
wild garden, even though not many
are native plants. Their flowers are
the first to cheer us, from the very
start of the year. Winter aconites,
snowdrops, *Crocus tomasinianus* and
Cyclamen coum are among the
earliest, often emerging through
snow-covered or frosted grass.

Others to flower during late winter
and spring are scillas, anemones,
dog's tooth violet (erythronium),
narcissi and fritillarias. Remember,
also, to include a few clumps of
primroses, which thrive in the same
grassy, uncultivated surroundings.

For the autumn, after the grass has
been cut, a planting of *Cyclamen
neapolitanum* will produce delicate
little flowers that vary between pink
and mauve.

Grass-trimming

Leave the grass and wildflowers uncut
until mid-July. Trim it back quite
hard and cut it again a month or so
later – before the cyclamen flower.
These should be over by November,
when a final trim will prepare the
grass for the spring bulbs.

Always remove the cut grass,
otherwise it will stifle new growth.
Net the pool each autumn to collect
falling leaves, first removing dead
plant growth before it can sink to
the bottom. Use secateurs to keep
the hedge in check.

These small chores apart, enjoy
your wild garden for what it is – a
place where the annual cycle looks
after itself and your main tasks are
simply to observe and wonder.

A PAVED COURTYARD

The smaller the garden, the less relevant becomes the standard formula of lawn, beds and a linking path. On heavy soil, and especially where children play, a tiny lawn seldom prospers. Better by far to omit it altogether and extend the area of paving. There is an advantage, too, in keeping beds to a minimum, making greater use of containers in their place. The overall effect is that of an extended patio garden.

In this instance the all-weather possibilities have been enhanced by an open-ended conservatory, an unusual arrangement that deserves wider consideration. Its uses include that of rainproof porch for the back door, sheltered accommodation for pot plants and a protected place to sit and take meals during "in-between" weather. The hindrance of a closed end was thought hardly worthwhile in what was already an enclosed yard. Nevertheless, a conventional conservatory or sunroom would have the advantage in a less sheltered situation.

Large paving slabs, spot-bedded on mortar, speeded this part of the garden-making. Note, though, that some smaller ones have been included to vary the overall effect. Some spaces have been left, mainly away from the direct route between house and back gate, for planting with prostrate plants and ground cover.

Another ploy to relieve the sameness of overall paving is the slightly raised area along the back and side boundaries. Consisting of a single course of bricks, laid on concrete and mortar, this slight upstand shows off container plants to better effect and adds to the overall character.

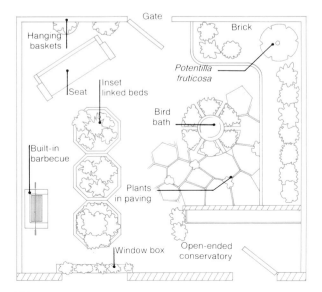

Laying paving slabs

Concrete paving slabs come in a number of sizes, colours and finishes. There is certainly no need for them to look like street paving. Laying is a relatively speedy business if the base is firm and if fairly large slabs are chosen. Even so, consider working some smaller ones into the design to vary the effect.

The easiest way to lay this sort of paving is on blobs of mortar. On a really firm surface the mortar may be laid directly on the soil. Otherwise, or if it is essential for the surface to remain absolutely even, a concrete sub-base is advisable.

Preparing the surface

Skim weeds, rubbish and roots from the surface with a sharp spade, disturbing it as little as possible. If necessary, remove a little topsoil to allow for the thickness of the paving plus another 13mm (½in) for the mortar. Rake the soil level and trample it well, if necessary leaving it for some weeks to settle even more.

If loose or unstable ground calls for a concrete sub-base you will have to remove sufficient extra soil for a slab 5–8cm (2–3in) thick. Firm the soil as thoroughly as you can before laying this. Use a mix of 1 part cement to 5 parts sand and stones.

Laying the slabs

For bedding the slabs you will need a mix of 1 part cement to 5 parts concreting sand. You will also need several dozen slips of wood, each 13mm (½in) thick, to help space the slabs evenly. Start laying from the far side of the area so that you will not have to walk on newly-laid slabs.

Bed each large slab on five blobs or mounds of mortar, one in the middle and one near each corner. The four corner mounds are sufficient for smaller slabs. Place the slab evenly on the mortar, then tap it level (using a spirit level) with a mallet. When setting further slabs alongside,

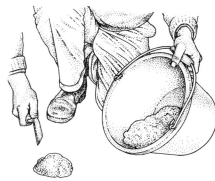

Laying paving slabs

1 Place each slab on five blobs of mortar, one near the middle and one inside each corner.

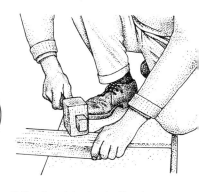

2 Tap the slabs level with a heavy hammer, using a block of wood between to avoid damage.

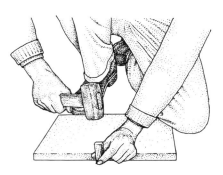

3 To ensure accurate spacing, tap in pegs of suitable thickness before placing adjacent slabs.

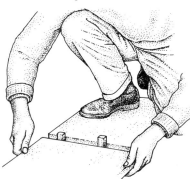

4 Lay the surrounding slabs on blobs of mortar, tap them level and then carefully remove the pegs.

insert two spacing strips in each joint. Straddle the slabs with a plank placed on edge, laying the spirit level on this, to ensure that the slabs have an even surface overall.

When cutting slabs, use a broad chisel and a heavy hammer to score both faces and edges along marked lines. Continue around the slab several times, working progressively deeper. When a clear groove has been formed, a series of sharper blows should give a clean break.

Filling the joints

Avoid walking on the slabs for couple of days. After this, remov the spacers and fill the joints. Kee the mortar on the dry side to hel avoid staining the slabs; wipe off an surplus from the paving. Alterna tively, make a wooden jig with a slo the same width as the joints an insert the mortar through this.

Firm the mortar thoroughly, finish ing off by smoothing it with a offcut of hose.

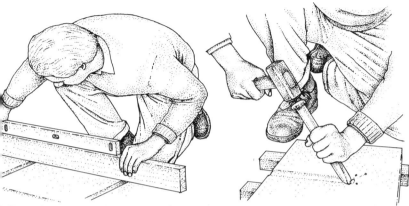

Check frequently, while the mortar is
till soft, that the slabs are in overall
lignment, using a level.

6 To cut a slab, score all around with a
hammer and cold chisel. Finish with
several harder blows.

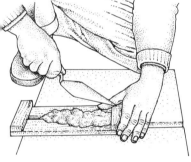

Make a simple wooden jig, with a slot
he width of the joints, for accurate
lacement of the mortar.

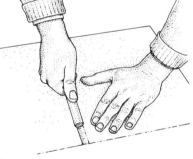

8 A short offcut of hosepipe provides a
simple means of forming a smooth,
recessed joint.

Growing plants in paving

Quite small spaces will do, as the
plants will spread over the paving
immediately around. Each gap needs
o be large enough, though, to allow
everal inches of soil to be dug out
vith a trowel and a gritty compost
placed there instead. Use a good
bought potting mix, with grit or
harp sand added to increase its bulk.

Place the plants where they will be
but of the direct line of traffic.
Occasional treading does little harm,
but no plant appreciates repeated
flattening. Watering should seldom
be necessary.

The plants to choose are those
with a spreading, carpeting form of
growth or a compact, bushy habit.
Among the best are *Acaena microphylla*, *Achillea*, *Ajuga*, *Alyssum
saxatile*, *Arenaria montana*, dwarf
campanulas and dianthus, some
Dampiera, helichrysums, raoulias,
saxifrages, *Silene acaulis*, *Thymus
nitidus* and *T. serpyllum*.

Seats and benches

A garden bench is always a welcom-
ing sight. Its positioning forms a
subtle element of garden design.

The main choice rests between
wood and cast metal, or a combination of the two. Teak is the most
popular choice. At most they need
treatment with a proprietary dressing; but some experts advise no maintenance at all. Softwoods include
redwood and western red cedar.

Cast aluminium is lighter than
iron and does not rust. It stays
attractive and serviceable with
minimum maintenance.

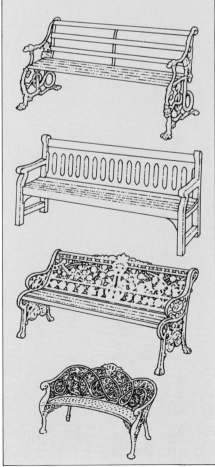

Conservatories and sun-rooms

A simple, open structure, as in our courtyard garden, would best be built on the spot, making it easier to tailor it to the site – in terms of appearance, as well as shape and size. Most conventional conservatories, though, are prefabricated and a choice has to be made from the many makes and models on offer.

Their uses vary from that of plant house and sheltered sitting area to providing an additional living room for year-round use. Without double-glazing, though, heat loss and condensation may cause problems during the winter.

The need for planning permission depends on the size of the structure and its position. Check this, as well as current building regulations, with your local authority. Its effect on house ventilation, in particular, and also the position of drains are points that may give rise to problems.

Laying the base

A concrete slab will be needed to support the structure and serve as a floor. A typical thickness is 10cm (4in) of concrete laid on top of a well-rammed 10cm (4in) bed of broken stones or hardcore. Formwork will have to be set up and it will save much time if pre-mixed concrete is ordered.

In this case be sure to have everything ready – helpers, barrows and tools – awaiting delivery. Access can be a problem and it is a wise precaution to ask for a retarder to be added to the concrete mix to slow down the setting rate.

Should you prefer to work at your own pace, or if there are likely to be certain difficulties, hire a concrete mixer instead.

Heating

Some form of heating will extend the season of use into early spring, and late autumn, in cooler areas. One possibility is to extend the

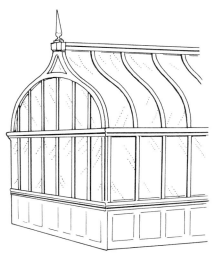

Though of classic shape, modern conservatories of this type can have all the latest design features.

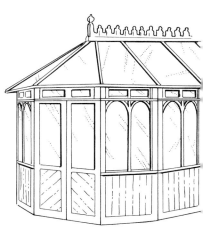

Conservatories built end-on to the house admit the most daylight but also lose the most warmth.

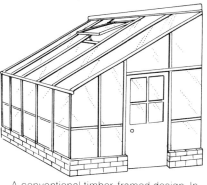

A conventional timber-framed design. In effect, a lean-to greenhouse and an ideal environment for plants.

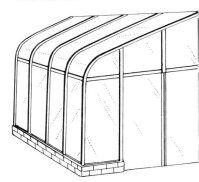

A modern, metal-framed structure, equally suitable for plant-growing as for a home extension.

household central heating, though the position of the controlling thermostat may well not suit the conservatory. The wisest course is to consult a local heating engineer, who should be able to adapt the system to your needs, assuming that it has sufficient capacity.

Electricity is favourite of the other forms of heating. Tubular heaters, fan heaters or storage radiators are all suitable. Unless the conservatory is strictly for plants, gas heaters are

better avoided due to the condensation they promote.

Ventilation and shade

Efficient ventilation is no less important than heating. It is a great advantage to fit hinged lights and louvres with automatic openers, so maintaining a relatively even temperature. Made primarily for greenhouse use, they are most effective. Even more efficient is a thermostatically-controlled extractor fan

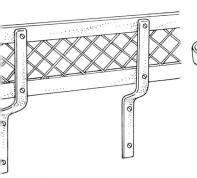

snow-guard fixed to the eaves above conservatory prevents sudden amaging falls.

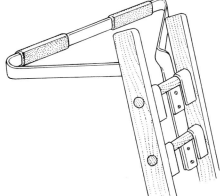

Access to the roof above a conservatory is marginally easier with the aid of a ladder stay.

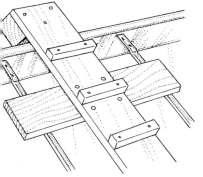

crawling board helps to spread the weight during roof maintenance. Fix a rop beneath.

Secure the bottom rung of a ladder that has to be erected at a dangerously shallow angle.

ounted in an end wall.

Shading is another need, especially the structure faces south. Slatted inds mounted outside the glass are robably the best solution. A little ss efficient, though more convennt, are window blinds mounted side. These may also be used to mit heat loss on winter nights.

lants for shade

bed on the shaded side of a wall or nce needs planting with some care, because the planting possibilities are obviously more limited than on sunny sites. The choice rests principally between biennials and perennials, for most annuals need plenty of sunshine.

Among suitable biennials are *Bellis perennis* (double daisy), digitalis (foxglove), lunaria (honesty), myosotis (forget-me-not).

Shade-tolerant perennials are more numerous. The following is a selection of fairly compact types: a juga (bugle), alchemilla (lady's mantle), alstroemeria, aquilegais, astilbe bergenia, Clivia miniata, epimedium, erigeron (fleabane), euphorbia (spurge), geranium, *Geum* (borisii), helleborus (Christmas rose), heuchera (coral flower), hosta (plantain lily), inula, liriope (knotweed), primula, pulmonaria (lungwort), stachys, tiarella, trollius, viola (violet).

Barbecues

As one of summer's subtler pleasures, barbecued meals should be relaxed, no-fuss occasions. This is all the likelier if the barbecue itself is a permanent affair, ready for instant use whenever needed. The obvious place is a corner of the patio (or yard, in this instance), preferably where smoke is unlikely to blow across into the faces of the gathering.

The basic structure is three-sided, constructed with bricks or stone blocks. The fittings – a lipped base plate, charcoal grid and wire food grill – are available from barbecue suppliers. Also needed are support strips for placing in the mortar joints, enabling the components to be set at variable levels.

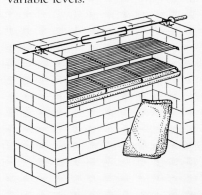

Using commercial fittings, a permanent barbecue involves only the simplest of bricklaying techniques.

A CHANGE OF LEVELS

A sloping garden may prove a mixed blessing. In its favour, the change of levels can often be used to advantage, giving greater prominence to a rock garden or some other eye-catching feature. But a sharp slope also means harder work, perhaps with the added problem of soil erosion. Grass may not be the answer, for steep banks are difficult to mow.

The solution in most cases has to be terracing, re-forming the ground into flat areas linked by steps. Carefully planned, the improvement in both workability and appearance can be dramatic. Though some hard work may be involved, at least it is a once-and-for-all job.

The less pronounced the slope, the easier the task. This is because there is little or no pressure of soil on retaining walls. In such a situation, peat blocks may be used instead of masonry. With an infilling of lime-tree soil and granulated peat, the resultant beds provide the acid conditions enjoyed by a wide range of attractive plants.

Elsewhere, a stronger wall may be needed to restrain the pressure of soil. Within reason it is possible for an amateur to tackle the job, but on a very pronounced slope it would be wiser to employ a professional, or at least to seek his advice.

Steps are constructed in a great many gardens, even where the ground is comparatively flat. We look at the possibilities and the principles involved. Establishing a lawn by seeding is another related topic, for many newly-formed terraces are put down to grass. It is a less expensive and, in some ways, more reliable method than turfing, which is described on p.92.

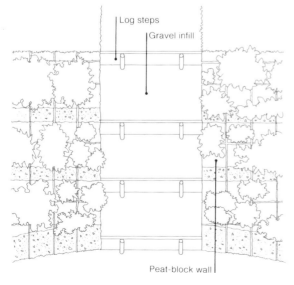

Log steps

Gravel infill

Peat-block wall

Terracing with peat

A peat garden, constructed to form one or more low terraces, should resemble a moorland hillside where erosion has resulted in marked changes of level. Either a sunny or lightly shaded site is best, though not one directly under trees. It is also a help if the garden soil tends towards acidity.

It is important to buy the right sort of peat blocks, especially to avoid the small, air-dried types sold as fuel. The best ones, which should still be damp, will measure about 30cu cm (1 cu ft) and will have been cut from near the surface. In this case they will have a markedly fibrous texture.

If the blocks turn out to be dry, soak them for a day or two. Start by digging out any perennial weeds from the slope, then form a trench about 8cm (3in) deep and just wide enough to take the first row of blocks. Slope the base slightly towards the rear, then place the blocks in it, packing them closely together. Fill in behind with a half-and-half mixture of granulated peat and lime-free soil, firming this thoroughly.

Place a second layer of blocks on top, staggering the joints. Some gaps may be left and the roots of plants inserted, with peat firmed around them. Because the trench was cut at a slight angle the wall will lean backwards, adding to its stability.

Fill in behind this second row of blocks with more peat and soil, finishing level with the surface of the blocks after firming. Rake a dressing of general fertilizer into the surface in the proportion of 16 gr per sq m (½ oz per sq yd).

If the upward slope continues beyond the back of the terrace, further walls and peat beds may be constructed in the same way. It is better to restrict each wall to 60cm (2ft) high, even if this means extra terraces, rather than have taller walls and fewer beds.

Before planting, place stepping

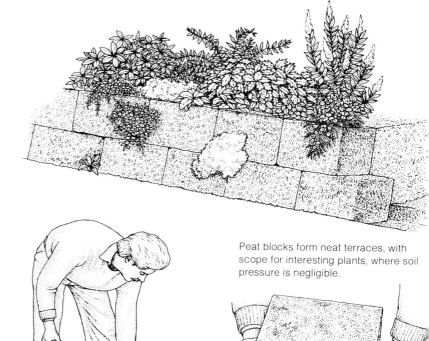

Peat blocks form neat terraces, with scope for interesting plants, where soil pressure is negligible.

Building a peat terrace

1 Dig out any perennial weeds. Then dig a trench 7.5cm (3in) deep, just wide enough to take the first row of blocks.

2 Place the blocks in the trench, packing them closely and with the tops tilted slightly backwards.

stones at intervals in the beds. This will avoid the exertion of too much pressure on the walls.

Once planted and established, the chief need is to keep the walls continuously moist. If allowed to dry, their stability will suffer. Top-dress the plants with peat and fertilizer each spring.

Plants to choose

There is no lack of plants suitable for peat beds. The following represents a small selection:

Adonis vernalis (yellow, early spring); *Astilbe glaberrima* (cream, summer); *Calceolaria tenella* (yellow, summer); *Codonopsis ovata* (blue, mid-late summer); *Cornus canadensis* (white, early summer); *Phlox adsurgens* (pink, summer); *Primula edgeworthii* (mauve, late winter); *Shortia uniflora* (white or pink, spring); *Uvularia perfoliata* (yellow, late spring).

Among shrubs, consider *Gaultheria*

After placing a second course of ocks, their joints staggered, fill in with ore soil and peat.

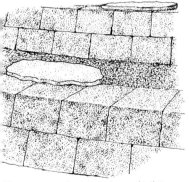

Place some stepping stones in the eat beds to help reduce the pressure n the retaining walls.

rocumbens (pink, summer); *Phyllo-oce aleutica* (green-yellow, spring); hododendrons and azaleas (dwarf pecies such as *R. keleticum* and *R. eucaspis* and a good many hybrids).

Sowing grass seed

1 Dividing the seeds into two equal groups, and sowing these at right angles, ensures even distribution.

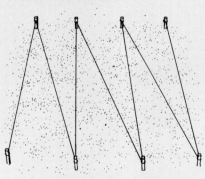

2 Black cotton zigzagged just above the surface of the seedbed will help to prevent birds eating the seed.

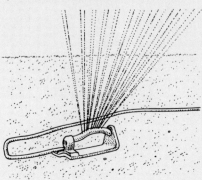

3 Use a fine sprinkler to soak the soil if a dry spell follows. Move it before puddles can form.

Sowing Grass Seed

Broad, shallow terraces, with brick or stone retaining walls, may be turned into a series of small lawns. For straightforward mowing, lay a mowing edge (see p.129) along the base of each retaining wall. Whether you lay turves or sow seeds and applies also to establishing larger lawns on level ground. Details are given on p.93. The timing is different, though, as the best times for sowing are spring and late summer, the latter for preference.

Allow 50 gr of seed per sq m (approx. 1½oz per sq yd), choosing a mixture to suit the sort of lawn required. For a luxury surface not subject to much wear, select one without perennial ryegrass. The latter, a relatively coarse grass, is an asset for hard-wearing, utility-type lawns. A compromise, suitable for the majority of lawns, is a mixture containing a dwarf, fine-leaved strain of ryegrass.

Sowing the seeds

Weigh out sufficient seeds for the area, then divide this into two equal amounts. First sprinkle one lot over the whole area, then sow the second at right-angles. As a guide to the sowing rate, a small, measured area may be sown first with the appropriate amount of weighed seed. Rake the seeds in very lightly with the tips of a wire rake, taking care not to draw the soil into ridges.

Black cotton stretched over the newly-sown lawn will keep birds off until the seeds have germinated. If the soil shows signs of drying out, either before or after germination, water it with a fine sprinkler. Give the soil enough water to soak right in but avoid puddling or disturbing the surface which might damage the seedlings.

Terraces with retaining walls

Dry-stone walls (see p.128) are one alternative to peat beds for gentle slopes where there is little downward pressure of soil. They look especially good when trailing alpines are planted in gaps in the stonework, in which case a sunny aspect is needed. Logs or old sleepers are another possibility in such a position.

In each case the soil will have to be formed into rough terraces before the retaining walls are built, though the front foot or two will have to wait until afterwards. This is where the hard work comes in, for it is necessary first to strip the topsoil from each terrace, then level the subsoil before replacing the topsoil at an even depth.

If a terrace is formed simply by shifting the topsoil, its rear half will consist mainly of exposed subsoil.

Dealing with half of each terrace at a time will avoid having to shift the soil uphill. The barrow can then be pushed sideways instead of up and down the slope.

On anything steeper than a gentle slope, each terrace needs the support of a well-made masonry wall. Bricks are a good choice, in which case construct it in English bond – that is, a wall 21.5cm (8½in) thick with alternate rows of headers and stretchers. It is advisable to seek expert local advice for anything more than a moderate gradient requiring walls up to approximately 1m (3¼ft) in height.

Dig the foundation trench 45cm 1½ft wide, 30cm (1ft) deep. This will allow for 15cm (6in) of concrete, together with the first two courses of brickwork. Finish the surface of the concrete at a slight angle to give the wall a gentle backwards tilt. Strengthening piers at 3m (10ft) intervals are a further safeguard.

Drainage

Build weep holes into the wall to release trapped rainwater. These

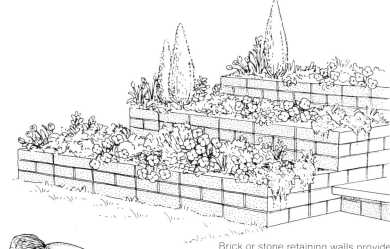

Brick or stone retaining walls provide a succession of raised beds for growing a variety of plants.

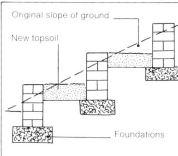

Original slope of ground

New topsoil

Foundations

Building brick terraces

1 Form the soil into a series of rough terraces before the retaining walls on each level are built.

2 It is important to retain the topsoil by shifting it to one side before adjusting the level of the subsoil.

should be situated about every 2m (6½ft) just above ground level and again a few courses higher.

Each weephole is formed by omitting the mortar from a vertical joint in the outer face of a stretcher course and cutting the bricks behind this to leave a gap 5–8cm (2–3in) wide. Fill the inner space with crushed stone or coarse gravel. When back-filling with soil, place some larger rubble immediately behind the gravel.

3 Leave weep-holes to release rainwater. Fill in behind with crushed stone or coarse gravel.

Building steps

Regardless of the materials chosen there are certain guidelines concerning the size of garden steps. A front-to-back measurement of 30cm (12in) is the minimum comfortable size for treads. Risers should not be more than 18–20cm (7–8in) high, including the thickness of the tread. About 60cm (2ft), is the narrowest convenient width.

Measuring and planning

To determine how many steps are needed and what their size should be first determine the height and depth (front-to-back measurement) of the slope. To do this you will need a helper to support a post vertically at its foot.

Place one end of a plank horizontally on top of the slope, its outer end meeting the vertical post. Check that the plank is level, then measure the height where the plank and post meet. Similarly, measure the distance along the plank from this point to the top of the slope.

Use these measurements to plan the number and size of the steps, in each case dividing the overall dimension into suitable units. For instance, if the slope is 1.2m (4ft) high, at least six steps will be needed if the riser height is not to exceed 20cm (8in).

Building

Of the several possible materials, among the easiest to build with are either bricks or blocks for the risers and slabs for the treads. Provide an 8cm (3in) concrete footing for the bottom riser; place subsequent risers at the rear of the slabs of the preceding tread.

Lay each tread on a layer of mortar, with the nose (front end) of the slabs projecting approximately 2.5cm (1in) beyond the riser. Aid the drainage by laying the treads so that they slope very slightly towards the front. Bricks make an attractive edging.

Cutaway view showing how steps are constructed. The bottom riser has a separate footing; subsequent risers are supported by the rear of the riser beneath. Give each tread a slight overhang.

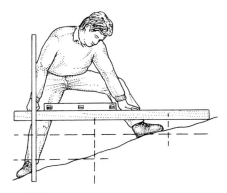

Building steps
1 Measure the overall height on a post by levelling a plank between it and the top of the slope.

2 Having calculated the number and depth of steps, dig out their rough shapes in the soil.

For both this and the risers use hard dense bricks that will not be easily crumbled by frost.

A simple but serviceable flight of steps can be formed by logs or thick planks, in both cases treated with preservative, retaining gravel treads. Drive stout pegs into the ground to hold the risers in place.

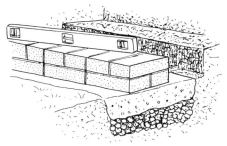

3 Lay the bottom riser on concrete, with a hardcore base. Allow for mortar beneath the tread.

A COTTAGE GARDEN

Planned informality, with a hint of nostalgia, lie behind this design. There are no paths as such, hardly a straight line to be seen, and most of the plants are "yesterday's favourites". The combination of a lean-to greenhouse and sun-facing wall mirrors in miniature the propagation department of many an older estate garden.

Drystone walling forms an unusual and sympathetic surround. It also increases the planted area by reason of the trailing alpines set between some of the stones. With this in mind, soil was included in the central in-filling during construction.

In practical terms, too, the design works well. Stepping stones reduce wear on the lawn at its most used point. An edging of bricks does away with the need for trimming.

Weathered old stone obtained for the tiny paved area forms a practical but mellow surface, a combination more difficult to achieve with concrete slabs or blocks. Small, cushion-like plants, including acaena, saxifrage and thrift, grow in random gaps between the stones.

Overall, it is the plants, of course, that give a garden its character. Around the lawn are such typical cottage-garden favourites as hollyhocks, lupins, larkspur and columbine. The ceanothus at one end is particularly well suited to these sheltered conditions, being a slightly tender shrub. Opposite the greenhouse, an amelanchier (snowy mespilus) provides an ever-changing display of flowers, bright leaves and berries.

The combined effect is simple, colourful and charming, the very qualities expected of a traditional cottage garden.

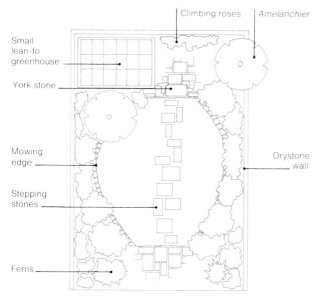

Climbing roses | Amelanchier

Small lean-to greenhouse

York stone

Mowing edge

Stepping stones

Ferns

Drystone wall

Constructing a drystone wall

A wall of this type, sometimes called simply a dry wall, may be free-standing or else used to retain a raised bed or terrace. No mortar is used in its construction – hence the name. Though building a dry wall is reasonably straightforward it is as well to gain experience with a low one first.

Hard stone, such as granite, is best. Building will be easier if the stones have some flat edges, not all rounded or irregular. A range of sizes is needed, from large ones that will span the width of the wall down to small pieces for in-filling.

After delivery the first job is to sort them into rough sizes, making at least four separate heaps. In particular, set aside pieces long enough to span the wall and others, evenly sized, to form the coping.

Laying the Foundations

Start by digging a foundation trench about 45cm (1½ft) deep and 60cm (2ft) wide. Try not to loosen the base; compact it well if you do.

Now place a layer of fairly large, flat stones around the edges of the trench, straight edges outwards. Fill in the space between with smaller stones that interlock as closely as possible. Continue with further layers, staggering the joints over the course beneath, until ground level is reached. Keep in-filling with small stones. The surface of the upper layer must be level.

Building the wall

The top of a dry wall is narrower than its base. To achieve this, both sides of a freestanding wall are given a "batter" – an inwards tilt – though only the outer face of a retaining wall need be angled.

Construct a pair of timber "batter frames" corresponding to the required cross-section. An inward tilt of about 10 degrees is adequate. Drive the uprights in at each end of the

A drystone wall is attractive, practical and not so very difficult to construct.

Constructing a drystone wall
1 First dig a deep foundation trench, disturbing the soil in the base of it as little as possible.

2 Place large, flat stones around the edges of the trench, each with a straight edge facing outwards.

foundation trench and stretch strings between as a guide to placing the outer stones. Simply slide the strings up as the wall grows.

For the above-ground courses use large, flat-faced stones on the outside and in-fill the centre with smaller pieces. Place each outer stone to span a joint in the wall beneath. Most important of all, place a number of large, "through" stones in each course to span the front and back leaves. Some should project beyond

the inner face on retaining walls.

To set plants in the wall add some soil to the centre filling. Plant as you build, leaving small gaps for the stems and firming soil or compost around the roots.

For a neat, strong finish, first lay a course of flat stones to span the wall from front to back. On top of these place a final layer of coping stones all slanted at the same angle. Choose flat stones with rounded tops, all of pretty much the same size.

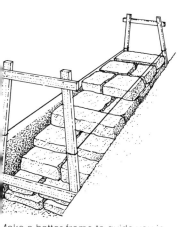

Make a batter frame to guide you in constructing a wall that narrows a little towards the top.

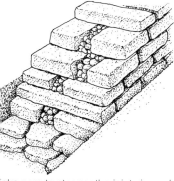

Take care to stagger the joints in each course and to bind the sides with "rough" stones.

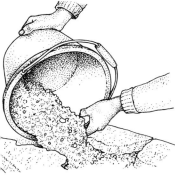

Add some soil to the centre filling of smaller stones if you wish to grow plants the wall.

Making A Mowing Edge

Trimming lawn edges is a tedious chore at a busy time of year. A permanent solution is to give the lawn a paved edge, laying this flush with the surface so that the mower can run over it.

Only quite small pieces are needed, forming a band as narrow as 22cm (9in). Bricks are ideal. The shorter the pieces of paving, the easier it is to follow a curving edge.

For maximum stability lay the paving or bricks on mortar. use mortar, too, to fill the triangular gaps between paving along a curved edge.

A band of paving serves the same purpose where a lawn abuts a wall or raised edge, as on a terraced slope put down to grass.

Laying stepping stones

Unobtrusive, inexpensive, easy to lay – stepping stones are a most effective means of reducing wear on lawns. They are especially valuable at the most used points, as where steps or a path lead onto the grass.

Pieces of natural stone, irregular in shape, are ideal. Manufactured paving, including circular pieces, may also be used, as may slices of log 5–8cm (2–3in) thick.

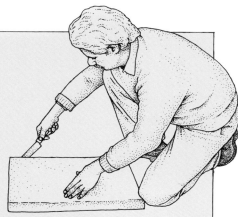

Laying stepping stones

1 Cut around the edge of the stepping stone, then remove the turf using a sharp spade.

2 Finish the base so that the slab fits snugly, its upper surface level with that of the turf.

Having positioned the pieces, cut around the outline with a heavy knife. Set the stepping stone to one side and remove the turf beneath to the appropriate depth. Replace the stepping stone in the cavity, its top flush with the ground.

SECTION THREE

BEST PLANTS FOR YOUR GARDEN

The choice of plants available today is staggering. As long as climate and space permit, you can often even alter your garden soil to accommodate a particular plant or tree.

Although the implications of the effects of colour spring to mind when considering plants for the garden, do not forget the power of pure shape and texture. Varieties in foliage can be one of the richest visual aspects of garden plant life, and its seasonal changes add dramatic colour interest throughout the year.

This plant guide seeks to give not a comprehensive list of plants, shrubs and trees, but rather a select list of plants for particular situations. Each plant has been specially chosen almost as a decorative feature to contribute to the overall design of a garden. The selection is here – the choice is yours.

Trees

The larger a garden, the more essential it is that it should contain trees, to provide the wider context in which the special world of the cultivated plot can be appreciated. A backdrop of mature, native trees places the garden in time as well as space, for most species take many summers to achieve their full height. Trees that fulfil this function are quite different from those "specimens" which are chosen and sited with great care, like living works of art, to occupy a particular place where their individuality can be admired. This is the place for exotic creatures like the flowering *Prunus* from the Far East, cone-bearing spruces from North America or Nepal, magnolias and koelreuterias. Because trees will be in their place for many years, it is important to prepare the site well, to plant the young tree with care and continue to care for it until it is safely established.

(D) = DECIDUOUS
(E) = EVERGREEN

Betula - Birch (D)

Birch trees are renowned for their graceful appearance and attractive bark, a feature particularly noticeable in the species *B. albosinensis* (height 5.4–6m [18–20ft]) where it is a glowing russet. *B. pendula*, the silver birch, has silvery bark that gives it an even more refined air. There are several named varieties of interest, notably *B. p.* "Youngii", (3–5.4m [10–18ft]), with elegantly weeping branches. Ordinary soil will suit, in sun or light shade.

Propagation: grafting
Diseases: various fungal diseases; rust.

Catalpa - Indian bean tree (D)

Catalpas have a fine profile: a slender, straight trunk with a roughly pyramidal head of branches and beautiful large heart-shaped leaves. *C. bignonioides* "Aurea" is a yellow-leaved form slightly smaller than the species at 7.5m (25ft) and holds its leaves later into the year. Upright spires of white flowers splashed with yellow appear in midsummer, to be followed by 38cm (15in) long seed pods. Any good garden soil is suitable in an open, sunny spot.

Propagation: by cuttings
Diseases: usually no problems

Corylus (D) - Hazelnut, cobnut

These trees are cultivated not only for their nuts, but also their yellow winter catkins and, in the case of *C. avellana* "Contorta", for their habit. In winter this species makes a curiously twisted silhouette against the cold sky. In 'Aurea' the oval, serrated leaves are yellow. Any well-drained soil is suitable, in sun or light shade, with some protection from winter winds.

Propagation: layering
Diseases: grey mould, honey fungus, powdery mildew

Davidia (Handkerchief tree (D)

The foliage of *D. involucrata* is its chief attraction, the oval leaves large, mid-green and drawn to a point. In early summer insignificant flowers appear, but each is surrounded by two large, papery, cream-coloured bracts. It is these drooping bracts that give the tree its popular name. Plant in sun or partial shade, in soil of any type, and keep well-watered.

Propagation: by layering or cuttings
Diseases: honey fungus

Eucalyptus (E)

Few people fail to identify a eucalyptus when they see it, although most would be taken aback to learn that there are over 600 species. The recognizable feature of species cultivated in small gardens, like *E. gunnii* is often the young foliage, which is silvery grey green, beautifully rounded and rather small – like thin coins. In maturity the leaves become much darker, longer and thinner, unless the young sapling is cut right back every year. The bark is the main point of interest in mature specimens, because of its warm brown colour. *E. niphophila* (4.5–6m [15–20ft]) has a clutch of virtues. It appears to have paused in a dance, swaying to one side; the bark is creamy but luminous, the leaves as fine as a willow's, and in midsummer numerous white flowers clothe the branches. Full sun, shelter from wind and well-drained moist soil are required.

Propagation: raise from seeds
Diseases: botrytis; silver leaf

Gingko biloba - Maidenhair tree (D)

The gingko grows to about 12m (40ft) and achieves that height in about 35 years. Its size prevents it being grown in many private gardens, for it needs to be seen at some distance to be fully appreciated – unless you sit directly beneath it and look up to enjoy its remarkable leaves. Not only are they beautifully shaped, very like a maidenhair fern, but a particularly fresh shade of green. A warm sunny site is best; any ordinary garden soil is suitable.

Propagation: from seeds
Diseases: usually no problems

Halesia (Snowdrop tree (D)

There are two species of halesias generally grown. Both reach at least 6m (20ft) quite quickly and their spread is wide. The foliage of the tree *H. monticola* is not dense and it does not cast a heavy shade. It is the white flowers of late spring which are distinctive and give both this and the shrubby variety *H. carolina* their popular name. The flowers are followed by 5cm (2in) long winged fruits. Halesias like lime-free soil that does not dry out and a sunny position, preferably with the protection of other nearby trees.

Ginkgo biloba originates in China, and its shape varies from sparsely covered "flagpoles" to lush columns

Propagation: long shoots may be layered in autumn
Diseases: usually no problems

Koelreuteria paniculata (D)

After 20 years, a koelreuteria will have reached about 6m (20ft) in height and be a handsome addition to any garden. The silhouette is in fine proportion, a sturdy straight trunk carrying a nicely rounded head of branches. The leaves, over 30cm (12in) long, are divided into numerous small leaflets of mid-green. Panicles of yellow flowers like laburnum blossom appear in summer, to be followed by green fruits flushed red.

Propagation: raise from seed
Diseases: usually no problems

Laburnum – Golden rain tree (D)

The blossoms of laburnum are breathtaking in their profusion and depth of colour – a strong yellow – as well as their pendulous habit of growth. Both the flowers and delicate leaves are light enough to rustle in the gentlest breeze. A single tree at about 4.5m (15ft) or more suits a small garden well; in larger spaces they are sometimes grown as miniature avenues to great effect. The best-looking species is *L.* x *watereri* 'Vossii', which flowers in early summer. Ordinary garden soil, if well-drained, is suitable, in sun or partial shade.

NOTE: all parts of the tree are poisonous. Since the seed pods will drop to the ground when dry they must be gathered and burnt if there is any danger to children.

Propagation: hybrids must be grafted on to species stock in spring
Diseases: honey fungus

Malus – Crab apple (D)

Edible apples belong to this family; in apple blossom time the relationship is obvious, and here it is indeed the blossom which is valued. The fruits too are admired, though more for their appearance than their usefulness, though they are edible (as preserves). There are several species in cultivation. "John Downie" certainly has the best fruits, but holds its own for beauty of blossom; "Echtermeyer" has weeping branches that sweep the ground, pale pink flowers and purple fruits; by contrast *M. tschonoski* is prized for its autumn foliage, a glorious medley of yellows, oranges and reds. Crab apples are ideal trees for small gardens, reaching about 5.4m (18ft). They like sun or partial shade and any well-drained garden soil.

Propagation: by budding or grafting
Diseases: apple mildew, apple scab, honey fungus

Picea (Spruce (E)

In addition to questions of size, colour and season of interest, which are taken into account when choosing trees, with conifers that of shape comes to the foreground. Their customarily unbending silhouette makes it difficult to blend them in many schemes. That

Laburnum is a dramatic and lovely addition which can easily dominate a garden

aid, the spruce includes some fine species, including the black spruce P. mariana with a conical rather than fastigiate habit and densely growing blue needles. It rises to 4.5m (15ft); there is a nicely curved dwarf form at 30cm (12in). P. pungens reaches up to 7.5m (25ft). The feathery needles of its variety "Glauca" are a lovely silvery blue-green; the weeping form is a fine and graceful little tree with a height and spread of 3m (10ft). All spruces need a little acid in the soil, which must be deep and moist. Sun or partial shade will do, but some shelter is necessary.

Propagation: raise from seed
Diseases: die back (after frost); honey fungus

Prunus (D)

This is a very large group of flowering trees that includes the flowering cherries, peaches and plums. For magnificence of blossoms the first of these three takes the prize, with P. subhirtella in the front running. It is covered in pale pink blossom in spring; "Autumnalis" and "Autumnalis Rosea" bear respectively white and pink flowers through the winter and they make excellent cut flowers. "Pendula" has graceful weeping branches. All these reach about 6m (20ft). Varieties of blackthorn, P. spinosa, make good trees for small gardens at only 3.6m (12ft). This is an ornamental plum but the fruits (sloes), can be used. The varieties are all spring-flowering; "Purpurea" is a good form with purple foliage and white flowers. Of the varieties of common peach, P. persica, which reaches 6m (20ft) and spreads as far, "Cardinal", with glowing red spring flowers, is very beautiful. All these are happy on ordinary well-drained soils, perhaps with a trace of lime. They need good light, it is important that they also have but some protection from winter winds.

Prunus subhirella "Stellata" is shown to best advantage in a large garden

Propagation: by budding and grafting
Diseases: honey fungus; chlorosis, bacterial canker

Robinia (False Acacia (D)

One of the compensations of living in the city is the occasional sighting of R. pseudoacacia, for this epitome of green refreshment is tolerant of atmospheric pollution. It makes an excellent specimen tree; the bright colour of its leaves is enhanced by their form – they are small, light and numerous, like the laburnum. In midsummer, the creamy and fragrant flowers appear in pendulous racemes 15cm (6in) long. R. pseudoacacia can reach 9m (30ft) in time; R. kelseyi is much more compact at 3m (10ft) high with a spread of 2.4m (8ft). As a standard, it makes a most elegant specimen with its dainty deep pink flowers. Robinias appreciate a sunny position; any well-drained garden soil will suit.

Propagation: raise from seed or detach and replant rooted suckers at any suitable time during the winter
Diseases: usually no problems

Magnolia (D)

The flowers of the magnolia are among the most beautiful of any plant and yet they appear in the relatively chilly days of early spring and persist for months. One of the earliest is M. denudata. This slow-growing tree eventually reaches 1.5m (15ft); the numerous white, sweet-smelling cup-shaped flowers are set off by oval mid-green leaves. The species often seen in town gardens is M. soulangeana whose lovely white flowers, flushed wine red at the base, appear before the leaves, a feature which adds to one's sense of admiration for these noble creatures. Named varieties include the purple-flowered "Picture". Where space is very limited M. liliiflora (at 2.4m [8ft] high, with a spread of 2.1m [7ft]) is the best choice. It bears crimson rather open flowers with narrow petals. Magnolias need to be sheltered from north and east winds and like a well-drained reasonably fertile soil.

Propagation: raise from seed or take heel cuttings in summer
Diseases: grey mould, honey fungus

135

Plants for a Dry Garden

Many gardeners must contend with dry conditions as a fact of life. Others will have a part of the garden where sharp (i.e. good, quick) drainage requires care in the choice of plants. Most will include in a scheme some plants that can survive a drought to ensure that, whatever the circumstances, their plot will have some element of visual excitement. Among the numerous plants that need little water to thrive are some so appealing that it is worth constructing a raised bed or wall – if you are not lucky enough to have one or more already – especially to cultivate them. Modest aubrieta and corydalis, though often seen, still charm. Rosemary and rue are among the fragrant herbs that suit these conditions, as do Spanish gorse, toadflax (*Linaria purpurea*), grand mullein and *Oenothera biennis* (a relative of the evening primrose). All of these have the gratifying habit of spreading generously.

Achillea – Yarrow

So many are the species of this hardy perennial, all sun-loving, that it is not difficult to find an example for every situation. But it is especially useful for the rock garden or herbaceous border. Most have fern-like leaves of grey-green from which straight stems rise to about 75cm (2½ft) bearing flat heads of yellow, white or, in the case of *A. millefolium* "Cerise Queen", cherry red flowers, throughout the summer. *A. ptarmica* "The Pearl", with its clusters of tight white blooms is aptly named. Alpine varieties such as *A. chrysocoma* reach 10cm (4in) in height.

Propagation: by division in early spring
Diseases: usually no problems

Antirrhinum majus – Snapdragon

Though perennial, antirrhinums are usually treated as annuals, since their natural span is short. The colour range is impressive, from showy reds, golds and vivid pinks, to pastel shades of lavender, primrose or faintly blushing white. No cottage garden would be complete without them, but they are just as comfortable in a formal bedding scheme, the velvety tubular blooms, like less exotic orchids, providing solid groups of deep colour from midsummer right through to the first frosts. The flowers are fragrant, and are formed in spikes. Pinching out the growing points encourages bushy growth. Sometimes antirrhinums will delight you by self-seeding in a wall or crevice, but generally it will be necessary to plant out seedlings in late spring. Because of a tendency to rust it is advisable to choose resistant types, which fall into three broad groups according to height. The tallest, *A.m.* Maximum, may reach 1.2m (4ft), and will need staking. As well as gracing the border, hybrids from this group make good cut flowers. If they are to be grown for this purpose, do not pinch out the growing points but remove the side shoots to leave a single good flower head. *A.m.* Nanum is the group which, at 45cm (18in) is best suited for summer bedding and in which some spectacular varieties may be found, such as "Black Prince" with deepest red flowers and bronze leaves. The Snapdragons from this group look well massed together in large containers such as half-barrels or other informal containers such as sinks, troughs or terracotta chimney pots. The baby of the family is *A.m.* Pumilum, only 15cm (6in) high, but as effective as its relatives in, say, a providing carpet of colour for the front of the border. They make a good subject for tubs, baskets or large window boxes as long as the growing medium is enriched with well-rotted manure or humus.

Propagation: sow seeds in early spring at 16–18°C (61–64°F) for planting out in early summer
Diseases: rust, downy mildew, grey mould

Cheiranthus – Wallflower

The familiar wallflower, *C. cheiri*, is an old favourite that has numerous qualities to recommend it. To the range of well-known shades of yellow, red and orange have now been added more subtle tones – white peach, pale yellow, pink, violet. Wallflowers bloom from spring to midsummer, and are often planted with tulips for a springtime display that contrasts the bushy, free-flowering aspect of the one with the straight stems of the other. To encourage the bushy habit, pinch out the growing tips. Wallflower blooms are cross-shaped, the petals rounded; many types are intensely fragrant. Though they make good cut flowers, they are at their best in the border, or massed together in glowing groups of a single colour. Taller varieties are well-suited to the cottage garden, while at 37–45cm (15–18in) dwarf types are ideal for rock gardens or in containers.

Propagation: set out young plants in Autumn for flowering the following spring. Dress acid soils with hydrated lime
Diseases: club root; crown and leafy gall; downy mildew

Dianthus

It's a blessing to gardeners that some of the most accommodating plants are also well-loved individuals that we would hate to be without. In this great family of pinks and carnations there are many perennial species that thrive on dry walls (or the rock garden), forming a neatly shaped cushion of grey-green, delicately pointed foliage as the perfect background for their old-fashioned flowers. *D. neglectus* is no more than 23cm (9in) high, with charming pink flowers, the depth of colour varying greatly. *D. deltoides*, the maiden pink, takes well to any sunny, open spot, and thrives even in the crevices of a paved path. It will set its own seed freely. The named varieties

Dianthus "Microchips" provides a stunning splash of colour in any dry garden

ange in colour from "Albus" (white), through "Brilliant" (clear pink), to "Wisley" (deep crimson). *D. caryophyllus*, the forefather of border carnations, has purple flowers on long straight stems of 60cm (24in) that may need staking; they exude the powerful scent of cloves associated with pinks. All of the species bear flowers which appear much simpler than the familiar, fussy, florist's carnations.

Propagation: sow seeds under glass in spring and set out young plants when developed. Cuttings may be taken in summer, or plants raised by layering side shoots
Diseases: foliage susceptible to a number of problems

Epimedium rubrum – Barrenwort
The other plants described in this list like dry soils and tolerate drought because they are happiest in the sun. What distinguishes *E. rubrum* is that it will cope with dry shade, such as occurs in soils sucked almost dry by the roots of overhanging trees. Even in such inhospitable conditions, this hardy perennial, which is half-

evergreen, bears its pretty heart-shaped leaves, fresh green tinged pinky red in spring, turning orange in autumn. Star-like bright pink flowers appear in spring. Plants reach about 30cm (12in); when grown in large groups they make very effective ground cover.

Propagation: divide and replant the roots between autumn and spring
Diseases: usually no problems

Erinus alpinus
On a drystone wall or in the rock garden, this diminutive (7.5cm [3in]) perennial will grow with no trouble at all, setting seed freely and bearing abundant vivid pink flowers like tiny stars. A long flowering period – from early spring to summer's end – is not the only reward. The erinus is evergreen, and little mounds of slender leaves remain the year round. Choose named varieties for colour – "Albus" is sharp white; "Dr Hanele" is a strong brilliant red.

Propagation: sow seeds in spring where they are required to flower
Diseases: usually no problems

Erysimum
It is the perennial species of this large family, closely related to wallflowers, which provide two members happy on dry soils, in rock gardens, at the front of the border or in wall crevices. *E. alpinum* reaches 15cm (6in) and its cross-shaped flowers of sharp yellow closely resemble those of the wallflower, though they are only 1cm (½in) across. Like its relative, erinus is a fragrant plant. "Moonlight" is a soft yellow variety; "K. Elmhurst" is taller at 45cm (18in), bushier, and pale lavender. "Bowles's Mauve" is seen flourishing in walls. *E. linifolium* is at its best in poor sharply drained soil, bearing lilac flowers in early summer. It makes good ground cover beside paths.

Propagation: take heel cuttings in summer. Overwinter in a cold frame and plant out the following spring
Diseases: usually no problems

Euphorbia
Euphorbias are a large and diverse family that includes the stunningly bright *E. pulcherrima* from Mexico, better known as poinsettia, and *E. lathyrus*, the caper spurge, that seeds itself freely in European woodland – a good subject for a wild garden. In so large a group there are inevitably species that are happy on thin dry soils. *E. characias* is such a one, and its rather exotic appearance is redolent of the sun-baked hillsides of the South of France. This herbaceous perennial grows to 1m (3ft) or so with an equal spread. The thickly clustered stems are clothed with numerous blue-grey narrow leaves and at the ends carry, not true flowers, but small flower-like papery bracts of acid yellow. These appear in early summer, but the density of foliage and pleasing proportion of the plant make it a point of interest all year round. It is worth growing three or four species at different points in the garden to provide harmonious contrast. *E.*

wulfenii is, in fact, very similar to *E. characias* but more intensely yellow. *E. polychroma*, at only 45cm (18in) high, has a much softer, fresher look, with bright green leaves and 7.5cm (3in) wide bracts of yellow in late spring. **Note**: all the species described are evergreen.

Propagation: set out small plants between late summer and spring
Diseases: root rot; grey mould on frost-damaged shoots

Genista – Broom

The golden-yellow pea-shaped flowers of *G. hispanica* (Spanish broom) make it one of the most brilliant summer-flowering shrubs. It reaches a maximum height of 1.2m (4ft) – usually less – but may spread its many, densely spined branches 2.4m (8ft) wide. On a bank, rock garden or as ground cover it provides a mass of colour. Its relatives *G. lydia* and *G. pilosa* are prostrate forms that do equally well in similar situations, the former particularly attractive if trained over a wall. None requires regular pruning, though to maintain the bushy habit the growing points should be pinched out after flowering.

Propagation: take heel cuttings in summer for planting out the following spring
Diseases: usually no problems

Gentiana –Gentian

Almost all members of this genus are hardy perennials and most have distinctive trumpet-shaped flowers. Although the colour most often thought of is briliant deep blue, some varieties are yellow, white or even pink. Small varieties are most suitable for a dry garden – or for a shallow rock garden, for instance. *G. clusii* is most commonly grown, but *G. kochiana*, *G. alpina* and *G. sino-ornata*, originated in the Far East and produces stunning blue flowers, with darker blue and pale

green stripes; the flowers are small and open from September to November – perfect for autumn colour.

Propagation: divide in spring
Disease: fungi which may lead to root rot

Gentiana acaulis is easily cultivated

Phygelius capensis – Cape figwort

If it can be given some support and the shelter of a wall, this half-hardy evergreen will reach 2m (6ft); in the border it will achieve half that height. In either situation its slender stems with numerous scarlet tubular flowers make a graceful display, and an extended one, from midsummer through to autumn. Its long straight stems and nodding flowers make it a favourite with flower arrangers.

Propagation: divide and replant the roots in spring
Diseases: usually no problems

Sedum – Stonecrop

Sedums have always been popular; they are generally undemanding and trouble-free, they form a satisfyingly dense hummock of succulent evergreen foliage, and some species are attractive to bees. Nevertheless only a handful of the large number of species available is commonly seen, such as the late-summer-flowering *S. spectabile*, at 45cm (18in) high with 12.5cm (5in) wide pink flower heads, or the hybrid "Autumn Joy", at 60cm (24in), with very wide flower heads of pink, gradually deepening to rust-red by late autumn. Particularly suitable for the edge of the border, for containers or dry walls is the diminutive *S. spathulifolium*. Like its larger relatives, this species has spoon-shaped leaves; they form little rosettes from which the stems emerge to no more than 10cm (4in). Named forms include "Cape Blanco", with grey leaves, stems of red, and bright yellow flowers in summer; and "Purpureum", which has reddish-purple leaves turning white at the centre as summer comes, when the yellow flowers appear.

Propagation: by division from autumn to spring; by stem cuttings in summer
Diseases: crown or root rot if soil is too wet

Tanacetum

Tanacetum haradjanii is the species of this large family which is generally grown. It bears thick clusters of minuscule yellow flowers in late summer; but many gardeners pluck them off to focus attention on the beautiful foliage. The leaves too are very small – the whole plant never reaches more than 20cm (8in) – and look just like feathers. Silvery grey in colour, they give out a sharp scent when crushed. The plant was formerly known as *Chrysanthemum haradjanii*.

Propagation: by division in spring
Diseases: usually no problems

Ground Cover Plants

ants that provide ground cover do
t necessarily do so at ground level;
tness stately species like *Astilbe*,
icket-forming types like *Gaultheria
allon* or shrubs like Rhododendron
dinomayo" whose branches spread
w. There are very many perennials
aching about 45–60cm (18–24in)
ich grow densely together,
oducing masses of attractive foliage
d delicate rather than ostentatious
ooms. Among this group are *Dicentra
mosa, Brunnera macrophylla*,
anesbills and hybrid anemones. The
niatures include familiar faces like
ssum, aubrieta and achillea as well as
lox subulata, creeping juniper and
sa paulii which are not so often
en. Ground cover plants reduce the
ount of work in the garden by
ectively smothering weeds (as long as
e site has been cleared of weeds
fore planting) and can be used to
cupy bare spaces between newly
nted shrubs while they are filling
t. In this situation it is important
t to select varieties that are
mpant, and will refuse to give up
eir patch when their useful days are
ne. Because so many accommodating
rennials fall into this group, offering
ch a wide range in terms of colour
d season, shape and size, it is likely
be the group from which the busy
rdener, who loves the look of a well-
ocked garden but has little time to
aintain it, might make his choice.

juga

he two perennial varieties of ajuga
ost useful for ground cover both
rive in moisture-retentive soil,
lerate shade, and reach about 23cm
in) in height. The first is *A.
ramidalis*, which is roughly conical in
ape with a spike of vivid blue
owers. *A. reptans*, commonly known
bugle, is the other. There are several
rieties in cultivation, distinguished
the colour of the leaves. "Rainbow"
s pink, gold and bronze leaves; those
"Variegata" are green and cream;

The chief beauty of *Alchemilla mollis* (Lady's mantle) lies in its foliage

"Atropurpurea" has purple foliage that
sets off the swirls of tiny blue summer
flowers particularly well.

Propagation: divide the plants at any
time
Diseases: usually no problems

Alchemilla mollis –
Lady's mantle

A. mollis is a hardy perennial which
grows to about 45cm (18in) high.
Plants should be set out 38cm (15in)
apart. The palmate leaves of light
green look especially pretty after

summer rain when the light down that
covers them tends to hold a few drops
of water on the surface. Modest, pale
yellow flowers no more than 3mm
(⅛in) wide appear in clusters at the top
of slender stems during the summer. In
flower arrangements the leaves are
much used alone. Alchemillas like sun
or light shade and any soil type as long
as it is moist and well drained.

Propagation: Alchemillas self-seed
readily but may also be increased by
division between autumn and spring
Diseases: usually no problems

Anthemis nobilis – Common chamomile

Chamomile is a perennial which has the distinction among plants prized for their ground-covering qualities of being grown alone to form a lawn. As long as the area to be covered is not great or subject to very hard wear, a chamomile lawn is a fragrant, attractive and labour-saving alternative to grass. The variety "Treneague" is the best choice for this purpose as it is sturdy and non-flowering. The leaves are fern-like, a subtler green than grass; to grow a lawn, set out plants in spring 15cm (6in) apart, on well-drained soil in an open sunny site. Once the lawn is established it may occasionally be necessary to mow it, say once or twice during the summer. Flowering chamomile can be used for ground cover at the front of herbaceous borders. It bears small flowers very like those of the common daisy, during the summer months. Both varieties reach about 15cm (6in) in height.

Propagation: divide and replant roots between autumn and spring
Diseases: usually no problems

Cyclamen coum

It seems that most plants suitable for ground cover are blessed with more than one virtue, and *C. coum* is no exception. As if clothing the bare earth with silvery green, heart-shaped leaves were not enough, it bears its lovely little flowers of pink or white in the unfriendly months of midwinter. They reach only 10cm (4in) high, and the corms should be set 10–15cm (4–6in) apart. Since woodland conditions suit this hardy plant best: moist soil, and a cool, shaded environment where they will not be disturbed, they are best used garden beneath trees.

Propagation: Raise from seed. Cyclamen corms do not produce offsets
Diseases: black root rot

Bergenia

The leathery, glossy quality of bergenia leaves gives them a rather exotic air which endears them to flower arrangers. Nevertheless they are hardy perennials, evergreen into the bargain, and diverse in their forms. All varieties reach about 30cm (12in) in height and should be planted at that distance one from another. The first to flower, in the middle of winter, is *B. crassifolia*, with pale pink bell-shaped blooms; but the most eye-catching is probably *B. cordifolia purpurea*, with flowers of purplish pink appearing in spring and leaves tinged sympathetically purple. These plants will grow in almost any soil, including limey soil, and in sun or shade. No attention is needed until they become overcrowded, when they can be lifted and divided.

Propagation: by division in autumn or spring
Diseases: leaf spot

Brunnera macrophylla

Anchusa myosotidiflora, the synonym of this hardy perennial, refers to the fact that its flowers are very like those of the forget-me-not (myosotis). Plants reach 45cm (18in) at most and should be set out at the same measure. The leaves are large in proportion to the plant as a whole, deep green and heart-shaped. The delicate flowers are deep blue, and appear in late spring. A shady situation is best, in soil of any type that does not dry out. Brunnera does well under trees, and is a suitable subject for a shaded town garden, perhaps at the side of a formal pool.

Propagation: divide and replant the roots in autumn or spring
Diseases: usually no problems

Heuchera sanguinea – Coral flower

Heucheras belong to the saxifrage family, and look very like their cousin London Pride, *S. x urbicum*, with a low

Tiarella cordifolia, or foam flower,

rosette of leaves, slender stems and bell-shaped flowers at the top. These flowers are vividly coloured, bloom right through the summer and last well in arrangements. Best for colour are the hybrids, including the gorgeous pink "Scintillation", the scarlet "Red Spangles" and "Pearl Drops" a gleaming white. All reach between 30 45cm (12–18in) and should be planted 45cm (18in) apart in light, well-drained soil, in sun or partial shade.

Propagation: Divide and replant the roots between autumn and spring, weather permitting
Diseases: leafy gall

Pachysandra terminalis

Even in deep shade, pachysandras

...ovides colour as well as dense ground cover all the year round

ground cover differ from each other mainly in size. V. major reaches at most 30cm (12in) in height, V. minor 10cm (4in). Both are hardy evergreens that have dark green oval leaves that spread by rooting from their trailing stems. Blue flowers with open petals appear in late spring and early summer. There are several named varieties of V. minor with flowers of different colours, such as "Atropurpurea", deep purple, "Alba", white, and "Burgundy", wine-red. While periwinkles are well-suited to a wild garden the foliage is good-looking enough to earn them a place in a shrubbery or mixed border, where they will effectively smother weeds. Any garden soil will do, in a shaded site.

Propagation: stem cuttings root with ease
Diseases: rust

Periwinkle creates a carpet of colour

...read rapidly, widening the carpet of ...eir decorative foliage. The leaves are ...d-green, oval, and neatly arranged in ...rays from the centre of which ...agrant creamy-coloured flowers ...pear in spring. These hardy ...ergreen plants have a shapeliness ...at is lacking in some carpet-forming ...ecies and look as much at home in ...rly formal schemes as in wilder ...ttings. Any soil is suitable except ...ose containing lime.

...ropagation: divide and replant in ...ring
...iseases: usually no problems

...iarella cordifolia – Foam flower
...ke heucheras, to which they are ...osely related, tiarellas are members of

the saxifrage family. T. cordifolia is the species best for ground cover, with large palmate leaves spreading low. In spring the slender stems bear spikes of tiny white flower which at 15cm (6in) long are half the height of the plant. Tiarellas, like other carpet-forming plants, require very little attention and are very easily established in any moist solid in cool shade. A good choice for a wild garden, tiarellas are perennials that keep their leaves through the winter.

Propagation: divide and replant the roots in autumn or spring
Diseases: usually no problems

Vinca – Periwinkle
The two species of periwinkle used for

Plants for Winter Interest

It is a cause for rejoicing that the number of plants which continue to bear leaves and blossom deep into the winter is so great, and that there are even more that burst into life in what seem to be unpropitious circumstances. Bulbs, shrubs and trees can easily be found to furnish a garden for all seasons. The temptation is to plan a garden primarily for winter interest, so varied are the plants that would fill it. Some give themselves away by their names – winter aconite (*Eranthis hyemalis*); winter sweet (*Chimonanthus praecox*), glory of the snow (*Chionodoxa*); snowdrop (*Galanthus nivalis*); and Christmas rose (*Helleborus niger*) – while others have become so familiar a feature of the winter scene that they would be badly missed: hedges of hornbeam to shelter the young bulbs, carpets of *Cyclamen coum* beneath bare trees, and heaths and heathers in abundance.

Callicarpa

The autumn berries of Callicarpa are an extraordinary shade of lilac-purple. Small, round and numerous, they appear in clusters in the axils of the leaves, which themselves turn from green to yellow and red. The species *C. rubella* is the tallest at 2.4m (8ft) and bears its berries for many months. Plants like a sunny sheltered position, but any good garden soil will do.

Propagation: by cuttings in summer
Diseases: usually no problems

Camellia

Exotic their appearance may be, but members of the camellia family form a hardy evergreen clan, barely waiting for winter's end to put out their enticing blooms. C. "Cornish Snow" is one of the most popular, with graceful arched stems and typically glossy dark green leaves. It flowers prolifically over its height and spread of 2.4–3m (8–10ft); the white blooms are pink in bud. C. x "Salutation" is a pink-flowered hybrid of smiliar height but more compact. For flowers throughout the winter, hybrids from the C. x *williamsii* group (height 1.8–2.4m [6–8ft] spread, 1.2–1.8m [4–6ft]) are unrivalled. There are many to choose from, but "Donation" has the greatest number of admirers, with semi-double, icy-pink flowers 10cm (4in) wide. For more colour, choose "J.C. Williams", lilac with saffron yellow stamens, a very hardy type; or "Philippa Forwood", blush-pink.
Note: Camellias will only grow in lime-free soil.

Propagation: take cuttings in late summer
Diseases: bud drop

Chaenomeles – Japanese quince

Of three species in this family the best known is C. *speciosa*, sometimes called japonica, which clambers in a rather gangly way over walls or fences to about 1.8m (6ft) and bears apple-blossom-like flowers in shades of white, pink or red. The small oval leaves are glossy green. After a long flowering period, beginning in midwinter, the golden-yellow fruits appear. There is a wide range of attractive hybrids, of which the red-flowered types make the most impact, like "Rowallane" or the dwarf "Simonii" with a spreading habit – useful for training over banks.

Propagation: take cuttings in summer or layer long shoots in early autumn
Diseases: chlorosis in excessively alkaline soils

Clematis

Few gardens can afford to be without at least one clematis, clothing a wall or fence or clambering over an old tree. The perennially popular "Nellie Moser" (pale pink with deeper stripe) and "Vyvyan Pennell" (violet) come into flower before most varieties and continue to bloom weeks after the others have faded. Both attain about 3.6m (12ft). There are two yellow-flowered clematis which go on to

Clematis viticella, a beautiful addition to any garden — as a climber or border plant

produce beautiful feathery white seedheads after the flowers have fallen. The first is *C. orientalis*, a vigorous species that can reach 6m (20ft). The summer flowers are scented, nodding and abundant. *C. tangutica* is similar but smaller, and equally vigorous despite its fragile appearance. Clematis like an alkaline soil and a sunny position with their roots in shade.

Propagation: by stem cuttings in summer
Diseases: clematis wilt

Colchicum – Autumn crocus

Apart from its later flowering period, the autumn crocus differs from the crocus proper in the size of its leaves, which are longer and wider, and which emerge after the flowers have faded, to grow on rather untidily. Because of this, one of their common names is "naked boys", for the flowers that appear unprotected by foliage. For this reason they are often set in clumps in rough grass. One of the showiest species is *C. autumnale* "Roseumplenum", with rose-pink double flowers that look like miniature water lilies nestling in the ground. Both this variety and hybrids of *C. speciosum* reach about 15cm (6in) with leaves about twice as high. Hybrids of white ("Album"), mauve ("The Giant") and purple ("Autumn Queen") are available.

Propagation: separate offsets from the corms in summer and replant in the flowering site
Diseases: usually no problems

Cornus – Dogwood

Cornus is an upright bushy shrub about 2.4m (8ft) high, spreading to 3m (10ft). Pleasant enough in summer, with green leaves and white flowers, it starts to earn its place in the garden as autumn draws on. The leaves turn golden red and the flowers are succeeded by white berries. In winter,

The brilliant scarlet branches of *Cornus*, or dogwood, provide welcome winter colour

all adornment gone, the plant comes into its own, revealing naked branches of vivid scarlet (*C. alba* "Westonbirt") or gleaming acid green (*C. stolonifera* "Flaviramea"). Cornus need moist soil in sun or partial shade.

Propagation: take heel cuttings in late summer
Diseases: usually no problems

Crocus

Crocuses are generally thought of as spring-flowering corms, but there are a number which are autumn-flowering. A good example is *C. longiflorus*. Not only does it bring a splash of colour – deep lilac with an orange throat – to

the gloomy days of late autumn, but it is strongly scented too. *C. imperati* actually flowers throughout the winter; another fragrant species, the outer petals are buff-coloured, those inside are purple. As it begins to fade, the earliest of the spring-flowering species is coming into bloom – *C. tomasinianus*, with lilac flowers, and the rich yellow *C. ancyrensis*, which is a little smaller than most types at 6cm (2½in), but produces up to 20 flowers from a single corm and is very long-lasting. It is possible to have crocuses in bloom for eight months of the year from early autumn to late spring, producing wave after wave of cheerful colour. They like almost any well-

A lawn covered with *Crocus tomasinianus* heralds the coming of spring

drained soil and produce flowers most readily in a sunny site.

Propagation: remove cormlets after leaves have died down and plant out or grow on in pots according to size
Diseases: gladiolus dry rot on corms

Euonymus – Spindle tree
The leaves of all deciduous varieties of this shrub have good autumn colour, but the most spectacular is E. *alatus*, which eventually reaches a height and spread of up to 2.4m (8ft). The branches spread outwards rather stiffly, but this only serves to draw attention to its stunning crimson foliage, and is no disadvantage. A further point of interest is provided by the tiny flat corky "wings" which are attached to the branches. Euonymus will grow in ordinary soil, in sun or partial shade.

Propagation: take heel cuttings of lateral shoots in early autumn
Diseases: honey fungus

Iris
A species of iris can be found for almost any situation. Three from the reticulata group are winter-flowering, best grown in a rockery or at the front of the border. None is taller than 15cm (6in), so it is important to put them where they can easily be seen – though the depth of colour of the velvety blooms is difficult to overlook; and the flowers, which are up to 8cm (3½in) across, are disproportionately large. I. *reticulata* itself is the easiest to grow, with deep blue flowers in the last weeks of winter. I. *historides*, in a pocket of the rock garden, produces bright royal blue flowers in the winter's depths; following on close behind is I. *danfordiae*, with wonderful, bright yellow, lightly scented flowers with an upward tilt to their lower petals.

I. *unguicularis*, not a reticulata, will grow in any well-drained soil as long as it is sited to get the most of any sun that is available. Its evergreen leaves at 60cm (24in) far outstrip the 23cm (9in)

flower stems, but they can be clipped for neatness in autumn. Through out the winter, 7.5cm (3in) wide lavender flowers streaked with yellow appear.

Propagation: divide the bulbs after flowering
Diseases: grey bulb rot

Jasminum nudiflorum – Winter-flowering jasmine
The innocent, bright yellow flowers of the winter-flowering jasmine will appear throughout winter in the most inhospitable conditions, only blowing to bitter winds. The shrub itself will grow even on a cold north-facing wall. It needs some support for its loosely climbing habit, whether a wall, pillar or accompanying sturdy shrub. It may reach 3m (10ft). The flowers are small – no more than 2.5cm (1 in) across and are borne on almost leafless twigs. The whole plant has a distinctly Oriental air to it, and indeed it originated in China. To prevent its becoming too leggy and sprawling, it should be pruned hard after flowering.

Propagation: by nodal cuttings in late summer
Diseases: usually no problems

Kochia – Summer cypress
In summer, the kochia forms a neat bush like an elongated egg about 75cm (2½ft) high of dense but delicate foliage, fresh grass green in colour. By late autumn, the variety K. *scoparia tricophylla* has turned deep crimson. The change in colour is striking; because the shrub is small enough to be used in summer bedding schemes, it is important to set it with other plants that look good with both its colourings. Plant in light soil in a sunny site.

Propagation: raise from seed sown in spring
Diseases: usually no problems

Narcissus – Daffodil

ike crocuses and tulips, the other
ell-loved ambassadors of spring, there
re many more species of narcissi than
re generally seen in parks and gardens.
ome of the lesser-known types are
miniatures, best raised under glass, but
. bulbocodium (5–15cm [2–6in] high)
ill flower out of doors at the end of
ne winter, planted in fine grass. It
aturalizes well, and in mild seasons
ay surprise you by springing up earlier
han expected. The same is true of the
oup related to N. cyclamineus, so
alled because of the way the outer
etals are turned back like those of a
yclamen. "February Gold" is a sturdy
riety, bright yellow and 30cm (12in)
gh. The flowering time of N. tazetta
ries very much according to climate.
mild districts its numerous, pale
umpets will bloom in midwinter; in
ery cold areas only greenhouse
ultivation will bring it into flower.
he variety "Paper White" 30–45cm
2–18in) high and scented, is the only
ne available.

ropagation: detach offsets and
plant in flowering site
iseases: virus diseases

osa – Rose

s well as the roses that go on
ooming bravely into early winter,
ere are several species roses whose
utumn fruits (hips) are highly
corative. R. moyesii reaches 3.6m
2ft) with a spread of 3m (10ft). The
mmer flowers are pink or vivid red,
e hips elongated and shiny scarlet.
he variety "Geranium" is smaller, but
th larger hips, and would be a better
oice for a small garden. R. pomifera
eight and spread 2.1m [7ft]), has
le pink flowers and dark red oval
uits. R. rugosa (2.1 by 1.2m [7 by
t]) is the best choice overall, since it
akes a good hedging plant, has a long
owering period, and strongly scented
ooms. The vermilion hips are almost
herical, R. r. "Alba" is a white

flowered variety; "Plena", also known
as "Roseraie de l'Hay", has double,
purplish-red blooms.

Propagation: by cuttings in late
summer
Diseases: black spot; grey mould;
powdery mildew

Stephanandra

Flower arrangers prize the foliage of
stephanandra not only because of the
autumn colour – yellow or orange –
but for the arching habit of the
branches and the pretty pointed shape
of each leaf. After the leaves have
fallen, the bare brown stems reveal
their curving shape. Both S. incisa and
S. tanakae reach about 1.5–2.1m (5–
7ft) but the latter spreads furthest, to a
maximum of 2.1m (7ft). S. incisa
prostrata (height 45–90cm [18ins–3ft])
is suitable for ground cover. All three
species bear panicles of tiny pale pink
or white flowers in summer. Any
garden soil will suit, in sun or partial
shade.

Propagation: detach and replant
rooted suckers between autumn and
spring or take hardwood cuttings in
autumn
Diseases: usually no problems

Tulipa – Tulip

The brilliant red of the earliest
flowering tulips brings the long
sentence of winter to a startling full
stop. The species that perform this
welcome task are T. eichleri (30cm
[12in] high), T. praestans (30–45cm
[12–18in] high), and the diminutive T.
pulchella (its name means "little
beauty") at only 10–15cm (4–6in). For
contrast, two white species are worth
cultivating, particularly T. biflora
(15cm [6in] high), which will continue
to produce flowers for years in a sunny
position. The flowers open right up to
reveal yellow centres. T. kaufmanniana
(10–25cm [4–10in] high) has earned
the name "water-lily tulip". Its pointed

petals, flushed with red and yellow,
open up to make a star 10cm (4in)
across.

Propagation: remove offsets after
flowering and plant out at depths
relative to size
Diseases: virus diseases; grey bulb rot

Vitis coignetiae – Vine

The autumn tints on the foliage of V.
coignetiae paint a breathtaking picture.
Large heart-shaped leaves of varied
sizes thickly cover this vigorous climber
– it can reach 15m (50ft) in favourable
circumstances – overlapping in shades
of green, yellow, orange and crimson.
This is one of the best ornamental
climbers for growing up a tree or to
cover a garden shed or garage. A moist
rich soil is needed, but almost any site
will suit.

Propagation: layer year-old growths in
autumn
Diseases: usually no problems

Vitis coignetiae: an ideal wall cover

Trees for Autumn & Winter Interest

Acer – Maple

There are numerous trees in the acer family which are suitable subjects for medium-sized gardens, as well as the small shrubs such as A. circinatum at 1.8 by 2.4m (6 by 8ft). Some have interesting bark, like A. griseum (eventual height 4.5m [15ft]); the smooth, grey-brown bark peels off in a thin layer to uncover rust-brown beneath, while in autumn the green leaves turn an astonishing scarlet. A. japonicum "Aureum" looks as fresh in summer, with light green and bright yellow leaves, as it is dramatic in autumn when the foliage turns to crimson. It eventually reaches 6m (20ft), but is slow-growing, like A. griseum. Both are lime-tolerant, and should be planted in sun or partial shade where they will be protected from cold winds, in moist but well-drained soil.

Pruning: not necessary
Diseases: honey fungus; scorched fungus

Amelanchier – June berry

A magnificent splash of golden organe in the autumn, these trees are a marvellous addition to any garden. They are hardy and grow easily. From april, A. candensis – properly a shrub, but quite tall – is covered with a shower of small white flowers, followed shortly by dark berries. Soil must never be allowed to go dry, but amelanchiers thrive in either a sunny of a shady situation.

Propagation: by layering or from seed
Disease: fireblight

Corylopsis

The deciduous trees and shrubs of this family have bright autumn foliage, and an elegantly twiggy outline in winter. In very early spring, before new leaves sprout on the branches, drooping racemes of yellow flowers appear, scented like cowslips. C. glabrescens reaches 3m (10ft); its shrubby relative C. platypetala (1.8–2.7 by 1.8m [6–9 by 6ft]) has the showiest flowers, in racemes about 7.5cm (3in) long. Corylopsis prefer lime-free soil, in sun or partial shade, but with the protection of a wall or surrounding shrubs.

Pruning: not necessary
Diseases: usually no problems

Hamamelis – Witch hazel

The half-dozen species and their varieties of witch hazel in common cultivation offer between them a number of interesting features. Most reach a maximum of 3m (10ft), the exceptions being the shrubby H. vernalis (1.5 by 1.5m [5 by 5ft]), which grows well near water, and H. japonica arborea, which sometimes reaches 6m (20ft). Almost all species have a pungent scent to their yellow, or yellow and red, spidery flowers that bloom in very early spring on naked branches – useful material for flower arrangers. Luxuriant summer foliage of mid-green turns yellow or red in autumn. Probably the best variety for autumn colour is H. x intermedia "Hiltingbury", the leaves of which take on a blaze of gold, russet, scarlet and red. Since Hamamelis can cope with a certain amount of air pollution they are a good choice for town and city gardens. They like neutral or acid soils, a sunny site and protection from winds.

Pruning: in maturity, branches that spoil the shape can be cut back after flowering
Diseases: usually no problems

Rhus – Sumach

Rhus typhina, the stag's horn sumach, is the best variety for brilliance of

Amelanchier hubbock provides a stunning splash of rich contrasting colour

The delicate coloured leaves on the *Rhus typhina* make it particularly decorative

autumn foliage, which takes on shades of violet, gold and red. The pendant leaves are of exceptional size, perhaps as long as 45cm (18in) and should be encouraged by hard pruning in early spring every year. After the leaves have fallen, the spreading outline of the branches explains the origin of the tree's common name. Tolerant of mild air pollution, *R. typhina* reaches 3–4.5m (10–15ft), but with a spread of 3.6–4.8m (12–16ft). A sunny position is best, on ordinary garden soil.

Pruning: prune hard in early spring
Diseases: verticillium wilt; die-back

Salix – Willow

Graceful willows are justifiably popular, but often too large for small gardens. Fortunately, the species most useful for winter interest are of manageable size. *S. daphnoides*, for example, reaches between 4.5–7.5m (15–25ft) with branches spreading to 4.5m (15 ft). It is known as the violet willow because of the colour of the shoots during winter. *S. caprea* "Kilmarnock", the goat willow, has a central trunk from the head of which numerous weeping branches cascade almost to the ground, making it a compact tree for its height, which may be anything from 3–7.5m (10–25ft). In very early spring it is covered with silvery catkins that turn yellow with pollen. If space permits, *S. matsudana* "Tortuosa" is an interesting choice for the outline of its twisting, outspread branches against a winter sky. It can reach 12m (40ft) or more and spread 7.5m (25ft). Willows like moist soil and a sunny position.

Pruning: cut away dead wood in winter
Diseases: anthracnose of willow

Sorbus

At all seasons trees and shrubs of this family, which includes the familiar mountain ash, or rowan, and the common whitebeam, are a delight to the eye. Bare in winter, their shapeliness is obvious; the leaves make a pretty foil to springtime flowers, which are succeeded by a profusion of bright berries and brilliant autumn foliage. For distinction of colour, *S. hupehensis* (6m [20ft]) cannot be bettered. Its numerous leaflets are blue-green; 7.5cm (3in) wide clusters of white, hawthorn-like flowers appear in midsummer, followed at the end of the summer by white or pink berries. In autumn the delicate leaves turn orange. The autumn foliage of *S. sargentiana* (5.4–6m [18–20ft]) is also very beautiful, flame red and plentiful. Sorbus will grow in any ordinary well-drained soil in sun or partial shade.

Pruning: not necessary
Diseases: honey fungus; apple canker

Stewartia (syn. Stuartia)

Chiefly represented by *S. pseudocamellia*, this is a small family of handsome trees with a strong silhouette, its attractive flaking bark in winter, beautiful white flowers in summer, and, orange foliage in autumn. The leaves, like the flowers, resemble those of the camellia. *S. pseudocamellia* is, however, a very large tree, up to 15m (50ft). Less common, but worth looking for, is *S. malacodendron*, at only about 4.5m (15ft) and with all the attraction of its larger relative. An acid soil in a site that provides protection from cold winds and from the midday sun is needed.

Pruning: not necessary
Diseases: usually no problems

Climbing Plants

Plants that scramble and ramble up over and sideways add an important extra dimension to the appearance of a garden. In an otherwise fairly formal design they can introduce a contrasting note of exuberance and movement. Where the atmosphere is relaxed or cheerfully crowded, covering a flat surface with foliage or flowers emphasizes the sense of pleasure in growing things. The variety of climbers is wide enough to offer something for every situation, whether the main purpose is to satisfy an aesthetic or practical demand – or more usually a combination of both. In purely functional terms the prime value of climbers is in covering unsightly features like sheds, dead trees or ugly fencing, or in beautifying blank walls. Fast growers like Virginia creeper (*Parthenocissus*) or Russian vine (*Polygonum baldschuanicum*) perform well here. Where boundaries or divisions within a garden are to be set, an easy solution is a climber-clad trellis, using a rose or clematis – or, temporarily, a vegetable screen of scarlet runner beans (first cultivated for their good looks rather than their usefulness) or Jerusalem artichokes.

Actinidia: a decorative climber

Actinidia

Actinidias are deciduous climbers whose chief attraction is their handsome foliage, though tiny flowers do appear in summer. The best example is A. *kolomikta*, which reaches 1.8 to 3.6m (6 to 12ft) – other species are much more vigorous. The leaves are heart-shaped, coloured a good dark green but tipped with coral pink fading to white. Very attractive in themselves, they provide a fine background for low-growing shrubs or bedding plants in a pink and white scheme. A. *kolomikta* grow best in a rich loamy soil; they dislike chalk. Plant against a wall in sun or partial shade.

Pruning: thin out in very early spring if necessary
Diseases: usually no problems

Clematis

There are so many clematis to choose from that, like roses, the best way to find one for a particular situation is to visit a specialist nursery and see them growing. "Nellie Moser" is a hybrid that deserves its widespread popularity and there are species with unusual seedheads. Other interesting species include C. *flammula* with bright white flowers much smaller than the better-known hybrids but sweetly scented and borne in great profusion at the top of the plant, which grows to about 3m (10ft). The flowers of C. *macropetala* (3.6m [12ft]) "nod" rather in the manner of fuchsias, pink or dark blue according to variety. Of the hybrids, the following are outstanding: "Jackmanni Superba", deep purple; "Ernest Markham", vivid red; "Dr Ruppel", bright pink edged white; and "Wada's Primrose", creamy-white with yellow stamens, good for a north wall. On average these varieties will reach about 4.5m (15ft), "Dr Ruppel" about half that height. All are hardy, and like to be planted in alkaline soil with their roots shaded from strong sun.

An abundance of Clematis is always

Pruning: cut down to 23cm (9in) the second spring after planting. In subsequent years remove all weak growth as soon as the buds appear
Diseases: clematis wilt

Ipomoea – Morning Glory

If there were some plants grown for the name alone, morning glory would surely be among them. Fortunately, it has more tangible virtues as well. I. *purpurea* is a half-hardy annual that quickly climbs to 3m (10ft). It bears purple flowers of open trumpet shape for 3 months in summer, set off by mid-green heart-shaped leaves. I. *tricolor*, a perennial usually treated as an annual, reaches 2.4m (8ft), with paler leaves. The flower petals are white at the centre, broadening out to lilac, with yellow stamens; each flower is about 12.5cm (5in) across, opening out at the beginning of the day and closing up at the end. Dead flowers

a spectacular garden feature

should be removed to prolong the flowering period. Ipomoeas advance by means of fine tendrils. They do best on walls or fences in full sun, out of the wind.

Diseases: cold night temperatures may damage young foliage

Jasminum – Jasmine
Gardeners lucky enough to have a sheltered south-facing wall may well devote some part of it at least to an elegant jasmine, and be rewarded with a generous springtime display of starlike flowers and delicate leaves. The flowers of *J. polyanthum* are white or pale pink, in panicles 5 to 12.5cm (2 to 5in) long; the plant reaches a maximum of 3m (10ft) and in favourable conditions is semi-evergreen. *J. primulinum* is of similar height, evergreen with 5cm (2in) wide yellow flowers. When these two have

faded, the common white jasmine comes into flower, and goes on producing innumerable pearly clusters until the autumn. This, the most vigorous species, may reach 9m (30ft) and is hardier than the other two. All will grow on ordinary garden soil as long as it is well-drained.

Pruning: after flowering. *J. polyanthum, J. officinale*: thin out shoots occasionally. *J. primulinum*: cut back flowering growths to within 5 to 7.5cm (2 to 3in) of the base

Lapageria rosea – Chilean bell-flower
This beautiful shrub requires tender handling, but if the right conditions can be provided the flowers are so exotic it is worth the worry. Those conditions are an acid to neutral soil (lapagerias are lime-intolerant), enriched with leaf mould, and a warm, sheltered wall with some shade from the midday sun. In winter, light protection is necessary, such as a covering of straw. The prize is a slender upright climber reaching some 4.5m (15ft) on its twining stems, with dark green, strong oval leaves and, for the length of the summer, 7.5cm (3in) long bell-shaped flowers of richest pink.

Pruning: not necessary
Diseases: usually no problems

Lonicera – Honeysuckle
Here is a thrice-blessed plant: generously covering wall, fence or archway, intensely fragrant, and with exceptionally pretty tubular flowers. *L. periclymenum* is perhaps the best known species, represented by the varieties "Belgica", the early Dutch honeysuckle, which flowers in late spring (and sometimes a second time in the late summer), and "Serotina", the late Dutch honeysuckle, which flowers midsummer to mid-autumn. The first has flowers of yellow and pink, the

latter yellow and red. Both reach about 4.5–6m (15–20ft). The complex flowers of honeysuckle are well set off by its simple oval leaves, but they too are attractively fragile, and seen at their best in the fresh green of *L. japonicum* "Halliana", a vigorous evergreen variety, with yellow and white flowers that can reach 6m (20ft). As the shoots can be pegged down, "Halliana" can be used for ground cover. Honeysuckles like any ordinary, enriched soil, sited in light shade.

Pruning: thin out old shoots after flowering
Diseases: leaf spot; powdery mildew

Passiflora caerulea – Passion flower
Like lapageria, the passiflora is South American in origin, and not fully hardy in cooler climes. *P. caerulea*, however, may be grown outdoors in mild districts against a protective wall with the support of a trellis or wires to which the tendrils can cling. Evergreen, the leaves are palmate (like a hand, but in this case divided into three parts); the extraordinary flowers, some 7.5cm (3in) across, are like the sun and its rays, but pinky-white with a halo of blue filaments around the centre. There is a pure white form named "Constance Elliott". Both sometimes produce (inedible) fruits like little plums yellow. Ordinary well-drained garden soil is suitable; protection in winter is necessary, such as plastic sheeting.

Pruning: thin out overgrown plants in early spring
Diseases: cucumber mosaic virus

Rosa – Rose
Its beauty and unforgettable fragrance may have inspired the deepest attachments in its devotees, gardeners and poets alike, but the rose family is still an extremely useful group of shrubs as well. The climbers, as distinct

from ramblers which have supple stems, fall into two groups, one being very vigorous and good for covering house walls and other large expanses quickly, the second better suited for smaller areas. Into the first group fall "Kiftsgate", white; "Mermaid", butter-yellow; and "Wedding Day", yellow in bud then white flushed pink. The second group is enormous. "Mme Caroline Testout" is an old pink rosegood for a north wall. The choice is wider on walls facing south and west, extending from the blushing salmon pink of "Shot Silk" to "Etoile de Hollande", a breathtaking deep red. "Schoolgirl" is orange-apricot, and suitable for training over a pillar, as are "Paul's Lemon Pillar" and "Handel", cream, flushed pink. The best way to choose roses is to visit a specialist nursery or garden. Pruning roses is worthy of a book on its own, not because it is especially difficult, but because opinions differ. And like all plants that have been long in intense cultivation, they are subject to certain diseases – most of which have their remedies – and a favourite with pests like greenfly, which should be kept under control.

Schisandra

S. rubrifolia is a hardy, deciduous climber that achieves a height of 4.5m (15ft) or more against a south- or west-facing wall in good light but not direct sun. It has a charm reminiscent of Oriental paintings, with its dark branches, glossy, rounded leaves and small, cup-shaped crimson flowers in spring. In gardens where colour has been kept to a play on shades of green the better to concentrate on shape, this might be the plant to introduce a more relaxed note. Any ordinary soil is suitable, if well-drained.

Pruning: not necessary, except to retain a good shape. Remove unwanted branches in winter
Diseases: usually no problems

Thunbergia alata – Black-eyed Susan

Wide-eyed might be a better epithet for the open, orange flowers of *T. alata* with their piercing dark brown centres. This tender annual reaches 3m (10ft) in a season and bears flowers all summer, as long as it is given a sunny sheltered position, preferably against a wall. It will grow well in a container, given a supporting system of wires.

Diseases: usually no problems

Wistaria

Most of us probably think of *W. sinensis* when we imagine a wistaria blooming in early spring, its aged stem and branches climbing to the roof of a fine old house, draped with long racemes of fragrant lilac flowers. It is certainly one of the loveliest of all climbing plants. There is a white form, "Alba", which is even more sweetly scented. *W. sinensis* can reach 30m (100ft) in time. *W. floribunda* is its equal in beauty but only attains a third of that height, and there are several varieties, notably "Macrobotrys", with 60–90cm (2–3ft) long racemes of deep lilac flowers and *W.f.* "Rosea" with pink flowers tipped purple. Wistarias need a good loamy soil and the protection of a south- or west-facing wall.

Pruning: cut back all growth in very early spring. Where space is limited, pruning of the season's young growth may be necessary in midsummer
Diseases: bud-drop; chlorosis; honey fungus

Wistaria sinensis adds a touch of old-fashioned grace to walls and archways

Hedges

Some say there is no better "finish" to garden than a neatly trimmed hedge, giving the same sense of prevailing order and care as a well-kept lawn.

Certainly as a long-lived boundary there is no better alternative, unless it be a particularly fine old wall. And for the many who prefer a living boundary above all, a hedge is a lovesome thing, as versatile within the garden as around it, making screens, creating secret rooms, defining particular areas,

Buxus sempervirens, neatly clipped, can emphasize differences between planted areas

151

maintaining privacy – a function better performed by a thorny rose like "Queen Elizabeth" than any fence or wall. Shrubs usually grown on their own can often be used in groups to make colourful, informal hedges, tall like Forsythia or waist-high with Fuchsia (a hardy species like *F. magellanica*).

Arundinaria – Bamboo

Of all the bamboos, *A. variegata* is best suited to small gardens, where it forms not so much a hedge as a thicket to signify a boundary or surround a given area such as a water garden. The canes and leaves are green striped randomly white, and the whole plant reaches about 1.2m (4ft). The leaves move with every breath of wind, making a lively contrast to more formally clipped hedges. Any ordinary moist soil will do, and the roots should not be permitted to dry out. Site in sun or partial shade.

Propagation: by division in spring
Diseases: usually no problems

Berberis – Barberry

The two evergreen hardy berberis best suited to hedging are *B. darwinii* and *B. x stenophylla*. Both grow to about 2.7m (9ft) and should be trimmed in early summer, after flowering. *B. darwinii* has glossy dark green leaves which set off to perfection the thick clusters of bright yellow spring flowers, followed by blue berries. *B. x stenophylla* is dense-growing with arching branches, yellow flowers and purple berries. For a lower, deciduous hedge, *B. thunbergii* is a good choice at 1.2m (4ft). It is shapely, with small rounded leaves that turn scarlet in autumn. "Atropurpurea" is a handsome variety with red, flushed purple leaves in summer, an invaluable addition to the colourist's palette – and armed with sharp thorns. All these are easy to grow, preferring a sunny position, though the evergreens will tolerate light shade.

Propagation: by 10cm (4in) cuttings in late summer
Diseases: honey fungus

Buxus sempervirens – Box

The dwarf form "Suffruticosa", an evergreen, is the variety often used for edging. Dark green and dense, with tiny shiny leaves, it is suitable for clipping and will give a very neat appearance. In formal gardens such as public parks or some of the great Italian gardens this facility is employed to great effect, but box hedges are versatile creatures. Even a country cottage garden may need its vistas and perspectives, its dividing line between kitchen garden and flowers for cutting, and box can fulfil that need as well. Any ordinary garden soil will suit, in sun or light shade. Clip to shape in summer.

Propagation: take 10cm (4in) cuttings in late summer
Diseases: leaf spot; rust

Crataegus monogyna – Common hawthorn

It is the hawthorn's toughness that makes it so effective a hedging plant. After five or six years it will have reached about 1.8 (6ft) in height, and provided it is clipped twice a year will be thick and thorny. The dark green leaves are glossy, with a toothed edge. The summer flowers and subsequent fruits produced on hawthorn trees are fewer when it is trained as a hedge. Any ordinary garden soil is suitable for this deciduous species, in sun or partial shade.

Propagation: increase by seeds
Diseases: fireblight; honey fungus

Escallonia

For an informal flowering hedge the hybrid *E*. "Donard Seedling", with long arching branches, is ideal. Evergreen in mild areas, it ultimately reaches 2.4m (8ft) as a shrub. Deep green and shiny, the small rounded leaves effectively set off flowers like pink apple blossom in summer. The species *E. macrantha* is often used as a hedge in seaside districts where it sturdily withstands coastal winds. With a long summer flowering period and deep rose flowers, it easily recommends itself. Both these species grow well in any ordinary garden soil, and will tolerate lime. Flowering growths should be removed when the flowers have faded. A light trim encourages flowering, but established hedges may need more severe pruning to shape which will reduce the number of flowers in the following season.

Propagation: by cuttings in late summer
Diseases: silver leaf

Fagus sylvatica – Beech

Grown as a tree, beech is a magnificent, broad-leaved specimen. To train as a hedge it is necessary to create a strong bushy base by cutting the young plants hard back for the first two years. A well-established beech hedge makes a handsome boundary to any garden and is as effective in a formal setting, next to a path or clipped lawn, as it is in a flower garden guarding the herbaceous border. Any well-drained soil is suitable. Trim in summer and the golden leaves of autumn will stay on the plant right through the winter.

Propagation: sow seeds in autumn
Diseases: coral spot; scorched foliage

Griselinia

Griselinia deserves better than a name like a fairy-tale witch, for its leaves are very beautiful, oval, leathery and a gleaming pale green, up to 7.5cm (3in) long. A tender evergreen, *G. littoralis* i restricted to mild and maritime districts, where it is much valued as a hedging plant. Plant in any soil, in sun or shade. Young plants will need some

Griselinia littoralis will thrive in a mild climate, particularly by the sea

winter protection – such as layers of straw or bracken – to help them get established. Trim in midsummer; remove straggly growth at the end of the summer.

Propagation: heel cuttings in late summer
Diseases: usually no problems

Ilex – Holly
In order for holly bushes to bear berries, male and female plants should be grown together. A holly hedge is a good way to achieve this, and creates by its very nature an interweaving of different coloured leaves which is very effective visually; and, given those daunting prickles – an effective barrier too. Evergreen, a holly hedge will reach 2.4m (8ft) in height after about six years. *I. aquifolium* is the species to choose, with the pair "Golden Queen" (male) and "Handsworth New Silver" (female) for a show of berries. Plant in sun if the variegation of gold and silver on the leaves is to be maintained. Any garden soil is suitable. Pruning and

trimming are not easy – protective gloves and jacket are recommended – but the hedges should be clipped to shape in spring.

Propagation: take 5 to 7.5cm (2 to 3in) cuttings in late summer
Diseases: honey fungus; leaf spot

Olearia – Daisy bush
In summer, when daisy bushes are in bloom, they seem to be covered in little white flowers, a very pretty sight. Because they withstand salt-laden winds so well, they are often used in seaside gardens. The best species is O. *macrodonta*, with holly-like leaves, which grows in a dome-shape to a maximum of 3.6m (12ft). Those tough leaves help O. x *haastii* resist atmospheric pollution too, making it a good choice for an urban garden. Its production of flowers is copious when compared with its relative, and it blooms later in the summer. Both have a strong scent. Pruning and trimming are unnecessary; but dead shoots should be removed in spring.

Propagation: take cuttings 10cm (4in) long in late summer
Diseases: usually no problems

Prunus lusitanica – Portugal laurel
Portugal laurel is an evergreen member of the cherry family, probably the largest and most beautiful group of ornamental flowering trees and shrubs. *Prunus lusitanica*, however, is grown for its handsome leaves, large, smooth and pointed, a fine foil for the creamy, scented flowers of summer, which are followed by purple berries. There are several named variegated forms available. With a potential height and spread of 4.5–6m (15–20ft), pruning may be necessary to keep older plants in check. Trimming should be carried out in spring or late summer. Any ordinary well-drained soil is suitable.

Propagation: take 7.5–10cm (3–4in) heel cuttings in late summer
Diseases: powdery mildew

Rosmarinus – Rosemary
An aromatic herb of upright to spreading habit, a good subject for container growing, a comfortable companion for many other garden plants, and not difficult to grow; rosemary has much to recommend it. It lends itself to different settings with ease. As a hedge it is best within the garden or where an ornamental rather than impenetrable boundary is called for. Rosemary bears tiny lilac flowers from spring through to the very end of summer. The upright branches are thickly covered in narrow, pointed dark green leaves. It will grow on any ordinary well-drained soil in a sunny position. Any necessary pruning should be carried out in the in spring in order to prevent the plant from becoming too straggly.

Propagation: take 10cm (4in) cuttings in summer
Diseases: usually no problems

Plants for the Mixed Border

Choosing plants for the mixed border is governed by a number of criteria. Getting it right from planning stage to finished product, so to speak, is complex enough for a successful result to earn marked regard. Given that the site is favourable it is essential to choose plants that like broadly similar conditions, as well as others that can be relied upon to thrive no matter what, leaving you free to devote a little extra care to one or two delicacies. The mixture comes from a blend of colour, height, plant type (shrub, perennial, annual, bulb and so on) and points of interest arising from differing habits of growth or flower form. The mixed border is a convention that offers great scope for individual expression. Whatever the theme, a successful combination in full flower is a deeply satisfying sight.

Agapanthus – African lily
Prized by flower arrangers for the straightness of the stems and the deep blue of the trumpet-shaped flowers, which are borne in round umbels at the top, agapanthus are hardy perennials that flower in high summer. The attractive seedheads can be dried for winter arrangements. They reach 60–75cm (2–2½ft) and like any fertile soil that is well-drained. Keep the plants well-watered during the growing season; after flowering, cut the stems right down. "Headbourne Hybrids" are hardier than the species. For a white type, choose A. orientalis.

Propagation: divide and replant in spring
Diseases: usually no problems

Allium
Alliums are decorative members of the onion family (with a smell to prove it) but offer a wide variety of species within the group. The tallest is A. giganteum at 1.2m (4ft), with plummy-pink umbels of tiny flowers 10cm (4in). wide at the head of erect stems that

rise well clear of strap-shaped leaves. A. narcissiflorum is a favourite, only 23cm (9in) high, with nodding, pink, bell-shaped flowers. A. moly has bright yellow flowers in open umbels on 30cm (12in) stems. All these summer-flowering bulbs are easy to grow on well-drained soil, but they like sun.

Propagation: divide in spring or autumn and replant immediately
Diseases: white rot

Alstroemeria – Peruvian lily
Alstroemerias are herbaceous perennials that make good cut flowers as well as enhancing the border. Ligtu hybrids are the hardiest of the group. They reach 60cm (2ft) on stems clothed to the top with narrow leaves.

Aquilegia brightens any border

The flowers are roughly trumpet-shaped, in lively shades of pink, orange and red as well as white. They look best in large groups and flower right through the summer if regularly deadheaded. Like all lilies they need protection from wind, but are not fussy about soil type, as long as it is fertile and well-drained. A sunny site is best.

Propagation: divide and replant in spring
Diseases: virus disease distorts the leaves

Aquilegia – Columbine
Aquilegias for the border, as opposed to the rock garden, include the popular hardy perennial species A. vulgaris, also a good candidate for the cottage garden. Its old-fashioned flowers are trumpet-shaped and the foliage is fern-like. Long spurred hybrids are available in a variety of colours from white, cream and yellow to lilac and crimson, and are 90cm (3ft) high. A moist but well-drained soil is required, in sun or partial shade. Aquilegias self-seed quite easily if dead flower stems are not cut.

Propagation: raise from seed or divide in winter
Diseases: leaf spot

Arctotis
With their clean-cut separate petals and clarity of colour, arctotis seem to epitomize the daisy type of flower, though they outdo the meadow prototype for size, with blooms some 10cm (4in) across and stems 30–60cm (12–24in) long. They are half-hardy and treated as annuals. The measurements given are for A. x hybrida, for the flowers last best and are best for colour too: white, yellow, red, deep pink, orange, often with a contrasting centre. Any soil is suitable; a sunny site is best.

Propagation: raise from seed
Diseases: grey mould

Camassia

Camassia flowers are an intense blue, carried in erect racemes at the top of slender 90cm (3ft) stems. These bulbs are hardy and will flower in summer over many years if left undisturbed. C. *lichtlinii* is the most widely cultivated species with white or blue flowers. They like heavy soils that do not dry out during the growing season.

Propagation: remove offsets in early autumn and replant immediately
Diseases: usually no problems

Chrysanthemum

There are great numbers of chrysanthemum species and hybrids and many complex techniques involved in their cultivation as houseplants, for florists, or as showpieces. But, simply for the ordinary garden the annual species are excellent, especially varieties of C. *parthenium*, which give a good showing of white or yellow flowers like slightly flattened pompoms for the whole summer. They need a light soil and a sunny position, but are not overly fussy, and flower well in containers. Height ranges from 20 to 75cm (8in to 2½ft) according to variety. Also good for containers and the front of the border is C. *multicaule* "Gold Plate" at 30cm (12in), whose flowers look like a ring of overlapping gold coins around a boss of stamens.

Propagation: sow seed in spring in the flowering site
Diseases: leaf spot

Collinsia

Collinsias fall into that precious group of hardy annuals which are easy to grow, long-flowering and yet rather beautiful plants with interesting lilac and white flowers, a little like snapdragons. The stems are straight, about 60cm (24in) and slender enough to need a little support. They are abundantly furnished with pointed green leaves. The variety "Salmon Beauty" has rosy-coral flowers. Collinsias like some shade and will grow on any well-drained soil.

Propagation: Sow seed in spring in the flowering site
Diseases: usually no problems

Crocosmia

Sometimes confused with montbretia, crocosmias are bulbs of African origin. The straplike leaves grow in a fan shape very like an iris. Though the drooping racemes of flowers are coloured intense vermilion, orange or golden yellow, they escape gaudiness by the gracefulness of their form. Flowering time is summer, and the newly introduced mixed hybrids are fully hardy, reaching 60–90cm (24–36in) in height. They like sandy soils but plenty of water, and a sheltered site in sun.

Propagation: raise from seed or divide established clumps in spring before flowering
Diseases: usually no problems

Doronicum – Leopard's bane

These hardy perennials exemplify the innocent gaze of the daisy-like flowers, all the more elegant with their carefully drawn, slim golden petals and heart-shaped leaves. D. *cordatum* "Finesse", with tapering petals and long (50cm [20in]) stems, flowers in spring and lasts well when cut. D. *grandiflorum* at 30cm (12in) is a good choice for the front of the border. Give them a site in sun or partial shade; moist soil is best.

Propagation: divide and replant the roots in winter
Diseases: powdery mildew on leaves

Echinacea – Cone flower

Very similar in appearance to doronicums, the vivid pink of echinaceas and the raised cone at the centre make an interesting contrast in a mixed planting. E. *purpurea* is the only species of this hardy perennial in general cultivation and several varieties and hybrids are available. "The King" is vivid pink. Given a sunny position in rich soil, echinaceas will flower all summer, reaching 90cm–1.2m (3–4ft).

Propagation: divide and replant the roots in winter
Diseases: usually no problems

Echium – Viper's Bugloss

Grown in large groups, echiums provide a sweep of colour for the front of the border and are very attractive to bees. These hardy annuals of the species E. *plantagineum* reach 30cm (12in), are bushy in habit and are available in mixed colours of white, lilac, pink and blue. The flowers are like upturned bells, the leaves pointed. They are easy to grow but best on light soils in a sunny site.

Propagation: sow seed in the flowering site in spring and – **or early autumn**
Diseases: usually no problems

Eremurus – Foxtail lily

For impressive height this hardy perennial outstrips its rivals, and is a refreshing alternative to delphiniums (glorious as they are). E. *robustus* can reach 3m (10ft), with spires of apricot flowers. E. *bungei* at 90cm (3ft) is more manageable, with bright yellow flowers. Since the leaves wither while the plant is still flowering in the early summer, the planting scheme should provide some surrounding cover for the bare stems. Well-drained rich soil is best, in a sunny site.

Propagation: divide and replant the roots in early autumn
Diseases: usually no problems

Eryngium – Sea holly

The metallic sheen on these hardy

Striking *Eryngium maritimum*

This expanse of fuchsias provides a splendid backcloth for the mixed border

perennials of silvery blue makes them something of a curiosity, with spiky thin petals and raised centres, and narrow pointed leaves. The flowers appear in high summer, and could either be partnered with *Rudbeckia fulgida* "Goldsturm" for colour contrast, or softened by a surrounding of rosemary, lavender, senecio, and *Dianthus neglectus* in front. E. x *olivierianum* reaches 90cm to 1.2m (3 to 4ft) and has a long flowering period. *E. maritimum*, the true sea holly, is only 30cm (12in) high and silvery green. Ordinary well-drained soil in a sunny position is suitable.

Propagation: sow seed in spring in a cold frame. Root cuttings may be taken in very early spring
Diseases: usually no problems

Fuchsia

There are numerous species, varieties and hybrids of fuchsia, some hardy, some half-hardy, some rather tender. The hardy shrub *F. magellanica* is a bushy specimen about 1.5m by 90cm (5

by 3 ft), which can be used at chosen points to provide a rich texture to the border and a good background for tall, slender or leggier plants. Of the hardy hybrids which can be trained as standards to provide focal points (at 1.5m [5ft] high) or left as bushes (60cm [2ft] high), there is a good choice. Fuchsia flowers are very showy, pendant with the outer petals reflexed. Typically they are bright pink like "Mission Bells" or pink and purple like "Mrs Popple". Any well-drained soil is suitable, especially if enriched with leaf mould. Among the tender hybrids, which can be introduced into summer bedding schemes, some more refined examples can be found, like the slender-flowered "Thalia", orange-red,

or "Lyes Unique", white and salmon. Choose a site in sun or light shade.

Propagation: (outdoor varieties only) take tip cuttings in spring
Disease: usually no problems

Galtonia – Summer hyacinth

G. candicans is the only species of these hardy bulbs in general cultivation. The white flowers are distributed much more loosely on the stem than those o the familiar spring hyacinth and more closely resemble snowdrops – except that they are 1.2m (4ft) high and flower in late summer. They have a refreshing air about them which lightens what might otherwise be an overblown phase in the border. Plant

shaped. G. *tricolor* is taller (60cm [24in]) and has creamy petals with blue centres. All like a sunny position best, on light soil, but are not difficult to grow in most situations.

Propagation: sow seeds in the flowering site in spring or late summer
Diseases: usually no problems

Heliotropium – Cherry pie
For a dramatic purple heliotrope flowers cannot be bettered; they are tiny, but massed in 7.5cm (3in) wide corymbs to great effect against dark green, slightly wrinkled leaves. *H. x hybridum* is a tender evergreen which is raised in the greenhouse but can be used in summer bedding schemes. They reach about 60cm (2ft) and need the support of canes. Any fertile soil will suit but sun is essential.

Propagation: greenhouse plants may be increased from cuttings taken in early autumn
Diseases: usually no problems

Incarvillea
I. delavayi is a herbaceous perennial with clear pink flowers loosely carried in the manner of primulas. It reaches 60cm (24in) and flowers in the early part of the summer. The leaves, like a buckler fern, appear at the base of the stems after the flowers have already opened. A sunny, open site is essential, on fertile soil that is well-drained.

Propagation: sow seeds in spring outdoors
Diseases: usually no problems

Lagurus ovatus – Hare's tail grass
There are several grasses prized by flower arrangers. This is one that enhances the border as well as the set piece, with its fluffy white "flowers" in bobbing groups that last right through the summer. A hardy annual, it reaches 30cm (12in) in a sunny position on fertile soil.

Propagation: raise from seed under glass
Diseases: powdery mildew

Lilium – Lily
In spite of their exotic appearance, most lilies are not difficult to grow, as long as the bulbs have good drainage and are set on a site in full sun. Because they are very popular and many varieties have been produced, they are divided into different groups and some nurseries are devoted to lilies alone. Typically, lilies are tall and straight, the stem clothed all the way up with narrow leaves, and at the top is a number of trumpet-shaped waxy blooms with reflexed petals. These are stately plants, richly coloured, often fragrant and with enormous blooms in summer. As with roses, any selection is arbitrary, and new varieties are constantly being introduced to rival old favourites like *L. regale* (1.2m [4ft]) a creamy white species, or "Empress of India", crimson and white flowers 25cm (10in) across. More modest is the stem-rooting species *L. mackliniae*, which likes semi-shade and moist well-drained soil to produce its pale lilac flowers. Depending on conditions it will grow to between 23 and 90cm (9in and 3ft).

Propagation: depending on type; it is possible to remove scales from bulbs without lifting them and raise new bulbs from these scales
Diseases: fungal and virus diseases

Lychnis – Campion
Lychnis are hardy perennials producing a variety of pretty, old-fashioned flowering plants in the red, pink- and orange-colour range. *L. coronaria* is bushy in growth with silvery-grey leaves and open-faced bright pink flowers in high summer, height 60cm (24in). *L. flos-jovis* carries its reddish-purple flowers candelabra-fashion at the same height, but comes into bloom a little earlier. The flower heads of *L.*

fertile soil in full sun, and do not ⏤ow the soil to dry out during ⏤wering.

⏤opagation: remove and replant ⏤sets in autumn and replant ⏤mediately
⏤iseases: usually no problems

⏤ilia
⏤here are three hardy annuals of this ⏤ecies useful in the border. G. *capitata* ⏤s blue flowers very like cornflowers, ⏤n-like foliage and delicate stems ⏤out 45cm (18in) long. It flowers all ⏤mmer. G. *lutea*, at 15cm (6in) is ⏤od for the edge of the border (or ⏤acks in paving). The flowers are ⏤ight yellow, orange or pink, and star-

The vivid red of *Lychnis chalcedonica*

chalcedonica are a startling scarlet 12.5cm (5in) across and carried at about 90cm (3ft), a very striking plant. All will grow in any fertile garden soil in sun or light shade.

Propagation: sow seed in spring under glass for planting out in autumn
Diseases: usually no problems

Malva moschata – musk mallow

The rose pink flowers of M. *moschata* look rather like cosmeas, but the plants are less tall at 60cm (24in) and are easily grown perennials with a long flowering period. A poor soil is an advantage, and sun or partial shade will suit. M. *moschata* "Alba" is a white-flowered form.

Propagation: sow seed under glass in spring for planting out in autumn or take 7.5cm (3in) cuttings also in spring
Diseases: rust

Meconopsis

A brief life but a ravishly beautiful one: many species of meconopsis, though they are classified as hardy herbaceous perennials, flower only

once before they die. In that flowering they produce poppy-like blooms 7.5cm (3in) to 12.5cm (5in) wide, of celestial blue on stems at least 60cm (24in) tall. M. *betonicifolia*, the Himalayan blue poppy, reaches 1.5m (5ft). M. *regia* is a yellow-flowered species, M. *napaulensis* red or pink. Plant in semi-shade where some protection from wind is provided. Staking may be necessary. Light, moist, well-drained soil is essential.

Propagation: sow seeds under glass in late summer for planting out the following year
Diseases: downy mildew on foliage

Molucella – Bells of Ireland

Molucellas' other popular name is shellflower, referring to the shape of the green calyces which are much larger than its tiny white flowers and curve around them protectively. The flowers cling to the top half of 60cm (24in) stems, interspersed with leaves not much larger than the "shells". In late summer, this half-hardy annual looks like a green spire of little bells. Molucellas like light soil and a position in full sun.

Propagation: sow seeds under glass in spring for planting out in early summer
Diseases: usually no problems

Myosotis – Forget-me-not

Its popular name, its heady blue colour, its summer fragrance: three good reasons for finding a place at the front of the border for M. *sylvatica*, which reaches 30cm (12in). Bushy in habit, this perennial bears its tiny azure flowers in sprays; the mid-green leaves are pointed and narrow. Forget-me-nots like partial shade and a rich moist soil (there is an aquatic species, M. *scorpioides*).

Propagation: sow seeds in spring outside, for planting in their permanent site in late summer
Diseases: grey mould on flowers

Nemesia

Nemesias bring splashes of bright colour to the mixed border – from lively reds and oranges to subtler blues, pinks and cream. These half-hardy annuals are easily raised from seed and their little funnel-shaped flowers on 30cm (12in) stems strike a cheerful note in high summer. They like light soils on a sunny site and should not be allowed to dry out in the growing season.

Propagation: sow seeds under glass in spring for planting out in early summer
Diseases: root rot

Nemophila insignis – Baby blue eyes

Blue flowers in the border have a stilling influence on the mixed palette; it is not surprising that their common names should be as endearing as this one, or love-in-a-mist, or forget-me-not. Nemophilas are bushy, hardy annuals about 15cm (6in) high, which bear saucer-shaped blue flowers with white centres and have delicate pale green leaves. Flowering in high summer, they like moist soils, and should be set in sun or partial shade.

Propagation: sow seeds in early autumn or spring in the flowering site
Diseases: usually no problems

Nierembergia

At a height of 15cm (6in) and with a habit of forming bushy hummocks of abundant lavender flowers N. *caerulea* is useful at the front of the border. Its 2.5cm (1 inch) wide cup-shaped blooms set amid a mass of narrow leaves continue right through the summer. Though a perennial by nature, it is usually grown as an annual, and needs a sheltered spot to protect the flowers in windy weather. Moist, well-drained soil is best, and a position in sun.

Propagation: sow seed in late winter under glass for planting out in late

pring. May also be increased by
uttings taken in summer
Diseases: usually no problems

Ornithogalum –
tar of Bethlehem
Chincherinchee (O. thyrsoides) is the
ender member of this family of bulbs,
ften seen in florists' displays. It has
hree hardy relatives, only the first of
hich needs full sun. This is O.
alansae only 10–15cm (4–6in) high,
nd flowering in spring at the same
me as late crocuses. A little later O.
utans, height 38–45cm (15–18in)
ears its pendant, bell-shaped white
owers and will tolerate some shade.
. umbellatum reaches 30cm (12in)
nd bears numerous white star-like
owers in spring. Any ordinary soil will
it, if well-drained, and a site in
artial shade.

ropagation: remove offsets in
ummer and replant immediately
Diseases: fungus may blacken the
aves

aeonia – Peony
o one could deny that the showy
ummer flowers of the peony are
xtravagant, but they are not vulgar.
White, yellow, pink, red or deep
rimson, they threaten to bend their
ng supple stems to the ground if
nsupported. These shrubby
erennials, once established, flower for
any years and dislike being disturbed.
here are numerous species of great
eauty in cultivation. P. lutea, its forms
nd hybrids, is a shrub which reaches
bout 1.5m (5ft) in height and bears
olden cup-shaped flowers about 5cm
in) across in early summer. Some are
ented, as are the hybrids of the
erbaceous perennial P. lactiflora, of
hich "Bowl of Beauty", soft pink,
Solange", cream, and "Lovely"
armine with double flowers are
ecommended. Peonies like moist well-
rained soil in sun or light shade. They
ust be well-watered in dry summers

Paeonia suffrutcosa "Duchess of Kent"

and should be deadheaded regularly.

Propagation: divide and replant in
early summer
Diseases: peony wilt

Penstemon
The individual blooms of penstemon
(also given as pentstemon), resemble
snapdragons, but they are more densely
distributed along the plants' stems,
more like hyacinths. Perennials usually
grown as annuals, they are an eye-
catching sight in the border at about
45–60cm (18–24in) in all hues of red
and pink. P. heterophyllus "True Blue"
is a brilliant blue variety with grey-
green leaves. Plant in any well-drained
soil in a sunny site.

Propagation: take cuttings in late
summer for planting out the following
spring
Diseases: usually no problems

Phlox
There are annual and herbaceous
perennial species of phlox suitable for
the border. Best-known of the first is
P. drummondii, which grows upright to
38cm (15in) and bears a cluster of little
open flowers, each one like a cross
between a wild rose and an old-

fashioned pink. White, pink and purple
form the basic colour range but many
variations are available. Tallest of the
perennials is P. paniculata. The many
garden varieties of about 90cm (3ft)
include cherry reds and claret forms.
Fertile well-drained soil in a sunny site
is best.

Propagation: Annuals: sow seed in
spring for planting out in early summer
Perennials: take root cuttings in early
spring
Diseases: leaf spot

Scabiosa causacica
A hardy perennial, S. causacica would
be as much at home in the cottage
garden. Its 7.5cm (3in) wide lavender
flowers, flatter than cornflowers and
frilly edged like love-in-a-mist, are
carried on slim 60cm (24in) stems and
appear through the summer.
"Bressingham White" is a fine variety,
and the slightly taller "Moonshine", a
delicate shade of blue. S. causacica likes
fertile well-drained soil in a sunny site.

Propagation: take cuttings in spring
for planting out in early autumn
Diseases: root rot

Thalictrum – Meadow rue
Thalictrum flowers, which appear
throughout the summer, are extremely
pretty, but small and delicate; the
stems are very fine. It is primarily for
their leaves that they are cultivated,
leaves closely resembling the popular
maidenhair fern. In fact, foliage and
flowers complement each other well,
and the plants are an enhancement to
any border. T. dipterocarum at 1.2 to
1.5m (4 to 5ft) is available in yellow-,
white- or pink-flowered varieties. This
herbaceous perennial likes moist fertile
soils best, but will tolerate some shade.

Propagation: sow seed in spring for
planting out in the permanent site a
year later
Diseases: usually no problems

Plants for the Rock Garden

Unless you inherit a site which naturally lends itself to the cultivation of alpines and which, therefore, will probably already be host to a few well-known species, you will be faced with two alternatives if you want to raise plants of this kind. One is building an alpine house, a kind of living museum which will, of course, extend the range of tender plants you have in your collection. The other is to construct a rockery, no easy task, if it is to look "natural", as it must to be successful. But the sweat and tears are well worth it if the result is the opportunity to grow and enjoy some of the most exquisite of cultivated plants. Their miniature perfection inspires the kind of admiration Elizabethans must have held for miniature portraitists, masters of the finest brushstrokes and brilliant colours. For alpines are a vivid coloured group, intense, like jewels – and often no bigger than a pearl.

Armeria – Thrift

The narrow pointed leaves of armerias form low hummocks; the slender stems are straight, carrying dense, spherical heads of tiny flowers. *A. caespitosa* is a hardy, evergreen perennial which reaches 5–7.5cm (2–3in) and is almost completely covered by pink flowerheads in late spring; the whole spreads to about 23cm (9in). *A. maritima*, found around the coast on rocks and grassland, is 15–30cm (6–12in) high with a correspondingly wider spread and larger pink flowerheads that appear from late spring to high summer if regularly deadheaded. The varieties "Alba" and "Vindictive" are respectively white and fuchsia pink. Grow in ordinary, well-drained soil in full sun.

Propagation: divide and replant the roots in spring
Diseases: rust on leaves and stems

Campanula – Bellflower

Campanulas are typically a glorious

The magic of a rock garden lies in the mix of colour, size and texture

blue in colour, or purple or white. Some pink forms of border species are available. The varieties suitable for the rock garden, all hardy perennials, include *C. carpatica*, with open bell-shaped flowers in high summer on 23cm (9in) stems and *C. garganica*, with innumerable star-shaped flowers right through the summer (height 12.5–15cm [5–6in]). *C. allionii* needs some encouragement but if in scree conditions produces pale lavender 2.5–4cm (1–1½in) bell-shaped flowers in midsummer. *C. portenschlagiana*, by contrast, is almost invasive, perhaps best suited to crevices or cracks in paving where it will settle down to a long and robust life. It reaches 15cm (6in), spreads at least three times that distance and carries very small, deep

blue bell-shaped flowers set amid thick clusters of rounded leaves from midsummer to the first frosts.

Propagation: sow seeds in autumn for planting out the following spring or in spring for the autumn of the same year. Plants may be raised from cuttings of basal shoots taken in spring
Diseases: rust on leaves and stems

Cerastium – Snow-in-summer

Like snow, cerastium covers all – or it will do, if its invasive tendencies are not kept check. It is useful in larger rock gardens where it can be kept apart from finer specimens. *C. bierbersteinii* and *C. tomentosum* both bear star-like white flowers in early summer, reaching about 15cm (6in) high. Their mat-forming woolly leaves, which in the case of *C. tomentosum* turn a shimmering blue-green in winter, spread 60cm (24in) wide. They like a gritty soil and a sunny position.

Propagation: divide and replant in spring
Diseases: usually no problems

Dianthus – Pink
Of the dianthus species suitable for the rock garden, many are also good subjects for the front of the border. All range in colour from white through pink to red. These low-growing hardy perennials belong to a family of flowering plants that have been popular for centuries. The clove-scented pink, *D. caryophyllus* or gillyflower, was known before Shakespeare's day as the epitome of the fragrant flower, lending its name to wall-flowers and stocks before plants were more rigidly classified. Of its descendants, *D. caesius* (Cheddar pink) is a particularly good rock garden plant at 10–30cm (4–12in) high, spreading up to 60cm (24in) on rooting stems to form a typical mat of leaves. These are narrow, pointed grey-green, studded with perfumed, pink flowers about 2.5cm (1 in) across, from late spring to high summer. *D. chinensis* (Indian Pink) comes into bloom as the last flowers of *D. caesius* are fading, and keeps going to the first frosts if regularly deadheaded. "Bravo", 23cm (9in) high, is a bright red form, vivid against its pale green leaves as the winter closes in. *C. deltoides* also lasts all summer, and though it seeds itself freely is easy enough to keep in check. The colour range is wide, including the sumptuous carmine "Wisley Variety". All these need full sun, and dislike acid soils. Good drainage is essential.

Propagation: sow seed in spring for planting out later the same year. In summer, take cuttings or layer side shoots.

Diseases: damping off, foot rot, leaf spot.

Draba – Whitlow grass
The flowers of draba species may be as little as 0.5cm (less than $\frac{1}{4}$in), but they are a glorious yellow and have a very attractive habit of rising up on thin stems from a neat cushion of miniature leaves which sits humbly on the ground beneath. In the case of *D. mollissima* (meaning: the tenderest), height and spread are 2.5cm (1 in) and 15cm (6in) respectively, proportions to invite tender feelings indeed. The cross-shaped flowers appear in late spring. *D. rigida* is twice the size but still a miniature and flowers about a month earlier. Both like a sunny site in well-drained soil. As the leaves grow so densely together it is important not to let them stay wet for long periods. Water around plants, not over them.

Propagation: detach rosettes of leaves without flowers in midsummer and treat as cuttings for planting out one year later
Diseases: usually no problems

Fritillaria latifolia – Fritillary
A group of these exquisite bulbs, members of the lily family, will provide a focal point in any rock garden. Unlike their relative, the snake's-head fritillary, found wild near streams, these fritillaries like well-drained sites in full sun. *F. latifolia* grows to between 1–20cm (4–8in), its flower heads like nodding tulips. *F.l.* "Aurea" has golden flowers chequered brown; the petals of *F.l. nobilis* are more noticeably chequered, a dark wine-red outside but lime-yellow inside. When planting bulbs, put them on their side so that the dimple on top does not collect water which could lead to rot.

Propagation: carefully detach offsets after flowering and plant in pots; plant out when large enough to flower
Diseases: usually no problems

Geranium – Crane's bill
Geraniums are among that well-loved group of plants that give a great deal in return for very little attention. The finely cut leaves are as attractive in their own right as the saucer-shaped flowers. They have all the appeal attached to cottage-garden plants, which is where the taller species of these would be perfectly at home. *G. reynardii* has particularly pretty leaves of grey-green that form clumps up to 23cm (9in) high, 30cm (12in) across and bear small lilac flowers from late spring to high summer. For quick cover, *G. pylzowianum* is a good choice, 7.5cm (3in) high, though its bright pink flowers in midsummer are not many. *G. subcaulescens*, on the other hand, produces an abundance of vivid magenta flowers from late spring right into autumn. Each plant reaches about 10–15cm (4–6in) and spreads a generous 30cm (12in). The hybrid form

Delicate *Fritillaria uva-vulpis*

"Russell Prichard" is a little larger, with a trailing habit that makes it useful for ground cover. All these like sun but will tolerate some shade; plant in ordinary well-drained soil.

Propagation: divide and replant in the flowering site between autumn and spring
Diseases: usually no problems

Leontopodium – Edelweiss

If there is a flowering plant that by its name alone conjures up the idea of alpine beauty, it must be this one. *L. alpinum* grows to about 20cm (8in) with a similar spread. Its tiny white flowers are surrounded by pointed white bracts; together they resemble white stars about 5cm (2in) across, and appear in midsummer. Edelweiss like an open sunny position in well-drained soil.

Propagation: sow seeds under glass at winter's end; grow on for planting out the following spring
Diseases: usually no problems

Limonium – Statice

The flowers of the perennial *L. latifolium* can be dried as everlasting flowers. Its 60cm (24in) high drifts of minuscule lavender flowers are seen to best advantage in the raised bed or rock garden in high summer. Its annual relative, *L. sinuatum* (height 45cm (18in)) is one of the best known everlasting flowers with much brighter, showier blooms available in almost every colour. Both these like full sun. The latter needs a light or dry soil.

Propagation: sow seed under glass in spring
Diseases: grey mould; powdery mildew

Picea – Spruce

P. abies "Pumila" is a dwarf-growing variety of the traditional Christmas tree which, with a habit more spreading than conical, makes a fine specimen in a rock garden, at 60cm (24in) high and spreading as far. The

Saxifraga is a excellent choice for filling any unsightly gaps in your rock garden display

small branches grow densely together, overlapping in horizontal fashion and completely concealing the stem. The overall effect is much softer than that of the ubiquitous fastigiate (upright columns) type dwarf conifer and much easier to incorporate into a successful design. Since spruces like moist, preferably slightly acid soil, care must be taken when choosing a position for this plant among alpines. Choose a sheltered corner in sun or partial shade. Frost damage must be avoided.

Propagation: raise from seed
Diseases: honey fungus; rust

Ranunculus calandrinoides

This tuberous-rooted plant, a perennial member of the buttercup family, is usually raised and grown in an alpine house, but may be grown in the open. Outside it will bear its white, bowl-shaped flowers in spring. The leaves are stalked and a little like those of a dwarf tulip. The whole plant reaches about 10–15cm (4–6in) and will grow in any ordinary garden soil in sun or partial shade.

Propagation: Sow seed in early spring for planting out from autumn to the following spring
Diseases: usually no problems

Sanguinaria

S. canadensis is a hardy perennial with cup-shaped, intensely white flowers that bloom in late spring. Each one opens up from enfolding leaves which provide it with a shapely foil. Choose the variety "Flore Pleno" for an extended flowering period and double blooms. Soil that contains leaf mould is best; in fact, S. canadensis will do as well under deciduous trees as it will in a sunny position.

Propagation: divide directly after flowering and replant, without damaging the roots, straight into the flowering site

Diseases: usually no problems

Saxifraga

Saxifrages are useful for packing into nooks and crannies between the rocks, from which they'll send forth drifts of little star-shaped flowers. S. aizoon baldensis, height 10–15cm (4–6in) has rosettes of silver lime-encrusted leaves and white flowers in midsummer. It forms a miniature dome shape. Yellow- and pink-flowered forms are available. S. x burnatii has extremely pretty colouring: silvery green leaves, with white flowers on red stems. Any of the varieties or hybrids developed from the mossy saxifrage, S. moschata, would enhance the rock garden. (They are equally effective as neat edging plants between a path and the mixed border.) All are between 2.5–7.5cm (1–3in) high and grow in cushion-forming fashion, bearing flowers ranging in colour from red to yellow, white or pink in late spring. For all these, sharp drainage is essential, and some lime in the soil is of benefit. Since they do not like to be baked by the sun, a south-facing aspect would obviously be unsuitable; the only exception would be in a chilly climate.

Propagation: divide after flowering and replant directly into the flowering site
Diseases: rust

Sedum – stonecrop

When Margery Fish was anguishing over what to plant in the rock garden at East Lambrook Manor she "came upon some stonecrop and pounced on it as an answer to prayer". Unfortunately, the species she had found was S. spurium, which, because it is naturalized in Great Britain, was soon rampant, its dense heads of flowers in high summer going in some way to induce forgiveness. A better choice would have been S. spathulifolium, height 5–10cm (2–4in), spread 23cm (9in). This evergreen perennial forms low mounds which bear cheerful yellow flowerheads in early summer. The leaves are succulent and spoon-shaped. In the variety "Purpureum" they are strongly flushed purple. Other alpines worth including for their evergreen foliage are S. acre, height 2–5cm (1–2in), spread 30cm (12in), with single yellow flowers in midsummer, and . album, slightly larger all around, with pink stems and abundant white flowers in summer. All these like full sun but are not fussy about soil type as long as it is well-drained.

Propagation: divide and replant from autumn to spring
Diseases: crown rot where drainage is poor

Sempervivum – Houseleek

There are few plants whose leaves so well befit the description "rosette-forming" as these little evergreen succulents. The leaves are indeed thought to be the main attraction, but their star-like flowers (and stems) are pretty too, and something of a curiosity as they perch on high like miniature versions of the foliage at ground level. Many of the species have variegated leaves. Those of the common houseleek, S. tectorum, are tipped with dark wine red, growing to 5–7.5cm (2–3in) with 15cm (6in) wide rosettes. S. arachnoideum is known as the cobweb houseleek because of the way the tips of the leaves are united by a network of very fine hairs. The rosettes are up to 4cm (1½in) across, and no more than 2.5cm (1 in) high, spreading to 30cm (12in). Stems of 15cm (6in) rise bravely up to bear tiny bright pink flowers in midsummer. Any well-drained garden soil is suitable, on a site in full sun.

Propagation: remove and replant offsets in autumn or spring
Diseases: rust on leaves

Plants for a Wild Garden

If a garden is a place where plants are cultivated according to the whim of the gardener rather than the laws of nature, then a wild garden is a contradiction in terms. Broadly interpreted, however, let us suppose it is a garden that *looks* as if it has occurred naturally, where there is no obvious artifice in the shape of thoughtfully placed statuary, paving or paths, carefully chosen specimen trees and shrubs, rare bulbs or nicely laid out beds of annuals. Here, in place of a modern rose trained over a pergola will be old man's beard or woodbine clambering over a moribund tree trunk; not a rectangular pool with exotic waterlilies, but a limpid pond, its ill-defined banks edged with primroses and clumps of yellow flags. "Holding the mirror up to nature" is not an easy thing for the gardener to achieve. Colour schemes must be subtle, mass plantings to achieve drifts of sympathetic hue the aim. The end result is a garden, or part of a garden, which is wonderfully restful to look at (perched on a thoughtfully provided log perhaps), and, once established, the wild garden mercifully easy for the gardener to maintain.

The delicate blushing hues of *Anemone nemorosa* bring softness to a wild garden

Anemone nemorosa – wood anemone

A. nemorosa is a fine spring-flowering anemone with bright white star-like blooms on 15cm (6in) stems. A native of Great Britain, it naturalizes itself readily in open woodland, and is perfectly appropriate to a wild garden. The variety "Robinsoniama" has lavender flowers slightly wider than the 2.5cm (1 in) blooms of the species. A site in sun or partial shade is best; the soil should be reasonably fertile, and well-drained soil.

Propagation: after foliage has died down, separate the offsets or divide the rhizomes
Diseases: virus diseases may stunt the plants

Astrantia – Masterwort

Astrantias are summer-flowering perennials well-suited to the wild garden, as they provide good ground cover and spread, without being invasive, by means of underground runners. Their flowers, however, are quite distinguished enough to be worth cutting, and they last well in arrangements. *A. major* reaches 60cm (2ft), and bears ruffled daisy-like flowers of a pretty pinkish green. *A. maxima* is between 45–60cm (18–24in), but its flowers are a clear pink and rather larger, about 4cm (1½in) across. The fine flower stems rise up from a dense clump of light green, three-lobed leaves. Ordinary, moist soil and a shaded site are best. The stems should be cut down after flowering.

Propagation: divide and replant the roots between autumn and spring
Diseses: usually no problems

Cimicifuga – Snakeroot, bugbane

Though they are tall plants, the flowering spikes of cimicifuga are so light and delicate that they are graceful rather than stately. Most species reach about 1.2m (4ft) in height. All are hardy perennials bearing creamy-white flowers at the end of summer, and all have highly decorative fern-like leaves. One of the best species is *C. racemosa*, with fragrant flowers suitable for cutting. *C. simplex* (syn. *C. foetida intermedia*) has the neatest flower spikes, rather like bottlebrush, and is good for waterside planting. Both like light shade and moist soil. Strong winds may damage the stems unless they are supported; it is better to site the plants in a situation which is sheltered from wind.

Propagation: divide between autumn and spring
Diseases: usually no problems

Galanthus nivalis – snowdrop

Almost any garden is enhanced by clumps of snowdrops, but what makes them particularly appropriate to a wild garden is their modest appearance, the coy way in which they hang their heads, snug in a little thicket of fresh green strap-shaped leaves (with the exception of *G.n. reginae-olgae*, which flowers before the leaves appear). The common snowdrop reaches anywhere between 7.5 and 20cm (3 and 8in) depending on the richness of the soil. The variety "Flore-plena" is double-flowered; "Viridapicis" has a dot of green on both sides of the petals. The varieties generally flower a little later than the species, which puts out its little blooms in the middle of winter. Snowdrops like most soils but prefer shade and should not be allowed to dry out.

Propagation: snowdrops self-seed, and seed can be collected for raising in pots until ready to plant out. Alternatively lift carefully and divide the plants immediately after flowering
Diseases: grey mould

Galega – Goat's rue

In contrast to cimicifugas, which like damp soils, galegas are tall, white-flowered perennials that need well-drained soil, and a sunny site or light shade. They flower in early summer. *G. officinalis* reaches up to 1.5m (5ft), with spikes of rounded lilac flowers and attractive foliage resembling laburnum (both are members of the pea family). *G.o.* "Alba" has numerous white flowers. *G. orientalis* produces mauve flowers in early summer and is about 90cm (3ft) high. All three, though well-suited to a wild garden, are attractive enough to merit a place at the back of an herbaceous border in any garden.

Propagation: divide the roots from autumn to spring
Diseases: usually no problems

Glaucium – Horned poppy

Few inhabitants of the wild garden bear what might be described as eye-catching flowers. These two biennial species are the exception. In early summer, G. *corniculatum* bears flowers as vivid as the poppies of the field which it so closely resembles. G. *flavum* is more rewarding, for its saffron yellow, 7.5cm (3in) wide blooms appear right through the summer and at up to 60cm (24in) it is twice the height of its scarlet-flowered relative. Both like an open, sunny position and ordinary, well-drained soil.

Propagation: raise from seed sown under glass in late spring and planted out in autumn
Diseases: usually no problems

Glaucium corniculatum: one of the more striking wild garden flowers

Heracleum mantegazzianum

If space permits, a wild garden is probably the only situation in which most gardeners would choose to accommodate this plant, which achieves Olympian proportions. It reaches a good 3m (10ft) in height, and the flower heads, spherical like the seedheads of dandelions, are up to 45cm (18in) across. The individual blooms are bright white, and appear in summer. A mound of mid-green, deeply cut leaves each 90cm (3ft) long, embraces the base of the stem. Heracleums like deep, damp soil in sun or partial shade. The stems should be cut back to ground level after flowering.

Propagation: raise from seed
Diseases: usually no problems

Iris foetidissima – Gladwyn iris

Many of the plants suitable for a wild garden are quickly established and spread easily. With a back ground of such plants, it is not difficult to wait for this hardy iris to get into its stride – and it will take over a year after planting to feel at home and start to flower. The blooms, when they appear in that first summer, are lavender, and about 6cm (2½in) across; they are not ostentatious, but the foliage is evergreen and after the flowers have died down the seed pods appear, soon to split open and reveal a clutch of vivid red seeds. The proper name refers to the unpleasant smell given off by the leaves if they are crushed. *I. foetidissima* likes moist, fertile soil and prefers a position in shade. It reaches about 50cm (20in).

Propagation: divide the rhizomes in autumn
Diseases: iris mosaic virus

Lamium – Dead nettle

Lamium belongs to the same family as many aromatic plants such as basil, hyssop, rosemary, lavender and mint.

Heracleum mantegazzi can be grown effectively in a spacious environment

Like mint it can be invasive, and for this reason is excluded from the garden proper. To the wild garden it brings a different note with its yellow, snapdragon-like flowers and variegated evergreen foliage which turns bronze in autumn. *L. galeobdolon* (yellow archangel) at 15–45cm (6–18in) is the most vigorous species and will thrive in almost any situation. *L. maculatum* reaches about 30cm (12in). The variety "Aureum" has beautiful, gleaming yellow leaves and bears pale pink flowers in late spring. It needs rich, moist soil to keep its good colour, but should be planted in shade.

Propagation: divide and replant the roots in autumn or spring
Diseases: usually no problems

Lavatera – Mallow

The biennial species *L. arborea* (tree mallow) is the best for wild gardens rather than the annual *L. trimestris*). It reaches an impressive 1.2–2m (4–6ft), with soft, velvety leaves and 5cm (2in) wide pink flowers that clothe the upper half of the stem in high summer. The flowers are trumpet-shaped, and the whole plant resembles a hollyhock. Lavateras do not do well in very cold areas; they like a sunny, sheltered site. Over-rich soils will encourage excessive leaf growth at the expense of flowers.

Propagation: self-seeds easily
Diseases: rust; leaf spot

Ligularia

These hardy perennials used to be classified under the species *Senecio*. The two described here might well be included in a list of plants for waterside planting, for both like damp or wet soils. *L. stenocephala* "The Rocket" is a tall (1.8m [6ft]) variety with plumes of yellow flowers on black stems rising from dense, flat green leaves with jagged edges. Less dramatic in form but beautifully coloured is *L. dentata* "Desdemona", 1.2m (4ft) high with clusters of daisy-like deep orange flowers and handsome purple-bronze leaves. Both flower from midsummer to early autumn, and like partial shade.

Propagation: divide and replant in spring
Diseases: powdery mildew (on leaves)

Limnanthes douglasii – poached egg flower

Should the wild garden possess a sunny stretch with a cool root run, and should the gardener feel disposed to raise the occasional annual from seed to add a touch of cheerful colour to a generally subtle landscape, this would be a good candidate. Limnanthes can be sown in the flowering site in autumn or spring to flower through the summer. They self-seed readily and

are highly attractive to bees. The flowers are funnel-shaped, white with an egg-yolk yellow centre, and are lightly scented. The pretty leaves clothe the length of 15cm (6in) stems.

Propagation: raise from seed. Self-seeds easily
Diseases: usually no problems

Smilacina – False Solomon's seal

The better known species of smilacina is *S. racemosa*, often cultivated for its decorative foliage. The abundant mid-green leaves closely resemble those of lily-of-the-valley (smilacina belongs to the lily family) and provide excellent ground cover. The erect stems rise to 90cm (3ft), arching slightly at the top, as if under the weight of the terminal spray of creamy-white fluffy flowers. The flowers, which appear in late spring – early summer, are pleasantly scented. *S. stellata* is a slightly smaller plant at 60cm (24in) high, and rather more delicate in appearance. It is sometimes known as star-flowered lily-of-the-valley. Both these perennial species are by nature woodland plants, at home in moist, shady places and tolerant of acid soils. They should be cut down in autumn.

Propagation: lift and divide established plants in autumn
Diseases: usually no problems

Ligularia dentata produces beautiful golden blooms in the summer

Specularia speculum-veneris (Venus's looking glass)

Like *Limnanthes douglasii*, specularia is an annual that recommends itself to the wild garden partly because it self-seeds readily, and at 30cm (12in) high provides a useful swathe of colour between the many very tall or almost prostrate plants that suit "wild" situations. The saucer-shaped flowers are very like campanulas of the star-flowered type in both form and colour – a lovely violet blue. They appear right through the summer, against a background of attractive oval leaves. Light soil is best, and a position in full sun or partial shade.

Propagation: sow seed in autumn or spring in the flowering site
Diseases: usually no problems

Tellima grandiflora

Tellima is a member of the saxifrage family, and like *S. X urbicum* (London pride) has a rosette of mid-green leaves displayed at ground level from which a thin stem rises, bearing tiny bell-shaped flowers at the top. Tellimas provide excellent ground cover, and look very graceful in late spring when the pale lemon-yellow flowers are in bloom. They flourish in partial shade, in any garden soil, but are highly adaptable and will grow in sun or in dry shade beneath trees. Flower arrangers will be tempted by the foliage of *T.g.* "Purpurea" which is a rich purple-bronze.

Propagation: by division
Diseases: generally no problems

Valeriana officinalis – Valerian

The red valerian the seeds of which are offered in most catalogues is *Centranthus ruber*, which flourishes on old walls. The plant described here is the one famed since medieval times for its medicinal qualities. The name comes from the Latin *valere*, to be healthy. Valerian is a hardy perennial

Tellima grandiflora provides year-round ground cover

that grows to about 90cm (3ft) in damp well-drained soil in a sunny position. The sharply divided, mid-green leaves are sometimes covered in fine hairs. In high summmer, clusters of pale pink flowers appear at the top of the tall stems. One of the plant's popular names is all-heal; another is cat's valerian, for it is very attractive to these creatures.

Propagation: by division
Diseases: usually no problems

Veronica spicata – speedwell

The flowering spikes of species of veronica do not differ greatly in form from cimicifugas or galegas, but they are less tall (between 15 and 45cm [6–18in]) and in a wider colour range – white, "Alba"; pink, "Barcarolle"; and ultramarine "Crater Lake Blue". What also distinguishes these hardy perennials is their foliage, a delicate grey-green. They flower for a good two months in summer, on moisture-retentive soils in full sun or partial shade. Cut down almost to ground level after flowering.

Propagation: divide the plants in spring
Diseases: powdery mildew (on leaves)

Plants for a Water Garden

From the great classical Italian gardens to the smallest urban plots, water is the element most often introduced into a garden to bring it life, to create a focal point, a place for reflection, for cool relief on a hot summer's day. Choosing plants that live in water or at the water's edge is a pleasant task, because they are for the most part as accommodating as they are attractive. It is a short step from the deliberately constructed water garden to the site which is boggy or simply endowed with wet soil. Even in these conditions it is possible to cultivate plants that are beautiful and interesting, rather than just filling a space, such as the eye-catching Kaffir Lily (*Schizostylis coccinea*); *Viburnum opulus* "Sterile" with round, pure white flowers, the little white aster "Snowsprite"; or *Fritillaria meleagris*, the snake's-head fritillary with its chequered flower heads.

(A) = AQUATIC

Aponogeton distachyus – Water hawthorn (A)

Aponogeton needs to have its roots in rich mud below about 45cm (18in) or less of slow-moving or still water. On the surface of the water its paddle-shaped mid-green leaves lie flat, overlapping each other to cover an area about 45cm (18in). In spring, white flowers with scent of hawthorn appear on fleshy stems 10cm (4in) long. They last right through to mid-autumn, sometimes even longer, changing from white to green as they fade. Their little waxy-white plumes of flowers are good in arrangements. Although the plants are more productive in sun, they tolerate shade well.

Propagation: by division in spring
Diseases: usually no problems

Aruncus – Goat's beard

A large clump of *A. sylvester*, in mid-summer with creamy plumes of tiny

Astrantia major and *lilium royale*

flowers rising to a height of up to 1.8m (6ft) is an impressive sight, especially if reflected in a pool. The leaves too make a good showing, thickly clustered together in a mass of light green pointed leaflets. "Kneiffii" is a smaller form (60cm [24in]) with more delicate leaves still. Both kinds usefully smother weeds; the female form of the plants has attractive seedheads.

Propagation: divide and replant in autumn
Diseases: usually no problems

Astrantia – Masterwort

The herbaceous perennial *Astrantia maxima* has particularly attractive leaves, almost divided into three, with noticeable veins, and bright green in colour. They are best appreciated

when in profusion, where they provide – as well as ground cover – a rich background for the small pink flower heads which appear on slender stems in summer. The whole plant reaches about 45cm (18in); to achieve the necessary massed effect, several plants should be set out 38cm (15in) apart. It is a good idea to support them with twiggy sticks if the site is open to winds. The long-lasting flowers are good in flower arrangements.

Propagation: by root division between autumn and spring
Diseases: usually no problems

Caltha palustris – Marsh marigold

The simplicity of calthas is what makes them so appealing. The rounded green leaves for a neat shiny tuffet about 38cm (15in) high, helpfully smothering weeds. The mass of yellow, cup-shaped flowers which appear in spring gives away their membership of the buttercup family. While the species grows in water up to a depth of 15cm (6in) the two named varieties prefer to be at the water's edge, with the crown just beneath the surface, or in very wet soil. "Alba" is the best of these; it bears flattened white flowers with bright yellow stamens in spring and again in the autumn. "Plena" is double-flowered, its yellow blooms looking very like the familiar garden marigold. Both grow to about 23cm (9in).

Propagation: by division in early summer, after flowering
Diseases: rust may appear as spots on the leaves

Eichhornia crassipes – Water hyacinth (A)

So beautiful are the lavender-blue flower spikes of eichhornias with equally splendid leaves, that it is well worth the little effort required to care for them. For these natives of tropical

America are tender, and must be lifted out of the water in autumn and overwintered indoors as wet soil. Plants should be set out on water 15–45cm (6–18in) deep in early summer, where they flot freely (the bottom mud, however, should be fertile). The glossy green leaves are shaped rather like those of the arum lily, curved protectively around 10cm (4in) stems which carry numerous blue flowers in hyacinth fashion. Since young plants establish themselves easily on stolons, one summer will see a great increase of eichhornias across the water.

Propagation: in summer, detach young plants when four or five good leaves have been produced
Diseases: usually no problems

Filipendula rubra – Queen of the prairie
Massed together at the water's edge, or equally content in a damp stretch of the garden, the herbaceous perennial *Filipendula rubra* is a rewarding sight. The mid-green leaves are like those of the maple, and almost reach the top of stems which rise to at least 105cm (3½ft), sometimes twice that height. In summer, nodding plumes of tiny but abundant rich pink flowers bloom at the top. Despite its size, the filipendula remains essentially elegant. *F.r.* "Venusta" is the form most usually seen. *F. ulmaria* (meadow sweet) is a species of lesser dimensions, but its flowering period is longer and the flowers themselves, creamy white in colour, are fragrant.

Propagation: divide and replant the crowns between autumn and spring
Diseases: powdery mildew may affect the foliage

Geum rivale – water avens
G. rivale is the only member of the family that likes moist soil. But like its relatives from the border or rock garden, this hardy perennial has vividly coloured flowers of rich red or coppery orange. Like little bells they hang at the top of stalks reddish about 45cm (18in) high, arising from rosettes of leaves reminiscent of young strawberry plants. They look well set against predominantly green plants, and when a light breeze moves along the water and rustles their stems, the effect is very pretty.

Propagation: raise from seed or divide plants in spring
Diseases: usually no problems

Hemerocallis – Day lily
All forms of the lily have their devotees, and to see the Day lily in full bloom goes far to explain the obsession. Ephemeral they may be – hence the name – but intensely beautiful, rich in colour and often fragrant. And each day, a new bloom opens to replace the last. Excellent at the edge of pools, or in the border in moisture-rententive soil, the arching strap-shaped leaves too are graceful in habit. Despite its exotic appearance, the hemerocallis is a hardy herbaceous perennial. Many hybrids are available, all about 90cm (3ft) high with flowers about 15cm (6in) across produced throughout the summer. "Marion Vaughn" is pale yellow; "Pink Damask", deep coral pink, "Burning Daylight", clear orange. Dwarf hybrids are a more recent introduction, only 38–60cm (15–24in) high with correspondingly smaller flowers but an equally wide colour range, from cream and apricot through to scarlet and burgundy red.

Propagation: divide and replant the roots between autumn and spring
Diseases: usually no problems

Hosta – Plantain lily
The hosta has become almost a cliché for plants with large shapely foliage, but its popularity is well-deserved and should not dim its real value. A hardy herbaceous perennial, there are more than 20 species worth investigating. All have the familiar broadly elliptical tapering leaves, but with many variations on that theme, and all make good ground cover that can be depended upon for years. As a member of the lily family, the trumpet-shaped flowers, which appear in summer, are charming but relatively modest, usually white or lilac. *H. sieboldiana* at 60cm (24in) is typical, with glossy, strongly veined, green leaves; *H. fortunei* "Albopicta" has pale green leaves splashed with yellow; in *H. crispula* the green leaves are edged with cream. *H. undulata* has wavy green leaves streaked silver. Plants with variegation on the leaves need some shade in order to retain their markings. Hostas are versatile in their favoured settings. Given moisture-retentive soil, they look splendid not only at the water's edge, but also alongside paths and at the front of the border, where they will easily overcome weeds.

Propagation: divide and replant the crowns in spring
Diseases: usually no problems

Iris
There are a great many species, varieties and hybrids of Iris. The group suited to cultivation in water or in bog conditions are known as laevigatae; the sibiricae group too flourish at the edge of pools. *I. laevigata*, which gives its name to the first group, is a hardly perennial that likes to grow in about 15cm (6in) of water. The leaves are narrow, pale green, and arch over very gracefully. On stems 60cm (2ft) high, deep blue flowers about 10cm (4in) wide are borne in early summer. Varieties include the lovely though unfortunately named "Monstrosa", with white flowers splashed deep blue. Yellow-flowered irises from this group are named varieties of the 1.2m (4ft) *I. pseudacorus*. "Golden Queen" flowers in late spring; "Variegata" is another

good choice with leaves also striped yellow.

I. sibirica is a waterside plant that will also grow in the herbaceous border if it is damp. Named varieties are easier to obtain than the species, and of these "White Swirl" is the finest, summer-flowering, 1m (3ft) in height and excellent as cut flowers.

Propagation: laevigatae: divide and replant as soon as flowering is over. Sibiricae: divide clumps every 4 years or so, separating into half-a-dozen pieces and replanting after the foliage has died down

Diseases: fungus may cause leaf spot; rhizome rot

Lysichiton – Bog arum

At the water's edge in spring lysichitons bring forth their splendid flowers, like waxy arum lilies with a thick green spadix inside. At 30cm (12in) high they are grand enough; but greater things are to come in the shape of the 1 to 1.2m (3 to 4ft) high glossy leaves. This feature may make them unsuitable for small gardens, but in larger informal schemes these hardy herbaceous perennials look magnificent. *L. americanus* has yellow flowers and will grow in 7.5cm (3in) of water; *L. camtschatsensis* prefers wet, fertile soil, bears white fragrant flowers and is somewhat the smaller of the two species.

Propagation: remove young plants from the base of old rhizomes and raise in pots until ready for planting out
Diseases: usually no problems

Menyanthes trifoliata – Bogbean (A)

The three-lobed olive-green leaves of these plants rise to about 7.5cm (3in) out of the waterlogged soil at the edge of ponds and streams, looking fresh and sprightly. In spring, pale pink starry flowers appear on 23cm (9in)

Lysichiton americanus: a striking plant to feature in any garden

stems. These hardy perennials look best massed together, and as they spread quite freely this effect is easy to achieve.

Propagation: by division in spring
Diseases: usually no problems

Nymphaea – water lily (A)

Waterlilies are one of the most admired plants – in soil or water – yet are not difficult to grow. There are a number of hybrids available which are long-lived, hardy and suitable for the depth of water which an average garden might provide. The roots take firm hold in the mud beneath. It is also important to provide the plants with enough space on the surface of the

water for the beautiful flat round leaves to spread out. The flowers appear in midsummer and like full sun.

One of the best white forms is "Marlicea Albida", which is fragrant and stands clear of the water. It needs a 60cm (2ft) depth of water. "Conqueror" is red splashed white with bright red stamens (45cm [18in] depth). "Rose Arey" has star-shaped very deep pink flowers, orange stamens, and purple leaves that turn green as they mature (45cm [18in] depth). For tubs and small pools where the water is only 30cm (12in) deep, "Aurora", rosy-red with marbled foliage or "Laydekeri lilacea", mauve and sweetly scented, would be good choices. The "pygmy" types like

"Helvola", bright yellow, or "Alba" snow white, will grow in tubs where only 15cm (6in) of water is provided.

Propagation: divide the plants in spring, or remove offsets and raise in pots of loam immersed in water until ready for planting out
Diseases: leaf spot; stem rot

Peltandra – Arrow arum (A)

Peltandras owe their common name to their pointed leaves, which may be as long as 75cm (30in). Flower stems like those of arum lilies appear in midsummer. *P. alba* has white flowers followed by handsome red berries; the flowers of *P. virginica* do not open fully, so they remain green, and green berries succeed them. These hardy perennials like to be set in clumps in shallow water at the edge of a pond.

Propagation: divide the roots in spring
Diseases: usually no problems

Pontederia cordata (pickerel weed) (A)

Blue-flowered plants like this one, eichhornia and *Iris laevigata* have a natural visual affinity with water. In this instance the effect is heightened by the glossy grass-green leaves one of which encloses each flower spike. Standing proud of the water, light streaming through them and reflected on them (for they like full sun), they look splendid in the shallows of a pond. Pontedarias are hardy perennials; they need to have their roots in water 15–23cm (6–9in) deep, with fertile mud beneath, and grow to 60cm (2ft). The flowering period is midsummer to late autumn.

Propagation: by division in spring
Diseases: usually no problems

Primula

Of the border primulas there are three, hardy perennials all, that may be grown in association with water.

The flowers of *Pontederia cordata* add a subtle touch of colour to a waterside setting

Though larger at 45cm (18in) and more colourful than the wild primrose to which they are related, each has a charm that recommends it to informal schemes in smaller gardens.

P. beesiana likes acid, permanently damp soil. It belongs to the Candelabra group, so called because of the way the flowers are arranged up the stem. It bears purplish flowers in early summer.

P. japonica is another Candelabra type, which starts flowering at the water's edge in late spring. The species bears red flowers; *P.j.* "Postford White" has white flowers with yellow centres and will also do well in lightly shaded woodland.

P. florindae bears yellow flowers shaped like bells in drooping umbels at the top of 1m (3ft) stems. Not surprisingly it is commonly known as the giant cowslip. Some types have orange or red flowers; all are fragrant and appear in summer.

P. rosea "Delight", properly an alpine primula, nevertheless thrives on boggy, acid soils, and looks quite at home on the banks of a natural pond. It is a beautiful, compact little plant: 15cm (6in) high, with intensely pink

he beautiful pastel colours of primulus work to advantage in a small landscape

flowers appearing in spring.

Propagation: after flowering, divide and replant into new positions
Diseases: crown, foot and root are susceptible to rot; virus diseases may stunt the plants

Trollius – Globe flower

As long as the roots are moist, in sun or light shade trollius readily produce flowers like marvellous golden orbs in early summer. There are several hybrids of this hardy herbaceous perennial worth cultivating, from the pale yellow "Canary Bird" to the true orange "Salamander", all growing to about 75cm (2½ft). The leaves as well as the flowers are characteristic of the buttercup family to which trollius belongs, and offer good ground cover (in the border as well as by water). If the water's edge can spare them from the clump in which they look best, trollius make good cut flowers.

Propagation: divide and replant the roots in autumn or spring
Diseases: swellings on stems caused by smut

Zantedeschia

One of these tender natives of southern Africa can be grown outdoors in mild districts. It is such a breathtakingly lovely flower that it is worth trying. That one is Z. *aethiopica* "Crowborough" which bears its exquisite flowers in late spring and early summer. Waxy-white and lily-like, the curving spathe of up to 23cm (9in) encloses a yellow spadix like a beeswax candle. The whole plant may reach 90cm (3ft). If this form is grown in containers it must be overwintered indoors; but if in water – at a depth of 15–30cm (6–12in) – it may well survive the winter, with a layer of straw as protection from frost.

Propagation: by division in autumn
Diseases: corm rot

Plants for a Fragrant Garden

Plants achieve enduring fame for their scent more readily than they do for their appearance, which says more about the power of our sense of smell than the beauty of flowers. We are very receptive to heady perfumes, and feel thankfully refreshed by the aroma of mint or lemon. Nevertheless most plants are chosen because of what they look like, their scent thought to be a bonus to their appearance. The list of well-known fragrant favourites naturally includes roses, honeysuckle, sweet peas, jonquils, violets and all the culinary herbs. Less familiar are the scented waterlily, the tulip "General de Wet", *Phlox maculata* "Alba", *Clematis recta*, a herbaceous species, *Romneya coulteri* (the tree poppy) and the glorious magnolia, M. *grandiflora* "Exmouth" with its scent of lemons. Scented foliage often needs to be bruised or crushed for the aroma to be released, and flowers often smell strongest either when it is very warm or as evening falls. Night-scented stock is an obvious example. A scented garden, or a scented corner in a large garden, is particularly appreciated by blind people.

Lavender: always a favourite, both for its coloration and its pervasive scent

Gaultheria procumbens – Creeping wintergreen

The scent of wintergreen is medicinal in the best sense; it is one of the plants traditionally used in infusions to relieve headaches and make it easier to breathe. This property is in the nicely rounded, glossy green leaves as well as the scarlet berries that appear in autumn. The summer flowers of pale pink are tiny and delicate. At only 7.5–15cm (3–6in) high, and with a creeping habit, this is an excellent ground cover plant, the more so as it is evergreen, but it will only flourish in soil that is free of lime. Preferably the soil should be slightly acid as well as moist. The site should be in shade, but not from overhanging trees which would drip on the plants in wet weather.

Propagation: take cuttings in summer
Diseases: usually no problems

Hyssopus officinalis – Hyssop

Hyssop – like mint, monarda and rosemary – is a member of the family *Labiatae*. Its aroma and flavour most closely resemble those of mint, though it is certainly not as pleasant in culinary terms; in appearance it is most like rosemary. As a purely ornamental plant it has more to offer than either. It grows much more densely than its relatives, so that it provides good ground cover; and because it grows quickly to about 60cm (2ft) in height it can be used to form a low hedge. Its blue flowers first bloom in midsummer and persist right through until the early autumn. The heavy scent

naturally makes hyssop a favourite with bees. It is one of the herbs used in the liqueur Chartreuse. Plant hyssop, which is a hardy perennial, in well-drained soil in full sun.

Propagation: hyssop will self-seed readily; it can also be increased by ster cuttings in spring or by dividing the roots in autumn or early spring
Diseases: usually no problems

Lavandula – Lavender

The scented old English lavender famed for its medicinal and cosmetic properties is *L. spica*, an evergreen perennial shrub that reaches 90cm (3ft) or more. Like hyssop, it makes a good low hedging plant, particularly fc a herb garden. Lavender, with its pale

lue flowers, is also a good companion
or rose bushes. Dwarf varieties (height
0–60cm [12–24in]) for container
rowing or for edging the border are L.
ana atropurpurea or L. stoechas
rench lavender). Both have deep
urple flowers, and the latter also has a
lume of papery purple bracts at the
op of each stem which remains after
ne flowers have faded. Lavender will
nrive in any well-drained soil, given
ıll sun. For hedging, set plants 23–
Ocm (9–12in) apart. To dry the
owers for pot-pourri or lavender bags,
ck the stems before the buds are fully
en, and dry them hanging upside
own in bunches in a cool airy place.

ropagation: take cuttings in early
ıtumn, and insert directly into the
e varieties of M. incana. The two
ost fragrant groups are "10-week"
ocks, half-hardly annuals flowering in
owering site
iseases: grey mould, honey fungus

latthiola – Stock
ne stocks familiar from florists'
ımmer and "Brompton" stocks, hardy
splays biennials treated as annuals
at flower in spring. Both are bushy
ints reaching about 45cm (18in) with
ıllflower-like leaves and stems
ensely covered with small but double
owers. The colour range is white,
nk, red and lavender, and 10-week
ocks are also available in yellow. As
ell as providing a marvellous display
the border stocks make excellent
ıt flowers, and are typical of the
ottage garden. The pale lilac-pink
owers of night-scented stocks, M.
comis are by comparison insignificant
appearance, but with an
comparable evening scent. They are
ten grown in conjunction with
alcolmia maritima; popularly know as
rginian stock, this 20cm (8in) annual
lightly scented and bears cross-
aped flowers of white, pink and
vender right through the summer
om successional sowings. The two

species of matthiola described need
good garden soil and the warmth a
sunny position will provide. Malcolmias
are easily raised in almost any soil and
site.

Propagation: raise from seed
Diseases: club root; grey mould

Mentha – Mint
Spearmint (M. spicata) left to itself to
invade the whole of a decent sized
flowerbed in the course of half a year,
is more of a liability than a blessing.
But there are a handful of much more
refined mints, superior in both
appearance and flavour, which would
be good subjects for container growing.
A large tub, an old kitchen sink, a
raised trough, would all make a good
home for a collection that included M.
piperata, peppermint, M. rotundifolia,
the apple mint with round leaves and
varieties of this species with leaves
splashed golden or white. Mints are
not at all fussy about soil and prefer to
be in shade. Most reach about 60cm
(24in) in height and bear pink or
lavender flowers in summer. As hardy
perennials, they die down in winter
and reappear the following spring.

Propagation: take cuttings or lift and
divide the plants in spring
Diseases: rust

Monarda didyma – Bergamot
One of the popular names of M.
didyma is Oswego tea, after the
soothing hot drink made from its
aromatic leaves by North American
Indians of that name. The aroma is
slightly minty. Both bergamot and
mint belong to the same plant family
and have similar pointed leaves. But
the flowers of bergamot are much
more showy, 7.5cm (3in) across on
their 90cm (3ft) stems, pink or scarlet
like unruly chrysanthemums, and
extremely attractive to bees. This
perennial plant likes moist soil and
should be set in sun or semi-shade.

Like mint, bergamot can be invasive.
This makes it a good subject for a wild
garden or for a container. Otherwise
restrict the root run by burying slates
sideways up around the plants.
"Cambridge Scarlet" is the best known
red-flowered variety; "Snow Maiden"
is a white form and "Blue Stocking" a
deep violet.

Propagation: divide and replant in
spring
Diseases: usually no problems

Myrtus communis – common myrtle
In Roman times the myrtle was held
sacred to Venus and was held as an
emblem of love. It is quite beautiful
enough to merit this honour, with
2.5cm [1 in]) wide flowers of the purest
white, saucer-shaped and with a boss of
prominent, very thin stamens. The
leaves are narrow and pointed, a dark,
glossy green. Both flowers and foliage
are fragrant. Because this evergreen is
a tender species, it is best grown in a
container so that it can be brought
indoors for the winter. Restricted in
this way, it will probably grow to 90cm
(3ft) in height and spread. There is a
more compact variety named
"Tarentina" with correspondingly
smaller flowers. Put the plants outside
for the whole of the summer; they will
bear flowers for the length of the
season.

Propagation: take heel cuttings in
summer
Diseases: usually no problems

Nicotiana – Tobacco Plant
The perennial N. affinis, syn. N. alata,
usually treated as an annual and grown
in borders or pots, is the taller growing
of the two species most often
cultivated, reaching about 60cm (24in)
or more. It has given rise to a number
of named varieties, none of which is
quite as heavily scented as the species.
The attractive flowers appear right

through the summer; they are tubular, and in a wide range of colours – white, pink, scarlet and a lime green which is sought after by flower arrangers. Most do not open during the day but emit their strong fragrance in the evening, when they at last open up. Named varieties that remain open during the day include "Nicki" and the F_1 hybrids "Domino" which only reach 30cm (12in). *N. affinis grandiflora* is a beautiful night-scented strain with large white blooms. *N. x sanderae*, the other popular variety, has all the appealing characteristics of *N. affinis* except, unfortunately, its scent. Tobacco plants need warmth to flower well and give their enticing scent. Give them a sunny site and rich, well-drained soil.

Propagation: raise from seed
Diseases: usually no problems

Philadelphus – Mock orange
Since it is the beautiful white cup-shaped flowers of mock orange which bear the heady scent, the variety most profuse in flower production is the most popular one. This distinction falls to the hybrid "Virginal", which at 2.4–3m (8–10ft) high is, all round, one of the largest forms of this hardy shrub. Much more compact at 90cm (3ft) is "Manteau d'Hermine". "Beauclerk" comes somewhere in between, about 1.8m (6ft), but has the loveliest flowers of all, very like those of myrtle with their prominent stamens. All these flower in summer; they are good plants for town gardens because they tolerate atmospheric pollution, and last well as cut flowers. The species *P. coronarius* flowers slightly earlier than the hybrids and does well on dry soils. For the rest, any ordinary well-drained soil is suitable, in a sunny site. Some shade is tolerated.

Propagation: take cuttings in summer after flowering
Diseases: leaf spot

Syringa – Lilac
Lilacs, renowned for their delicious perfume, may be grown as large shrubs or small trees. Most of the examples usually grown are hybrids of the common lilac *S. vulgaris*, growing to a height of 2.4–3.6m (8–12ft) with a spread up to 3m (10ft). Single- and double-flowered varieties of the familiar pyramidal blooms are available, most of which are deeply fragrant. The colour range is wider than lilac alone; two of the most heavily scented are the rose-red "Paul Thirion" and the pure white "Souvenir de Alice Harding". Both flower in early summer. The smaller species *S. microphylla* with a height and spread of 1.2–1.5m (4–5ft) and lilac-coloured blooms has the advantage of flowering twice, once in early summer like most lilacs but again at summer's end. *S.M.* "Superba", which produces flushes of rose-coloured flowers right through from late spring to early summer,

Syringa: beautiful and fragrant

reaches up to 2.4m (8ft). Lilacs thrive in any reasonably fertile soil, in sun or shade.

Propagation: raise from cuttings. Budding on to *S.vulgaris* or privet stock produces more vigorous plants
Diseases: die back; lilac blight

The graceful lines and delicious scent of *Philadelphus* are welcome in any garden

Plants for Containers

eople who are forever shifting the
urniture around to try out new
rrangements will be enchanted by
container gardening". As long as the
ontainers are not *too* enormous (and
herefore enormously heavy, once
lled with earth), there is a certain
argin for moving the scenery.
timulating though such an
nvironment might be, one of the
eat advantages of growing plants in
ibs or pots is that you can virtually
nore the restrictions imposed by the
te-and-soil parameter of a particular
rden. By filling the container with a
owing medium exactly matching the
ant's requirements and positioning it
the most favourable site it becomes
ossible to enjoy camellias,
ododendrons, deep blue hydrangeas
d other plants that otherwise would
ither away. This is also a good way to
ow tender plants like black-eyed
san or passion flowers for their brief
it glorious life. No matter how small
e space available, containers make it
ossible for everyone to have growing
ings around them. The urban
ndscape would not be the same
thout the glorious profusion of
olourful plants on windowsills, in
orways, on balconies and roof
rdens that spring into life with the
st bulbs – thanks to the versatility of
ntainers and the plants that are
appy to grow in them.

itrus
hile few modern gardeners have the
eans to sustain a full-scale orangery,
creasing numbers aspire to – and
hieve – a conservatory. Oranges, and
mons too, are ideal conservatory
ants. C. *mitis* is the calamondin
ange, which only grows to about
5cm (18in) but still bears fruit and
wers; C. *limon*, the lemon, reaches
2m (4ft); C. *neticulata*, the mandarin,
ows to 90cm-1.2m (3-4ft) and is the
rdiest of the three. All have the
miliar citrus foliage, dark green and
iny, which so perfectly sets off the

Fuchsia: a perfect container plant

bright, white fragrant spring flowers
and glowing summer fruits. Grow the
plants in 25cm (10in) pots or small
tubs of No. 2 compost. Keep them
under glass until summertime, when
they may be taken out to sit in full sun
until the end of the season.

Propagation: take cuttings in summer
Diseases: leaf drop

x Fatshedera
x *Fatshedera* is a hardy evergreen
hybrid between *Fatsia japonica* (*see*
Shrubs) and *Hedera helix* "Hibernica",
a variety of ivy, and has characteristics
of both: beautiful, large glassy leaves as
well as a tendency to trail which makes
it suitable for banks or as ground
cover. But just as ivy is often used
indoors as part of a mixed planting, so
x *Fatshedera* makes an excellent
companion in a tub or barrel out of
doors to other plants, especially
flowering kinds like camellia or fuchsia.
It bears flowers itself in autumn, pale

green in colour, but they are unlikely
to open up out of doors. Grow the
plants in No. 2 compost.

Propagation: take cuttings of side
shoots in summer
Diseases: usually no problems

Fuchsia
The fuchsia with its beautiful bell-like
hanging flowers never fails to excite
the eye. Hardy in mild areas, many f its
varieties are suitable for containers in
the garden. An upright variety such as
F. *fulgens*, for example, will strike a
dramatic note in any setting; while F.
procumbens, a native of New Zealand,
when planted outside in a hanging
basket, will give colour all summer and
survive all but the harshest winters.

Propagation: by cuttings in early
spring or from seed
Disease: usually no problems

Laurus nobilis – sweet bay
When grown as a half-standard or
standard in a tub and neatly clipped to
a spherical shape, laurel is one of the
most elegant plants to grace a patio or
doorway. That it is also a useful herb,
and was a symbol of triumph in
ancient Rome, makes it even more
desirable. The aromatic leaves are dark
green, narrowly oval and pointed.
Grow laurel in 45cm (18in) containers
in potting compost: No. 3. Set the tubs
in a sunny position out of wind. Clip
with secateurs two or three times
during the summer to keep the outline
neat.

Propagation: take heel cuttings in late
summer
Diseases: usually no problems

Lobelia
It is the annual species of lobelia, L.
erinus, which is often used in mixed
container plantings, for example
window boxes, hanging baskets,
troughs and tubs. It is a dense-growing

The distinctive foliage and flowers of *Pelargonium* make it a popular container plant

little plant with tiny blue and white flowers appearing from late spring right through to the first frosts. There are two forms, one compact, the other trailing (which also makes it suitable for raised beds). There are named varieties of each form varying in intensity of hue; "Rosamund" is a magenta and white variety. Often grown with pelargoniums, fuchsias and petunias – and, always to great effect, still other combinations than the familiar red and pink with pink or blue are worth trying. Blue lobelia with bright yellow tuberous begonias or with white hydrangeas for a summer scheme would be refreshing. Plant *L. erinus* in containers of No. 1 compost, keep them moist, and set in a sheltered position, in partial shade for

preference. Since pelargoniums and petunia like sun this may not be possible, but bear in mind that the larger plants themselves provide some shade for the little lobelias.

Propagation: raise from seed
Diseases: damping-off (of seedlings)

Pelargonium

Pelargoniums are far and away the most popular of all plants grown in window boxes, tubs, hanging baskets, troughs – containers of all shapes and sizes. It's not difficult to understand why: the colour range, broadly red, pink and white, but embracing lavender and burgundy, includes some of the most vivid and cheering shades to be in seen the garden (or, equally,

on a patio or tiny balcony). The flowering period is very long – from the early summer through to mid-autumn, and sometimes beyond in mild seasons. The foliage too is fine: sometimes flushed ('zoned') with deep red, cream, or yellow; sometimes scented; sometimes with the form of an ivy leaf rather than the customary rough fan shape; and always abundant. Although they are so striking, pelargoniums mix well with other summer-flowering favourites without overwhelming them. Every season there is a clutch of new varieties to be enjoyed, with the result that the range of flower form is very wide, from showy, large blooms like "Grenadier", an F_1 hybrid that reaches 30cm (12in), to rather delicate flowers that provide glints of colour against profuse foliage. "Red Fountain" falls into this group, a semi-cascading variety which is ideal for hanging baskets. Pelargoniums are widely available as young plants for bedding out. They are not difficult to raise from seed, however, and by doing so you greatly extend the range of your display. Both in garden centres and in seed catalogues they are still often and mistakenly called geraniums. The plants should be grown in No. 2 potting compost. They like full sun, and should be kept well-watered during the growing period. As tender perennials, they must be taken indoors before the first frosts.

Propagation: take cuttings in early spring from overwintered plants
Diseases: (of foliage) oedema, rust

Petunia

"Blue Danube", "Flounce", "Purple Pirouette", "White Swan", "Fluffy Ruffles", "Cascade Fandango": the names given to modern varieties of petunia alone tell you that the flowers resemble nothing so much as the skirt of a ballerina, though the colour range is certainly not limited to a classical white. Single-coloured forms may be white, salmon, lipstick pink, scarlet, or purple. Bi-coloured forms have either a white edge to the petals, which may be ruffled, or a white stripe running down the centre. Huge double-flowered varieties in all colours are also available: the F₁ hybrids "Bouquet" are among the best of these. At the other end of the spectrum are single-flowered dwarf hybrids of great delicacy, such as the pale pink "Chiffon Magic" or the pure white "Prio White". The largest petunia reach 30cm (12in) with 7.5cm (3in) blooms; the dwarfs are half that size. Trailing varieties of the "cascade" group reach about 23cm (9in). Less often seen are yellow petunias, but here are several named varieties – "Summer Sun" and "Brass Band" among them – which are reliable and look particularly pretty interplanted with white pelargoniums and blue obelia. The flowering period of petunias is right through the summer to early autumn. Regular deadheading of the plants encourages flowering. Some of the pink and purple strains have a light, vanilla-like scent. Petunias are perennials but invariably grown as half-hardy annuals. They may be bought in as bedding plants or raised from seed without difficulty. They do best in No. 1 compost and should be set in a sunny spot, sheltered from wind, which can damage the flowers.

Propagation: raise from seed
Diseases: foot rot

Sanvitalia procumbens – Creeping zinnia

Dazzled by the pinks and purples of petunias and pelargoniums, the little sanvitalia is undeservedly overlooked. One of the most attractive characteristics of this 15cm (6in) annual is that it is so easy to grow: another is that with its trailing stems it is a graceful summer-flowering plant well-suited to all kinds of containers including hanging baskets. The daisy-like flowers are a cheerful yellow with a black centre; those of the species are only 2cm (¾in) across, but there is a double-flowered variety "Flore Pleno", and a new strain with 2.5cm (1 in) double, orange flowers called "Mandarin Orange". Sanvitalias show up well against dark green foliage or with other flowers of orange or yellow. An unusual combination for a sunny porch or patio could include the climbers *Tropaeolum peregrinum* (a yellow nasturtium) with black-eyed Susan (*Thunbergia alata*) and containers of x *Fatshedera* and sweet laurel (*Laurus nobilis*) with sanvitalia spilling over the edge. Sanvitalias like sun and should be grown in pots of No. 1 compost.

Propagation: raise from seed sown in the flowering site in autumn or spring
Diseases: usually no problems

Tropaeolum – Nasturtium

The best nasturtiums for pot culture are the smaller varieties of the annual species *T. majus*. At 38cm (15in), the "Gleam" nasturtiums are the largest of these, with trailing stems that particularly recommend them for use in hanging baskets. "Golden Gleam" is a bright yellow-flowered example; "Indian Chief" has scarlet flowers with purplish leaves. For an explosion of colour and flowers "Jewel Mixed" is the best choice, slightly smaller at 30cm (12in) high. For brightening up a windowsill or to be grown in conjunction with other plants, dwarf plants are the solution. The "Tom Thumb" strain fits the bill at 25cm (10in). All of these kinds have the characteristic bright papery petals and almost circular, light green leaves. The leaves have a mild peppery taste and can be used in salads. The flowers appear right through the summer. In the garden, nasturtiums need poor soil if they are to produce plenty of flowers; in a pot, they should be grown in No. 2 compost, and set in the sun.

Propagation: raise from seed
Diseases: virus diseases affect foliage

Tulipa – Tulip

Dwarf varieties of spring-flowering bulbs such as iris, daffodils and hyacinths can all be grown in containers, whether window boxes outside or small pots indoors. This is the best way to enjoy some of the exquisite species of tulips, too, which are best seen at close quarters, like *T. batalinii*, height 15cm (6in), with pointed cream petals, *T. tarda*, which is the same height but bears up to 5 white flowers on each stem, or *T. greigii*, which bears 7.5cm (3in) long red flowers on 30cm (12in) stems and has beautiful pointed leaves dappled with bronze-brown. What distinguishes tulips from other spring-flowering bulbs is their soldier straight stems and upright, uniform blooms. A large half-barrel containing nothing but tall tulips, all of the same colour, all chosen so that their height is in perfect proportion to the container, all equally spaced – this is a piece of design *par excellence*; and because the tulips are in a container, in the context of the garden itself they can be placed exactly where you want them. Lily-flowered species that reach 60cm (24in) merit such special treatment, such as the golden yellow 'Arkadia'; better still, revive some of the cottage tulips, renowned for their stiff stems and impressive height – 90cm (3ft) – such as "Greenland", green flushed with pink; "Viridiflora", green; or the stately "Bacchus", wine red. Plant the bulbs in late autumn to flower in spring, about 15cm (6in) deep in soil lightly dressed with lime. Lift and store the bulbs after the foliage has died down.

Propagation: detach offsets when lifting bulbs and store until ready for planting in autumn
Diseases: virus diseases; mould in poor storage conditions

Shrubs

Shrubs provide the landmarks in a garden, permanent fixtures in an otherwise changing miniature landscape where annuals come and go, perennials rise and fall. Even where trees are present to offer an even more solid set of focal points, shrubs are welcome because of their size – often equal in height to a human being, neither towering overhead nor crouching at one's feet. You can walk up to a rose or rhododendron and be presented at eye level with a handful of marvellous blossom. Even shrubs that come to waist level look sturdy enough to bear the touch of an inquisitive hand as it strokes a glossy leaf or cups a feathery flower head. While shrubs may be small when they first come from the nursery, it is important to know what its eventual requirements in terms of height and spread are likely to be, so that it is not, by being too restricted, prevented from achieving its natural size and shape. The shape of a bushy plant is, after all, an integral part of its charm, whether rounded or spreading, upright or weeping. Successful arrangements are often made with thoughtful combinations of these shapes, or by choosing a colour theme, using flowering shrubs with others that have striking foliage or stems or winter berries. Do bear in mind that it is wise to have a look at plants in which you are interested in their mature state before going to the trouble of buying and planting them – with luck they will populate your garden for a good many years.

Amelanchier – Snowy mespilus

If there is room to accommodate it – the mature height and spread is 3m (10ft) – A. canadensis is a fine shrub; hardy and undemanding, it is covered with racemes of white flowers in spring, which are followed by round black edible berries. In autumn the foliage turns a glorious glowing orange.

The subtle beauty of Ceanothus makes its careful cultivation well worthwhile

Propagation: layer branches in autumn; from autumn to spring suckers that have rooted may be separated and replanted
Diseases: usually no problems

Ceanothus
Most ceanothus species are best trained against a south-facing wall to give them the protection and shelter they need. The radiant blue of their flowers is one of the glories of any garden and they should be planted where it has no gaudy competitor. Of the evergreens, C. thyrsiflorus is the toughest as well as the most vigorous (height and spread 3m [10ft]). It flowers in early summer. C.t. "Repens" is neater in habit and half that size. The hybrid "Autumnal Blue" is another vigorous evergreen with the advantage of a long flowering period, from midsummer to the autumn. If a sheltered sunny wall is available one deciduous variety that would particularly like its care is C. azureus, which shows its appreciation from midsummer to early autumn with feather panicles, up to 15cm (6in) long, of tiny blue flowers. It is a nicely proportioned shrub at a height and spread of 1.2m–1.8m (4–6ft). Light soil is best, without too much lime.

Propagation: take cuttings in high summer
Diseases: chlorosis; honey fungus

Choisya – Mexican orange
Choisyas are evergreen, and a rather soft green at that, which makes them welcome in the winter garden when other plants are flowering either on bare stems like Jasminum nudiflorum or have rather dull foliage, like Viburnum tinus. What's more, the glossy leaves are aromatic when bruised, and are excellent in floral arrangements. Flowering time is spring, when the rounded shrub (height 1.5–1.8m [5–6ft], spread 1.8–2.4m [6–8ft]) bears fragrant white flowers very like

philadelphus (mock orange) blossom. The flowering sprays last well when cut. This plant will do well in any type of soil but to protect the leaves from frost damage in cold areas it needs a position in full sun, say against a south-facing wall.

Propagation: take cuttings in late summer
Diseases: honey fungus

Daphne
The flowers of daphne species are renowned for their sweet fragrance as well as their charming appearance. Four petals are arranged in a rough cross shape, and may be white, pink, magenta or red. The leaves too are very fine and shapely whether oval, like those of D. blagayana or more pointed, as with D. odora. There is some diversity of size in this group. D. cneorum (garland flower) is a prostrate evergreen only 15cm (6in) high; it spreads about 60cm (24in) or more and produces numerous pink flowers in early summer. "Eximia" is a good variety, of slightly increased proportions. D. blagayana, another low-growing species, brings a distinctly Oriental air to the garden with its almost naked branches stretching up to 1.8m (6ft) across, with heavy clusters of white flowers in late spring. Most daphnes are rather slow-growing, but D. burkwoodii "Somerset" is an exception, and reaches 60–90cm (2–3ft). A half-evergreen, its profusion of pink and white flowers appears in early summer. Daphnes are not difficult to grow; any soil will do, even chalk, but it must be well-drained. They thrive in sun or partial shade.

Propagation: take cuttings during the summer after flowering
Diseases: honey fungus

Deutzia
Deutzia scabra is a widely grown species from this deciduous family, rather

upright in habit and with interesting bark that peels away. It is tall in maturity, up to 3m (10ft) – with a spread up to 1.8m (6ft). The named varieties bear 15cm (6in) long panicles of white or pink and purple flowers in summer. With elegantly pointed pale green leaves, this is a handsome plant. For a smaller garden, however, D. elegantissima at 1.2–1.5m (4–5ft) may prove to be the better choice. Its stems arch gracefully from the branches and the abundant flowers which appear in early summer are scented. There are many hybrid deutzias, with "Perle Rose" perhaps the prettiest, and "Mont Rose" the most vigorous, the first a pale, the latter a keep pink, both reaching about 1.5m (5ft). No special soil requirements apply. Although they like full sun, deutzias are also happy in dappled shade.

Propagation: take cuttings of side shoots in summer, or hardwood cuttings in autumn
Diseases: usually no problems

Dierama – Angel's fishing rod
In an island bed, where it can rise to its full 1.8m (6ft), D. pulcherrimum "Windhover" is a picture of grace. Long arching stems spring from a cluster of grassy leaves. At the top, bell-shaped pink flowers shimmer in the breezes of late summer. There are white, deep red and purple-flowered varieties. All are evergreen. Enrich the soil with peat or leaf-mould and any ordinary soil will do. Choose a site in sun or partial shade.

Propagation: Lift and divide the bulbous rootstocks after flowering and detach offsets. Grow on for planting in the permanent site the following autumn
Diseases: usually no problems

Erica – Heath
The ericas, all evergreens, probably contribute more than any other species

to keeping colour and cover in the garden than any other plant. Because the range of colour and height is so wide, correspondingly complex schemes can exploit all the possibilities. There are varieties of *E. carnea*, which reaches no more than 30cm (12in) and spreads 60cm (24in) for every taste, showy and subtle. "Aurea" has yellow leaves and pink flowers from midwinter to spring: the vigorous "December Red" flowers through the winter; one of the best, and trailing in habit is "Springwood White", from midwinter to spring. Among the taller-growing heaths is the Dorset heath, *E. ciliaris*, up to 45cm (18in), with bell-shaped flowers; good varieties include "Corfe Castle", with deep cerise flowers. All are in bloom for half the year, no less, from midsummer onwards. The Mediterranean heath can reach 3m (10ft) but the named varieties (with the exception of "Superba") stay at a more manageable metre in height and spread (3–4ft). "Brightness" lives up to its name, with bronze-green leaves and rosy-pink flowers. It is a good hedging plant.

Ericas are so varied that it is well worth visiting a specialist nursery or garden centre to see them growing. They are best planted in groups together, preferably on peaty, acid soils, but this is not always essential.

Erica carnea provides effective cover

The *Hebe* hybrid 'Midsummer beauty': a popular and attractive shrub

Full sun is important, and while the soil should be well-drained, if it were allowed to dry out it would be disastrous for the plants.

Propagation: take cuttings during the summer
Diseases: fungus discolours the leaves

Fatsia japonica
Also known as aralia, *F. japonica* is an evergreen with wonderfully glossy, dark green palmate leaves, the veins clearly marked in creamy yellow. Its sculptured silhouette makes it an ideal shrub for a formal or urban garden, particularly since shade or sun will suit and it needs some protection from the worst of the weather. Fatsias look handsome in pots or large tubs, and in

autumn long panicles of spherical white flowers appear to add to the dignified picture. Any good garden soil is suitable.

Propagation: suckers can be detached in spring and treated as cuttings
Diseases: usually no problems

Hebe
Hebes are justifiably popular shrubs, for though they are in fact half-hardy, they have an air of permanence which lends substance to a planting scheme. The leaves of the hybrid "Autumn Glory" (height and spread 60–90cm [2–3ft]) are oval and dark green, the stems purple and the flower spikes, which are produced from midsummer right through to the autumn, are blue.

Hydrangea macrophylla produces beautiful quilted blooms in the summer months

best blues will be "Générale Vicomtesse de Vibraye" or "Gentian Dome", the deepest pink, "Westfalen". An outstanding white variety is "Mme. E. Moulliére", for neutral soils. All these are Hortensias; a good blue Lacecap is "Bluewave"; the best pink "Mariesii". *H. macrophylla* flowers in high summer; in height and spread it reaches 1.5m (5ft) or more and is an impressive shrub. Remove the dead flower heads and thin out 3-year-old flowered shoots at ground level to encourage vigorous new growth. Give them a sheltered position in sun or partial shade.

Propagation: take cuttings in late summer
Diseases: chlorosis in over-alkaline soil; honey fungus

Hypericum – St John's Wort
The three best-known hypericums, semi-evergreens all, have in common their bright yellow flowers, five-petalled and star-shaped with prominent stamens; dense, mid-green foliage, and unusually accommodating natures. *H. calycinum*, the Rose of Sharon, will grow almost anywhere but at 30–45cm (12–18in) with an indefinite capacity to spread it might properly be regarded as ground cover, rather than a decorative shrub. No such qualifications apply to *H. patulum* "Hidcote", named after the great garden where it was raised. It reaches 90cm–1.8m (3–6ft), spreads about 1.5m (5ft) and, like its relatives, bears masses of yellow flowers for 3 months in high summer. This is a beautifully proportioned plant. It is unfortunate that *H. elatum* "Elstead" is prone to rust, for its individual flowers are probably the most elegant of the trio, the narrower petals almost overcome by feathery stamens. Bright red berries follow in autumn. Moister conditions help combat the rust problem.

Propagation: divide roots of *H.*

H. x franciscana "Blue Gem" is a rewarding choice as it bears its violet flowers for most of the year. Useful for ground cover is *H. pinguifolia* "Pagei" which only reaches 23cm (9in) but spreads 90cm (3ft). The rounded leaves are a grey blue and the white flowers appear in early summer. Most well-drained garden soils are suitable, and a site in full sun.

Propagation: cuttings should be taken in high summer for planting out the following autumn
Diseases: downy mildew

Hydrangea
The common hydrangea is *H. macrophylla*. It divides into two groups, the Hortensias with mop flower heads and the Lacecaps with flatter heads of fertile, closed, florets in the centre ringed by open, sterile blossoms. For form perhaps the Lacecaps are prettier; but neither group enjoys the admiration it deserves because all too often both groups are grown without enough attention being paid to their soil. And this precise requirement must be met if the varieties are to bloom true to colour. To stay blue, blue varieties must not be grown on alkaline soils; the soil must be dressed with peat, and the pH level kept low with annual applications of aluminium sulphate. Pink varieties, on the other hand, need alkaline soils to maintain their colour. On acid soils, they turn an unhealthy-looking purplish blue. With their needs properly satisfied, the

calycinum from autumn to spring; take cuttings of the taller species in summer
Diseases: usually no problems

Pieris

Pieris are evergreens with precise needs as to soil, which must be lime-free and moisture-retentive, and situation – they must be sheltered from frost, wind and early morning sun. If you can offer such a spot, there are few shrubs that so well merit it as *P. formosa forrestii*. It is very slow-growing, although ultimately makes 1.8–3m (6–10ft). Even in infancy it is extremely beautiful, with long pointed glossy leaves, flushed crimson early in the season and gradually turning green. Great panicles of white flowers like lilies of the valley appear in early summer

Propagation: in late summer, take cuttings or increase by layering
Diseases: usually no problems

Potentilla – Shrubby cinquefoil

To paraphrase – slightly – William Morris, have nothing in your garden that you do not know to be useful or believe to be beautiful. That many gardeners believe potentillas comply with one or both of these strictures is clear to see. This compact shrub, neatly and sweetly made in all its parts, gets its familiar name from the five leaflets in the compound leaf. The flowers are like a tiny species rose. It has long been in cultivation, originally for medicinal purposes. There are numerous named varieties of the shrubby species *P. fruticosa* from which to choose, all flowering from the beginning of summer well into the autumn. One of the tallest is "Farreri", (1.2m [4ft]), with golden yellow flowers; "Mandschurica" at 30cm (12in) makes good ground cover with silvery leaves, purple stems and white flowers; better still for that purpose is "Tangerine", 60cm (24in) high but spreading to 1.5m (5ft) with buds and

flowers of red-orange. Light soil which is well-drained and a site in full sun are best.

Propagation: raise from seed or take cuttings of side shoots in the autumn
Diseases: usually no problems

Rhododendron

Rhododendrons range in size from diminutive azaleas to vast bushes that can only be accommodated in huge gardens or in woodland. As a group they like acid soils. Many species are spring-flowering, but there are some that bloom in the middle of winter (like *R. lutescens*) and others that wait until the height of summer (*R. viscosum*). They include some of the most magnificent and colourful flowering plants known – indeed this is their popular image; but there are more refined examples worth cultivating too. One such is the azalea "Narcissiflorum", (height 1.5–2.4m [5–8ft]), with yellow, daffodil-like flowers on almost leafless twiggy branches. This fragile looking blooms smell of honey. This is one of the so-called Ghent hybrids and very hardy. More conventionally clothed are the hardy evergreen hybrids, which on average have a height and spread of 3–5m (10–15ft). The colour range is almost infinite. A good white is "Mrs A.T. de la Mare"; in strong contrast is "Purple Splendour". "Goldsworth Orange" is more of a peach, with a height and spread of 1.5–1.8m (5–6ft). Some rhododendrons of the azalea type make good ground cover if planted in groups; "Addy Wery", 90cm (3ft) high with brilliant vermilion flowers is one such. For all, a sheltered semi-shaded site is to be preferred. They must not be allowed to dry out.

Propagation: raise from seed sown at the end of winter; or layer young stems at any time
Diseases: azalea gall; chlorosis; honey fungus

Rosa – Rose

The list of roses of all types is long and always being extended. Among those which are repeat-flowering and which will reach at least 1.2m (4ft), the following are recommended: "Boule de Neige", white bourbon; "Chinatown", yellow tinted pink, a good hedging shrub; "Eroica", dark red hybrid tea; "Cornelia", strawberry pink hybrid musk; "Kathleen Ferrier", vermilion orange modern shrub; "Lucy Cramphorn", geranium red hybrid tea; "Queen Elizabeth", clear pink floribunda; "Schneezwerg", pure white hybrid rugosa, good for seaside gardens; "Super Star", pure vermilion, hybrid tea. But there are countless more, which should be seen at specialist nurseries or the gardens of rose-growing societies.

Roses need good drainage, an open sunny site, rich soil and must not be allowed to dry out. Deadheading is important during the flowering season, and pruning should be carried out to dispose of weak branches.

Propagation: It is possible to raise some types of roses from cuttings, but budding is the most reliable method and is carried out in high summer
Diseases: black spot; grey mould; powdery mildew and others

Spartium junceum – Spanish broom

The long summer-flowering period of *Spartium junceum* is one of its greatest assets, and the quality of its graceful green stems means that, though it loses its leaves quickly, it is attractive all year round. The small yellow flowers, which are scented, resemble laburnum blossom, another member of the pea family. Because it likes sandy or alkaline soils it does well in seaside gardens. It reaches 2.4–3m (8–10ft) and spreads 1.8–2.4m (6–8ft).

Propagation: Take cuttings in spring
Diseases: usually no problems

Rhododendrons, whether small or well-established, are always sought after for their beautiful varied blooms

INDEX

ACKNOWLEDGEMENTS

The Paul Press Limited would like to thank the following organizations to whom copyright in the photographs noted below belongs:

Heather Angel 144; Arcaid/Richard Bryant 10/11, 13, 46/47; Michael Boys 16/17, 35, 42/43, 51; Camera Press/Hauser 15, 38, 44; EWA 14, 28/29, 32, 40/41; John Glover 50, 138, 161, 182(b); Jerry Harpur 24 (designer Anne Dexter), 36/37 (designer Michael Branch), 39 (designer Michael Branch), 45, 48, 49, 134, 142, 143, 145, 148, 158, 159, 173 (designer Anne Steven), 176(t), 177, 185; Neil Holmes 148/9(t), 178; Peter McHoy 135, 137, 153, 172; Tania Midgeley 20/21, 22/23, 27, 139, 140/1, 146, 147, 150, 151, 154, 156 (tl), 160, 162, 164, 165, 167, 169, 174, 180; Harry Smith 156/7(t), 182(t); David Squire 171, 176(b); Michael Warren 133, 166, 168, 183.